Dog Is My Co-Pilot

Dog Is My Co-Pilot

The Editors of *The BARk*

Great Writers on the World's Oldest Friendship

THREE RIVERS PRESS
NEW YORK

Complete text for permissions appears on pages 278–280.

Published by Three Rivers Press, New York, New York.
Member of the Crown Publishing Group, a division of Random House, Inc.
www.crownpublishing.com

Originally published in hardcover by Crown Publishers, a division of Random House, Inc., in 2003.

Printed in the United States of America

Design by Lynne Amft

Illustrations by Mark Ulriksen

Library of Congress Cataloging-in-Publication Data
Dog is my co-pilot / the editors of the Bark.
1. Dogs—United States—Anecdotes. 2. Dog owners—United States—Anecdotes.
3. Human-animal relationships—United States—Anecdotes. I. Bark (Berkeley, Calif.)
SF426.2.D644 2003
636.7—dc21 2002155044

ISBN 1-4000-5053-7

10 9 8 7 6 5 4
First Paperback Edition

Contents

Lessons

Passages

Introduction

Our life with dogs, and the history of *The Bark,* starts with a familiar human-meets-dog story. Around seven years ago a stray foundling came into our lives. We already had a gaggle of quasi-feral felines who had staked claim to us, so we weren't looking for another pet. But when a prescient and persistent friend introduced us to an adorable mixed-breed pup needing a new home, our resolve started to melt. We wondered how a dog would fit into our cat-filled household and commute-driven lives, but Cameron, my life partner (and *The Bark*'s cofounder), was an art director for Autodesk, a software company famous for its friendly pet-in-the-workplace policy, and my consultant's job came with a courtyard office in San Francisco and a fairly tolerant boss, so the care-giving duties could be divvied up between us. Then the gentle Nell displayed due deference to the cats, and they, in turn, ignored her. So, in short order we joined the ranks of the dog people—satisfying Nellie's needs and anticipating her every desire came to be the central focus in our lives.

We began *The Bark* with a small group of like-minded, dog-crazed individuals who walked and played with their dogs at a local park. The inaugural issue, in 1997, was a mere eight-page newsletter, fittingly called *The Berkeley Bark.* We were hoping to legalize our off-leash cavorting and needed a medium that could serve as a call to action to other dog people and carry our cause to city hall. "Dog Is My Co-Pilot" became the motto. It perfectly expressed our attitude toward our canine companions, plus it livened up the debate with a playful cheekiness. We were novices at political campaigning but somehow came up with a winning formula for pamphleteering. While keeping our eye on the dog-park message, we tackled other subjects with zeal and fresh enthusiasm. We started to notice the emergence of a new "dog culture," and it enthralled and fascinated us. With *The Bark* we set out to explore this growing phenomenon in our pages.

The world's oldest friendship evolved over the millennia, and is undergoing a remarkable transformation today. Life with dogs has taken on new meaning in our society, with dogs moving out of the backyard and into our homes, our communities, and the center of our lives. Dogs are everywhere, in places never before seen—in the workplace, schools, and hospitals—plus their image and symbolism permeate every form of media. Their heightened presence cannot be denied—37 percent of American households include dogs, meaning dogs can be found in more households than children. Their influence affects every facet of daily life. In a survey of pet owners conducted by the American Animal Hospital Association in 2002, 97 percent of respondents said that their pet makes them smile at least once a day. Another 76 percent believe that their pet eases their stress level, and about half of the respondents have taken their dog to work and plan most of their free time around their dog! A new breed of dog people has emerged, and a new set of operating instructions has been issued. We have applied our concern for our own enrichment and well-being to our dogs, creating a bevy of dog walkers, day-care facilities, spas, dog parks, and canine-human activities such as agility, flyball, and dog dancing. But the implications of integrating another species into society's daily fabric goes well beyond how we nurture *our* dogs. It calls for revamping the standard etiquette—and respecting the concerns and interests of society at large. This new relationship, along with an appreciation for our rich past and unbound future, comprise what we call today's dog culture. This is what *The Bark* set out to chronicle.

So we filled our newsletter with smart writing, insightful interviews, hard-hitting reporting, great fiction, topical cartoons, humor, poetry, reviews, book excerpts, and more. It was everything we wanted to read, and its canine-centricity inspired the best from contributors. Also, *The Bark* simply looked different—the design and layout were cutting-edge and hip, mirroring the fun and liveliness emanating from this new subculture. We took pride in publishing a periodical that not only reflected its time but one that also showcased the esteem that we felt for all dogs. But it wasn't just about dogs—we looked more broadly at our relationship with dogs through culture, art, and politics. We knew that we were on to something special when we started to attract attention and interest from contributors and readers from across the country. *The Bark* grew, and after two years we dropped *Berkeley* from the masthead, gradually morphing from newsletter to tabloid to magazine. Since then, accolades have been garnered, awards won, and friends made with thousands of readers worldwide.

As for Cameron and me, we adopted two more dogs, stopped commuting, became full-time magazine publishers, and now are proud to spearhead this book. Back in Berkeley, the dog-park fight turned into a six-year-long campaign, but the city now boasts a spectacular 17-acre dog park that is a testament to the dedication of dog lovers.

As the title *Dog Is My Co-Pilot* suggests, this book celebrates the unique bond between humans and canines. Dogs have been our muses, our mentors, and our faithful companions. We've selected some of our favorite work from the pages of *The Bark,* as well as new writing from esteemed and award-winning authors that sees its debut in this tome. The essays, short stories, and expert commentaries explore the great complexity and depth of our relationships with our oldest friends. The collection is arranged into topics with broadly drawn categories: "Beginnings," "Pack," "Lessons," and "Passages."

The essays in "Beginnings" explore that first meeting, the initial murmurings when a dog-human relationship is formed. Whether selecting a puppy, taking in a rescued stray, or welcoming a second dog, the experience involves learning the "otherness" of another being (another species!)—we of them, they of us. Alice Walker chooses a new pup; Caroline Knapp and Ann Patchett offer odes to canine friendship; Margaret Cho's world gets turned upside-down when a second dog joins her household. Exploring, testing, nosing around for a fresh start together, and facing all the challenges that a new relationship brings: These are the themes that inspire this section.

We move from "otherness" to "togetherness"—the true theme of "Pack." Whether they concern a pack of two or a den of twenty, these writings pay tribute to the special dynamic of multiple personalities, habits, and approaches. Erica Jong salutes the many dogs in her life; Michael Paterniti ponders the unique social patterns of a dog park; and Carolyn Chute asks the question: How did the dogs come to rule? These writers explore the point of critical mass—when the whole becomes greater than the sum of the parts—how we relate with our dogs to become something entirely different and unique.

"Lessons" examines what dogs teach us. Who has not learned a little more about life from the wisdom of dogdom? Pam Houston lists "Ten Things My Dog Taught Me That Made It Possible for Me to Get Married"; Lama Surya Das reflects on enlightenment and the way of the dog; and Lynda Barry captures the meaning of it all in her wonderful cartoon strip.

Finally, "Passages" tackles those moments that change us forever, with Elizabeth Marshall Thomas's thoughtful examination of a dog's ability to transform, Maeve Brennan's quiet mediation on the shifting seasons in a dog's mind, and Rick Bass's and Tom Junod's poignant tributes to loss and friendship. Dogs often act as a vital life force, and the experiences we share with them that bring about a change in our thinking and being are captured here with great passion.

It is our hope that all the writing contained in this book expands on the subject of dogs and the special bond that exists between us and them. It has been our honor to work with this remarkable group of authors. We hope their tales entertain, enlighten, and engage you as a dog lover and fan of good writing.

beginnings

Crimes Against Dog

Alice Walker

For Wendy

MY DOG, MARLEY, WAS NAMED AFTER THE LATE MUSIC SHAMAN, Bob Marley. I never saw or heard him while he was alive, but once I heard his music, everything about him—his voice, his trancelike, holy dancing on stage, his leonine dread-locks—went straight to my heart. He modeled such devotion to the well-being of humanity that his caring inspired the world; I felt a more sincere individual had probably never lived. Considering his whole life a prayer, and his singing the purest offering, I wanted to say his name every day with admiration and love. Marley has grown up on his music; Bob, leaning on his guitar in a large poster on my living room wall, is regularly pointed out to her as her Spirit Dad.

Marley was born December 19, 1995. She shares a birth sign, Sagittarius, with my mother and several friends and acquaintances. At times I feel surrounded by Sags and enjoy them very much; they are fun to be with, outspoken, passionate, and won't hesitate to try new things. They also like chicken. Marley has all these qualities, though I didn't know that the morning I drove out to the breeder to look at the litter of Labrador Retrievers I was told had arrived.

Crossing the Golden Gate Bridge, a friend and I joked about whether I was in fact ready to settle down enough to have a dog. Who would feed it when I was distracted by work? Where would it stay while I was away on book tours? Had I lined up a reliable vet? I had no idea what would happen. I only knew this friend was about to go away on a journey of unknown length. I would be unbearably lonely for her. I needed a companion on whom to lavish my overflowing, if at times distractible, affection. I needed a dog.

My first thoughts are always about enslavement on entering a place where animals are bred. Force. Captivity. I looked at the black and the chocolate Labs who were Marley's parents and felt sad for them. They looked healthy enough, but who knew whether, left to themselves, they would choose to have litter after litter of offspring? I wondered how painful it was to part with each litter. I spoke to both parents, let them sniff my hand. Take in the quality of my being. I asked permission to look at their young. The mother moved a little away from her brood, all crawling over her blindly feeling for a teat; the father actually looked rather proud. My friend joked about offering him a cigar.

I was proud of myself, too, standing there preparing to choose. In the old days of up to several months before, if I were going to choose an animal from a litter I would have been drawn to the one that seemed the most bumbling, the most clueless, the most un-amused. I saw a couple like that. But on this day, that old switch was not thrown: I realized I was sick of my attraction to the confused. My eyes moved on. They all looked much alike, to tell the truth. From a chocolate mother and a black father there were twelve puppies, six chocolate, six black. I'll never get over this. Why were there none with spots?

I asked the woman selling them, whom I tried not to have Slave Trader thoughts about. She shrugged. They never spot, she said. That's the nature of the purebred Lab.

Well, I thought. *Mother. Once again doing it just any old way you like. Mother* is my favorite name for Nature, God, All-ness.

I settled on a frisky black puppy who seemed to know where she was going—toward a plump middle teat!—and was small enough to fit into my hand. I sometimes wish I had chosen a chocolate puppy; in the Northern

California summers the dust wouldn't show as much, but I think about this mostly when Marley rolls in the dirt in an effort to get cool.

After seven weeks I returned alone to pick her up, bereft that my friend had already gone on the road. It didn't feel right to pay money for a living being; I would have been happier working out some sort of exchange. I paid, though, and put Marley in my colorful African market basket before stroking the faces of her wistful-looking parents one last time. In the car, I placed the basket in the front seat next to me. I put on Bob Marley's *Exodus* CD and baby Marley and I sped away from Babylon.

We wound our way back through the winter countryside toward the Golden Gate Bridge and the bracing air of San Francisco. Before we had gone twenty miles, Marley, now about the size of my two fists, had climbed out of the basket and into my lap. From my lap she began journeying up my stomach to my chest. By the time we approached the bridge she'd discovered my dreadlocks and began climbing them. As we rolled into the city she had climbed all the way to the back of my neck and settled herself there between my neck and the headrest. Once there she snoozed.

Of the weeks of training I remember little. Dashing down three flights of stairs in the middle of the night to let her pee outside under the stars. Sitting on a cushion in the kitchen, before dawn, her precious black body in my lap, groggily caressing her after her morning feed. Walking with her zipped up in my parka around and around the park that was opposite our house. Crossing the Golden Gate Bridge on foot, her warm body snug in my arms as I swooned into the view. She grew.

Today she is seven years old and weighs almost ninety pounds. People we encounter on walks always ask whether she's pregnant. No, I reply, she's just fat. But is she really? No matter how carefully I feed her or how often I downsize her meals, she remains large and heavy. And she loves to eat so much that when her rations are diminished she begs, which I can't stand. This is one of those areas where we've had the most work to do. I've settled it lately by taking her off any slimming diet whatsoever and giving her enough food so that she seems satisfied. I did this after she was diagnosed with breast cancer, had surgery, and I realized I might lose her at any time. I did not want her last days to be spent looking pleadingly at me for an extra morsel of bread. To make up for giving her more food, I resolved to walk her more.

The friend who went away never really returned. Marley and I ceased expecting to see her after about the first year. Marley was an amazing comfort to me. What is it about dogs? I think what I most appreciate in Marley is how swiftly she forgives me. Anything. Was I cool and snooty when I got up this morning? Did I neglect to greet her when I came in from a disturbing movie? Was I a little short on the foodstuffs and did I forget to give her a cube of dried liver? Well. And what about that walk we didn't do and the swim we didn't take and why don't I play ball with her the way I did all last week? And who is this strange person you want me to go off with? It doesn't matter what it is, what crime against Dog I have committed, she always forgives me. She doesn't even appear to think about it. One minute she's noting my odd behavior, the next, if I make a move toward her, she's licking my hand. As if to say, Gosh, I'm so glad you're yourself again, and you're back!

Dogs understand something I was late learning: When we are mean to anyone or any being it is because we are temporarily not ourselves. We're somebody else inhabiting these bodies we think of as us. They recognize this. Ooops, I imagine Marley saying to herself, sniffing my anger, disappointment, or distraction. My mommy's not in there at the moment. I'll just wait until she gets back. I've begun to feel this way more than a little myself. Which is to say, Marley is teaching me how to be more self-forgiving. Sometimes I will say something that hurts a friend's feelings. I will be miserable and almost want to do away with myself. Then I'll think, But that wasn't really the you that protects and loves this friend so much you would never hurt them. That was a you that slipped in because you are sad and depressed about other things: the state of your love life, your health, or the fate of the planet. The you that loves your friend is back now. Welcome her home. Be gentle with her. Tell her you understand. Lick her hand.

The Color of Joy

Caroline Knapp

IMAGINE A SCALED-DOWN, DELICATELY BONED GERMAN SHEPherd dog, black and gray and tan instead of black and sable like a purebred, her face the color of ink with a faint gray mask. This is Lucille, a most ordinary-looking dog. She does have some exceptional features—her two forelegs are white, one halfway up from the paw, the other about a quarter of the way, which create the impression that she is wearing ladies' gloves; there is also the tiniest bit of white mixed into the fur at her chin, which makes her look vaguely like Ho Chi Minh if you catch her at the right angle. But for the most part, she is the kind of dog you might see pictured in the dictionary under *mongrel* or, if you happen to own a more politically correct edition, *mixed breed*. Unremarkable, in other words, but no matter. When you study a dog you love, you find beauty in every small detail, and so it is with Lucille: I have become enchanted by the small asymmetrical whorls of white fur on either side of her chest, and by her tail, which she carries in a high confident curve, and by her eyes, which are watchful and intelligent, the color of chestnuts. I am in love with the dog's belly, where the fur is fine and soft and tan, and I am charmed by her jet black toenails, which stand out against the white of her front paws as though they've been lacquered, and I am deeply admiring of her demeanor, which is elegant and focused and restrained. I seem to spend a great deal of time just staring at the dog, struck by how mysterious and beautiful she is to me and by how much my world has changed since she came along.

Before you get a dog, you can't quite imagine what living with one might be like; afterward, you can't imagine living any other way. Life without Lucille? Unfathomable, to contemplate how quiet and still my home would be, and how much less laughter there'd be, and how much less tenderness, and how unanchored I'd feel without her presence, the simple constancy of it. I once heard a woman who'd lost her dog say that she felt as though a color were suddenly missing from her world: The dog had introduced to her field of vision some previously unavailable hue, and without the dog, that color was gone. That seemed to capture the experience of loving a dog with eminent simplicity. I'd amend it only slightly and say that if we are open to what they have to give us, dogs can introduce us to several colors, with names like *wildness* and *nurturance* and *trust* and *joy.*

I am not sentimental about dogs, my passion for Lucille notwithstanding. I don't share the view, popular among some animal aficionados, that dogs are necessarily higher beings, that they represent a canine version of shamans, capable by virtue of their wild ancestry or nobility of offering humans a particular kind of wisdom or healing. I don't think that the world would be a better place if everyone owned a dog, and I don't think that all relationships between dogs and their owners are good, healthy, or enriching. "Dogs lead us into a kinder, gentler world." Honey Loring, a woman who runs a camp for dogs and their owners in Vermont, said this to me about a year after I got Lucille, a statement that struck me as rather flip. No: Dogs lead us into a world that is sometimes kind and gentle but that can be frightening, frustrating, and confusing, too. Dogs can be aggressive and stubborn and willful. They can be difficult to read and understand. They can (and do) evoke oceans of complicated feelings on the part of their owners, confusion and ambivalence about what it means to be responsible, forceful (or not), depended upon. They can push huge buttons, sometimes even more directly than humans can, because they're such unambiguous creatures, so in-your-face when it comes to expressing their own needs and drives: If you've got problems asserting authority, or insecurities about leadership, or fears about being either in or out of control, you're likely to get hit in the face with them from day one. In my view, dogs *can* be shamanistic, can be heroic and gentle and wise and enormously healing, but for the most part dogs are dogs, creatures governed by their own biological imperatives and codes of conduct, and we do both them and our relationships with them a disservice when we romanticize them. Writes Jean Schinto, author of *The Literary Dog,* "To deny dogs their nature is to do them great harm."

That said, I also believe that dogs can—and often do—lead us into a world that is qualitatively different from the world of people, a place that can transform us. Fall in love with a dog, and in many ways you enter a new orbit, a universe that features not just new colors but new rituals, new rules, a new way of experiencing attachment.

Everything shifts in this new orbit, sometimes subtly, sometimes dramatically. Walks are slower: You find yourself ambling up a city street instead of racing to a destination, the dog stopping to sniff every third leaf, every other twig, every bit of debris or detritus in your path. The clothes are different: Predog, I used to be very finicky and self-conscious about how I looked; now I schlepp around in the worst clothing—big heavy boots, baggy old sweaters, a hooded down parka from L.L. Bean that makes me look like an astronaut. The language is different, based on tone and nuance instead of vocabulary. Even the equipment is new and strange: You find yourself ordering unthinkable products from the Foster & Smith catalog (smoked pigs' ears, chicken-flavored toothpaste), and you find your living-room floor littered with sterilized beef bones and rawhide chips and plastic chew toys and ropes and balls, and you find your cupboards stocked with the oddest things—freeze-dried liver cubes, tick shampoo, poop bags.

The internal shifts are bigger, sometimes life altering. When you speak to people about what it's like to live with a dog, you hear them talk about discovering a degree of solace that's extremely difficult to achieve in relationships with people, a way of experiencing solitude without the loneliness. You hear them talk about the dog's capacity to wrest their focus off the past and future and plant it firmly in the present, with the here-and-now immediacy of a romp on the living-room rug or a walk in the woods. You hear them talk about joys that are exquisitely simple and pure: what it's like to laugh at a dog who's doing something ridiculous, and how soothing it is to sit and brush a dog's coat, and how gratifying it is to make a breakthrough in training a dog, to understand that you're communicating effectively with a different species. Above all, you hear them talk about feeling *accepted* in a new way, accompanied through daily life and over the course of years by a creature who bears witness to every change, every shift in mood, everything we do and say and experience, never judging us when we falter or fail.

Of course, not everybody gets this. Fall in love with a dog, and among non-dog people, you will see eyebrows rise, expressions grow wary. You'll reach into your wallet to brandish a photograph of a new puppy, and a friend will say, "Oh, no—not *pictures.*" You'll find yourself struggling to decline an invitation for a getaway weekend—to a hotel or a spa or a family home, somewhere dogs are not permitted—and you'll hear the words, "Just kennel the dog and come on down." You'll say something that implies profound affection or commitment, and you'll be hit with a phrase, dreaded words to a dog lover, "Oh, please, it's *just a dog.*"

More commonly, you'll get vacant looks. A married friend who lives in Los Angeles, someone I don't often see, was in town recently and came to my house for dinner. At one point, sitting in my living room, he looked around and asked me, "So what's it like living alone? What's it like getting up alone every morning and coming home every night to an empty house?" I was on the sofa, Lucille curled against my thigh. I pointed to the dog and said, "But I'm not alone. I have her." He said, "Yeah, but . . ." He didn't finish the sentence, but he didn't have to. He meant, Yeah, but a dog isn't the same as a human. A dog doesn't really count.

Attitudes like this can make dog lovers feel like members of a secret society, as though we're inhabiting a strange and somehow improper universe. Not long ago, over dinner with a nondog friend named Lisa, I started talking about Lucille, and how important her presence had been to me during the breakup of a long-term relationship. The breakup was recent, and it was long and painful and scary, as such things are, and at one point I said quite candidly, "I'm not sure I would have been able to face the loss if I hadn't had the dog."

This seemed like a perfectly reasonable statement to me—I tend to take my attachment to her for granted these days, as a simple and central fact of life—but Lisa's eyes widened a little when I said it. She said, "Wait a minute. You're scaring me."

Scaring her? I looked at Lisa, aware of a sudden sense of dissonance, as though I'd just exposed too much. It was an uh-oh feeling. Uh-oh, she doesn't live in that world, she probably thinks I'm wacko.

So I took a deep breath and tried to explain. This is a complicated task, trying to describe how a relationship with a dog can be healthy and sustaining and rich. It's hard even trying to explain that the attachment does, in fact, qualify as a relationship, a genuine union between two beings who communicate with, respect, and give to one another. Unless you fall back on the one or two pat explanations we routinely trot out in order to explain the canine place in the human heart—dogs give us unconditional love, dogs are "good companions"—it's hard to talk about loving a dog deeply without inviting skepticism. Many people, quite frankly, think intense attachments to animals are weird and suspect, the domain of people who can't quite handle attachments to humans.

So there was a good deal I didn't tell Lisa. I didn't talk about what a central force in my life Lucille has become in the years since I acquired her. I didn't talk about how I basically structure my life around the dog, organizing the day around the morning walk, the noon walk, the evening outing. I didn't tell her how much I think about Lucille, how much I hate leaving her alone when I have to go out, how I've either written off or vastly reduced my involvement in activities that don't include her—shopping, movies, trips that involve air travel. I didn't use words like *joy* or *love* or *affection,* although it's safe to say that Lucille has given me direct and vivid access to all those feelings.

Nor did I tell Lisa how much I *need* the dog, which might have been the most honest thing to say. Lucille came into my life in the aftermath of a period of enormous upheaval. In the three years before I got her, both my parents had died, my father of a brain tumor and my mother of metastatic breast cancer. Eighteen months to the day before I got her, I'd quit drinking, ending a twenty-year relationship with alcohol, and opening up a third abyss in my life. So I was wandering around at the time in a haze of uncertainty, blinking up at the biggest questions: Who am I without parents and without alcohol? How to make my way in the world without access to either? How to form attachments, and where to find comfort, in the face of such daunting vulnerability? Lucille has been a fundamental part of my answer to those questions: In her, I have found solace, joy, a bridge to the world.

But I didn't go into all that with Lisa. Instead, I used safe descriptions, clinical terms. I talked about loneliness, and how Lucille's presence had helped ease the fear and emptiness that accompany a major breakup. I gave the dogs-as-pack-animals speech, explaining how dogs' need for social structure really does turn them into family members of sorts, highly relational creatures who look to their owners for leadership and guidance and companionship. I talked about what a comforting presence she is, how much pleasure I get out of walking in the woods with her, watching her play, even just sitting beside her while she's curled up on the sofa at home.

Lisa seemed to respond positively enough to this line of thought—"Right," she said at one point, "they are good companions"—but I was aware as I talked of a gnawing frustration, a sense of my own compulsion to hold back when I talk about my dog and to offer up what's in effect a watered-down and fairly stereotypical view of the attachment: dog as man's best friend, dog as a loyal and faithful servant. There are elements of truth to that view—dogs can be wonderful friends, they can be enormously loyal and faithful creatures—but those factors represent only one part of the picture, a limited and really rather arrogant fragment that concerns only the way dogs serve us, not the ways we serve them or the ways we serve each other. Finally, I shook my head and said to Lisa, "You know, it's been really important to me to learn not to pathologize my relationship with Lucille. People have very powerful relationships with their dogs, and that doesn't mean they're crazy, or that they're substituting dogs for humans, or that they're somehow incapable of forming intimate attachments with people. It's a different *kind* of relationship, but it's no less authentic."

Alas, Lisa looked across the table and said, "You're still scaring me."

Dog love, popular wisdom suggests, should be limited love. Let on the depth of your true feelings about a dog—how attached you are, how vital the relationship feels—and you risk being accused of any number of neuroses: You're displacing human love onto the animal, which is perverse; you're anthropomorphizing, which is naive and unsophisticated; you're sublimating your unconscious wish for a baby or a spouse or a family into the dog, which is sad and pathetic. Children are allowed to harbor deep affection for dogs: That's seen not only as cute and normal but as morally acceptable, as caring for a pet can teach a child about compassion and responsibility, even about loss, given a dog's relatively short life span. The elderly and the infirm are permitted some degree of attachment, too, thanks in recent years to wide-scale acceptance of the use of therapy dogs in settings like nursing homes and hospitals. But the rest of us are expected to keep our feelings about dogs somehow contained and compartmentalized, in the box labeled "Just a Dog." And if we don't—well, as my friend Lisa said, we're a little scary.

In fact, more than one-third of all Americans live with dogs today—by most reliable estimates, that's about 55 million dogs—and it's safe to say that a good number of us don't contain or compartmentalize our feelings nearly so effectively. Suspect though dog love may be in the public eye, Americans are in the midst of a veritable love affair with dogs: We're spending more money on our dogs than ever before (the average owner can expect to shell out a minimum of $11,500 in the course of a dog's life); we're indulging them with an ever more elaborate range of goods and services (doggie day care, doggie summer camp, gold-plated Neiman Marcus doghouses); and in many respects we're treating them far more like members of the human pack than like common household pets. Depending on which study you look at, anywhere from 87 to 99 percent of dog owners report that they see their dogs as family members, figures that are certainly borne out by behavior. The American Animal Hospital Association conducts an annual survey of pet-owner attitudes. In 1995, 79 percent of respondents reported that they give their pets holiday or birthday presents. Thirty-three percent said they talk to their dogs on the phone or through an answering machine when they're away. If they were stranded on a desert island and could pick only one companion, 57 percent of owners said they'd choose to be marooned with the dog rather than a human. A more telling number: The following year, 48 percent of female respondents reported that they relied more heavily on their pets than on their partners or family members for affection.

I understand the temptation to pathologize such behavior, or at least to poke fun at it (dogs in birthday hats?), but I don't believe that dog owners are unilaterally engaged in displacement, sublimation, or rampant anthropomorphism. Nor do I see this apparent depth of attachment as a sad commentary on contemporary human affairs. This is another common view, that people turn to pets for love and affection by default, because "real" (read: human) love and affection are so hard to come by in today's fractured, isolated, alienating world. I think there is a kernel of truth to that—we live in lonely times, and dogs can go a long way toward alleviating loneliness—

but I think the more important truth has to do not with modern culture but with dogs themselves, and with the remarkable, mysterious, often highly complicated dances that go on between individual dogs and their owners.

That dance is about love. It's about attachment that's mutual and unambiguous and exceptionally private, and it's about a kind of connection that's virtually unknowable in human relationships because it's essentially wordless. It's not always a smooth and seamless dance, and it's not always easy or graceful—love can be a conflicted, uncertain experience no matter what species it involves—but it is no less valid because one of the partners happens to move on four legs.

"Love is love. I don't care if it comes from humans or from animals; it's the same feeling." Paula, a forty-seven-year-old children's book author who lives in Los Angeles with three Maltese dogs, said this to me with such simple candor that the words stuck with me for days. She continued: "When I'm feeling bad or thinking about something I can't handle, I pick up my dogs and it helps for that moment. It may not be the perfect relationship we all hope to have with a human, but it's a relationship. And love is love."

Indeed. Just this morning, I came into the house after being out for an hour or so and found Lucille nestled in a corner of the sofa, her favorite spot when I'm away. She didn't race across the room to greet me—she's sufficiently accustomed to my comings and goings by now that she no longer feels compelled to fly to the door and hurl herself onto me as though I've just returned from the battlefield—but when I came into the room and approached her, her whole body seemed to tighten into a smile: the pointed ears drew back flat, the tail thumped against the sofa cushion, the eyes gleamed, the expression took on a depth and clarity that suggested, *Happy; I am completely happy.* A friend says her dog seems to wake up every morning with a thought balloon over her head that says, *Yahoo!* That was precisely the look: *All is right with the world,* it said, *you are home.* I crouched down by the sofa to scratch her chest and coo at her, and she hooked her front paw over my forearm. She gazed at me; I gazed back.

I have had Lucille for close to three years, but moments like that, my heart fills in a way that still strikes me with its novelty and power. The colors come into sharp focus: attached, connected, joyful, *us.* I adore this dog, without apology. She has changed my life.

The Existence of Dog

Elena Sigman

MY YEAR-OLD SON, ISAIAH, SENSES AN APPROACHING DOG THE way I used to locate a sexy man in the vicinity: by shape, smell, and sound. If the dog is a block away or across the street, Isaiah's little back jolts upright, his arms extend and flap, and he tries to propel himself into the air, a dog-copter. His breath comes out in rapid sighs, eh-eh-eh. I push the stroller faster, fearful that the dog's master, oblivious to this drama, will steer his four-legged mate in another direction, and my son's heart will break. But no, we catch up with the dog, Isaiah leaps up, straining against the stroller's strap: Ahhhhyyyiii!

This instinctive attraction to dogs is the first significant way in which my child is different from me. There are many other things we do not share that might seem more important, including gender. But this strikes me as a very big difference: Isaiah loves dogs. He always has, and his love for them just keeps growing stronger.

I have never liked dogs. It's not just that I don't have a dog myself;

until a year ago, I ignored them out of existence. They didn't live in the same three dimensions that I inhabited. They occupied their own dog world, a planet of poops, pooper-scoopers, and pooper leavers; a planet of barking and biting, endless noises and secretions.

Now, suddenly, I have a child who is a dog lover, dog watcher, dog stopper, dog dogger. Dog is on Isaiah's mind even when a dog is not in sight. He is ready, prepared at all times for an encounter. He loves to get in the stroller, tolerates the belting in and sweatering up and whatever else must be gotten through in order to go outside. He longs to greet the world, knowing that the world is filled with dogs. He goes out, arms flung open and willing.

At first, I was skeptical. The passion that provoked Isaiah to crow with delight at the approach of a shaggy canine was completely foreign to me. But now, I am won over. I have witnessed the dog's heart-stopping hello, the wet nose, the long tongue meeting Isaiah's for a quick French kiss. I have smelled the various fur smells of wet, dry, oily, and hot dogs; seen a paw lifted in greeting; a tail draped provocatively across the bar of Isaiah's stroller like a cabaret singer's boa resting on a man's shoulder.

I have discovered the thrill of anticipating a dog, the excitement in the mere idea of a dog. Down any block, around any corner, exists the prospect of comfort, love, welcome, wet eyes, velvet muzzles, deep, deep fur to lose your fingers in. The possibility of nose pulls, yowps, tongue rolls, fists of fur, ear flicks, paw dances, a brush with ecstasy. Perhaps, for the dog, it's all about salt; for Isaiah, it's all about love. Love for something animated, roughly his own height, that runs to him as he runs to it. It? No, not an it. Not a he or a she either. A supreme being.

The power of Isaiah's joy is so strong I am converted. I believe in dog, and in this heightened, devotional consciousness, I, too, seek out dogs wherever I go. I am not so much a human being, woman, or mother as a dog finder. The extra three feet of height that I have over Isaiah is an adaptive trait that has evolved so I can spot dogs from farther away.

I know things now that I never knew I could know: I know that Basset Hounds have the long ears that drop like tablecloths to the ground. I know who's a mutt and who's not. I know that in a Cocker-Poodle mix, the brains come from the Poodle side of the family. The higher power is lower to the ground and walks on four feet.

Day by day, we log more encounters of the doggie kind: We pass a couple sitting on a bench, a dog sitting on his haunches between them. Isaiah's dog-alert goes off, the arms whirring up and down, the siren of delight, and the woman in this couple falls in love with my son.

"Here, want to feed Coco?" she asks. She gives Isaiah a dog biscuit. He holds it out to the dog, who licks it up. He laughs as the dog keeps licking, licking his empty hand and his wrist all the way to the elbow and beyond. Isaiah shrieks with pleasure and holds his hand out like a prize. Even after the couple leaves and the dog's tail wags away, he holds his dog-licked arm up like a trophy.

Why didn't I like dogs for so many years? Fear. And why, for so many years, didn't I want to have a baby? Fear. When I was a child, growing up in Los Angeles, a huge red dog lived behind my house. On my side of a very short chain-link fence grew some agapanthus and jade plants; on the other side was a fierce, salivating, jaw-snapping attack machine. I feared being eaten by that dog.

As an adult, I outgrew my fear of being eaten by a dog, but not the fear of being consumed. People with dogs, and babies, love them beyond measure. They are consumed with love. I never believed that I could survive such inordinate passion.

When I was a child, I never asked to have a dog. I thought that dogs were dirty, noisy, mean. I also believed that there was not enough time, energy, or space (love) in our house for children and a dog. What no one told me, until my husband mentioned it, is that love breeds more love. Love of a dog just makes room for more love. My husband can, it now appears, love me and our baby. More marvelous: I, too, love them both.

There is, of course, a developmental explanation for the phenomenon of dog love in both Isaiah's life and mine. The rationalist will point to Isaiah's growing capacity to retrieve memories over the course of his first year of life. Isaiah is not simply experiencing dog for the first time, over and over, but linking memories and fitting them into the concept of dog. Thanks to object permanence, Isaiah has, from six months, known that dogs do not cease to exist when he cannot see them.

I, too, have entered a new developmental phase, in which the ability to love a dog is connected to the experience of generativity that pulled me into parenthood. Yet science cannot explain everything. I managed to avoid my biological destiny for two decades, and might have avoided it permanently.

Instead, I have taken a leap of faith. I am listening to the part of me that says: Let's try it, let's see what happens. I feared I would not be even remotely decent as a mother. Now I am doing the thing I cannot do perfectly and loving myself a bit, loving Isaiah all the more. Why is it that I didn't see dogs before? I think I didn't know, didn't want to know, that I am like a dog, out in the world looking for scraps of food, warmth, and love, maybe some shade on a hot day.

I don't see sexy men on the street anymore. Like the invisible dogs of my past, the sexy men have been removed to some other dimension far from mine. Now I live in dogs' world, and I can sense that there is a dog out there now, already smiling, a bit of drool coming off his long tongue, waiting for me to notice and smile back.

This Dog's Life

Ann Patchett

IT HAPPENED LIKE THIS: AFTER A WALK IN THE PARK WITH A friend, I saw a young woman sitting in a car talking to a dog. Even from a distance, beneath the hard glass of the windshield, we could tell this was an exceptional animal. Never shy, I tapped on the young woman's door to ask her what kind of dog it was. We live in Nashville, where people do things like this and no one is frightened or surprised. The young woman told us the sad story: The dog, who on closer viewing was nothing but a mere slip of a puppy, had been dumped in a parking lot, rescued, and then passed among several well-intentioned young women, none of whom were allowed to have dogs in their apartments. Finally the dog had landed with the young woman in the car, who had been explaining to said dog that the day had come to look cute and find a permanent home.

The puppy was small and sleek and white. The sun came through her disproportionately large ears and showed them to be pink and translucent as a good Limoges cup held up to the light. We petted. She licked. We left the park with a dog.

I didn't think it would be this way. I thought when the time was right I would make a decision, consider breeds, look around. The truth is, I too was a woman who lived in an apartment that didn't accept dogs. But when fate knocks on the door, you'd better answer. "Let's call her Rose," my boyfriend said.

I was breathless, besotted. My puppy tucked her nose under my arm, and the hundred clever dog names I had dreamed up over a lifetime vanished. "Sure," I said. "Rose."

I was thirty-two years old that spring, and all I had ever wanted was a dog. While other girls grew up dreaming of homes and children, true love and financial security, I envisioned Shepherds and Terriers, fields of happy, bounding mutts. Part of my childhood was spent on a farm where I lived in a sea of pets: horses and chickens, a half a dozen sturdy, mouse-killing cats, rabbits, one pig, and many, many dogs, Rumble and Tumble and Sam and Lucy and especially Cuddles, who did justice to his name. Ever since that time I have believed that happiness and true adulthood would be mine at the moment of dog ownership. I would stop traveling so much. I would live someplace with a nice lawn. There would be plenty of money for vet bills.

At home, the puppy, Rose, played with balls, struggled with the stairs, and slept behind my knees while I watched in adoration. It's not that I was unhappy in what I now think of as "the dogless years," but I suspected things could be better. What I never could have imagined was how much better they would be. I had entered into my first relationship of mutual, unconditional love. I immediately found a much nicer apartment, one that allowed dogs for a ridiculously large, nonrefundable pet deposit. Since I work at home, Rose was able to spend her days in my lap, where she was most comfortable. We bonded in a way that some people looked upon as suspicious. I took Rose into stores like the rich ladies at Bergdorf's do. I took her to dinner parties. I took her to the Cape for vacation. As I have almost no ability to leave her alone, when I had to go someplace that foolishly did not allow dogs, I'd drive her across town and leave her with my grandmother. "Look at that," people said, looking at me and not Rose. "Look how badly she wants a baby."

A baby? I held up my dog for them to see, my bright, beautiful dog. "A dog," I said. "I've always wanted a dog." In truth, I have no memory of ever wanting a baby. I have never peered longingly into someone else's stroller. I have, on occasions too numerous to list, bent down on the sidewalk to rub the ears of strange dogs, to whisper to them about their limpid eyes.

"Maybe you don't even realize it," strangers said, friends said, my family said. "Clearly, you want a baby."

"Look at the way you're holding that dog," my grandmother said, "just like it's a baby."

People began to raise the issue with my boyfriend, insisting that he open his eyes to the pathetic state of maternal want I was so clearly in. Being a very accommodating fellow, he took my hand. With his other hand he rubbed Rose's ears. He loves her as blindly as I do. Her favorite game is to be draped over the back of his neck like a fox-fur stole, two legs dangling on either shoulder. "Ann," he said, "if you want to have a baby . . ."

When did the mammals get confused? Who can't look at a baby and a puppy and see that there are some very marked differences? You can't leave babies at home alone with a chew toy when you go to the movies. Babies will not shimmy under the covers to sleep on your feet when you're cold. Babies, for all their many unarguable charms, will not run with you in the park, wait by the door for you to return, and, as far as I can tell, know absolutely nothing of unconditional love.

Being a childless woman of child-bearing age, I am a walking target for people's concerned analysis. No one looks at a single man with a Labrador Retriever and says, "Will you look at the way he throws the tennis ball to that dog? Now, there's a guy who wants to have a son." A dog, after all, is man's best friend, a comrade, a buddy. But give a dog to a woman without children and people will say she is sublimating. If she says that she, in fact, doesn't want children, they will nod understandingly and say, "You just wait." For the record, I do not speak to my dog in baby talk, nor do I, when calling her, say, "Come to Mama."

"You were always my most normal friend," my friend Elizabeth told me, "until you got this dog."

While I think I would have enjoyed the company of many different dogs, I believe that the depth of my feeling for Rose in particular comes from the fact that she is, in matters of intelligence, loyalty, and affection, an extraordinary animal. In the evenings, I drive Rose across town to a large open field where people come together to let their dogs off their leashes and play. As she bounds through the grass with the Great Danes and the Bernese Mountain Dogs, I believe that there was never a dog so popular and well adjusted as mine (and yet realize at the same time that this is the height of my own particular brand of insanity). The other dog owners want to talk about identifying her lineage, perhaps in hopes that one of her cousins might be located. It is not enough for Rose to be a good dog. She must be a particular breed of dog. She has been, depending on how one holds her in the light, a small Jack Russell, a large Chihuahua, a Rat Terrier, a Fox Terrier, and a Corgi with legs. At present, she is a Portuguese Podengo, a dog that to the best of my knowledge was previously unknown in Tennessee. It is the picture she most closely resembles in our *International Encyclopedia of Dogs.* We now say things like "Where is the Podengo?" and "Has the Podengo been outside yet?" to give her a sense of heritage. In truth, she is a Parking-Lot Dog, dropped off in a snowstorm to meet her fate.

I watch the other dog owners in the park, married people and single people and people with children. The relationship each one has with his or her dog is very personal and distinct. But what I see again and again is that people are proud of their pets, proud of the way that they run, proud of how they nose around with the other dogs, proud that they are brave enough to go into the water or smart enough to stay out of it. People seem able to love their dogs with an unabashed acceptance that they rarely demonstrate with family or friends. The dogs do not disappoint them, or if they do, the owners manage to forget about it quickly. I want to learn to love like this, the way we love our dogs, with pride and enthusiasm and a complete amnesia for faults. In short, to love others the way our dogs love us.

When a dog devotes so much of herself to your happiness, it only stands to reason you would want to make that dog happy in return. Things that would seem unreasonably extravagant for yourself are nothing less than a necessity for your dog. So my boyfriend and I hired a personal trainer for Rose. We had dreams of obedience, of *sit* and *stay* and *come,* maybe a few simple tricks. She didn't really seem big enough to drag the paper inside. I was nervous about finding the right trainer and called my friend Erica for moral support, but she was too busy going on interviews to get her four-year-old son into a top Manhattan preschool to be too sympathetic. The trainer we went with was the very embodiment of dog authority figures. After a few minutes of pleasant conversation in which Rose jumped on his shoulder and licked the top of his head, he laid out the beginnings of his plan.

Number one: The dog doesn't get on the furniture.

We blinked. We smiled nervously. "But she likes the furniture," we said. "We like her on the furniture."

He explained to us the basic principles of dog training. She has to learn to listen. She must learn parameters and the concept of no. He tied a piece of cotton rope to her collar and demonstrated how we were to yank her off the sofa cushion with a sharp tug. Our dog went flying through the air. She looked up at us from the floor, more bewildered than offended. "She doesn't sleep with you, does she?" the trainer asked.

"Sure," I said, reaching down to rub her neck reassuringly. She slept under the covers, her head on my pillow, her muzzle on my shoulder. "What's the point of having a twelve-pound dog if she doesn't sleep with you?"

He made a note in a folder. "You'll have to stop that."

I considered this for all of five seconds. "No," I said. "I'll do anything else, but the dog sleeps with me."

After some back-and-forth on this subject, he relented, making it clear that it was against his better judgment. For the duration of the ten-week program, either I sat on the floor with Rose or we stayed in bed. We celebrated graduation by letting her back up on the couch.

I went to see my friend Warren, who, handily, is also a psychologist, to ask him if he thought things had gotten out of hand. Maybe I have a obsessive-compulsive disorder concerning my dog.

"You have to be doing something to be obsessive-compulsive," he said. "Are you washing her all the time? Or do you think about washing her all the time?"

I shook my head.

"It could be codependency, then. Animals are by nature very codependent."

I wasn't sure I liked this. Codependency felt too trendy. Warren's sixteen-year-old daughter, Kate, came in, and I asked her if she wanted to see the studio portraits I had taken of Rose for my Christmas cards. She studied the pictures from my wallet for a minute and then handed them back to me. "Gee," she said, "you really want to have a baby, don't you?"

I went home to my dog. I rubbed her pink stomach until we were both sleepy. We've had Rose a year now, and there has never been a cold and rainy night when I've resented having to take her outside. I have never wished I didn't have a dog, while she sniffed at each individual blade of grass, even as my hands were freezing up around the leash. I imagine there are people out there who got a dog when what they wanted was a baby, but I wonder if there aren't other people who had a baby when all they really needed was a dog.

Mutts

Maxine Kumin

WHEN I COME OUT OF THE GROCERY STORE, OF COURSE they've both jumped into the front. The white pseudo–German Shepherd, betrayed by his upwardly curling tail and misaligned biscuit-colored eyes, is in the driver's seat. The mostly German Shepherd with an all-black muzzle and a Collie's white vest sits at attention in the passenger seat. Staring straight ahead, both coconspirators ignore me.

"You're not driving," I always say to them. "Get in the back!" After I say it a second time, they do.

"What interesting-looking dogs!" people say if they pass by during these discussions. "What breed are they?"

"Generic farm dogs," I tell them. If my husband's answering, he says it more emphatically: "They're just a couple of mutts."

Both of them are foundlings. Josh, the white one, came to us first, while our last Dalmatian was still alive. He arrived as a four-month-old puppy, rescued by our new neighbors from a bad situation in which he was always confined, either penned or chained, and little handled. Our neighbors couldn't house him because they were already sharing close quarters with two teenagers, four cats, two dogs, and three birds, but it was summer and he had the run of their barn.

When he first came up the hill half a mile to live with us that fall, he made daily forays back to his Other Home. After he saw the girls off to school in the morning, he returned with something in his mouth: a halter, a leg wrap, a curry, or a brush. Often, a barn boot from the back stoop. We diligently returned each of the items at the end of the day. Gradually, the girls developed stricter barn-keeping habits and reduced the number of articles available for Josh to deliver.

Deprived of equine objets d'art, he learned to navigate the steep staircase up to a storage area in the barn loft and began to pilfer far more ambitious items. A bag of curlers, a baby doll, some winter socks. His most inspired retrieval was a pair of ice skates, tied together by their laces, which he laboriously fetched up the hill ten feet or so at a time, pausing in between to sit down and catch his breath.

Eventually, a door was installed at the top of the stairs and Josh slowly unlearned his foraging habits. For several months, though, he seemed to feel it his duty to trot downhill to see the scholars off to classes. Sometimes Gus, our aging Dalmatian, went with him, but for the most part he found it a long haul down and up and preferred to stay at the top, overseeing Josh's excursion.

Gus tolerated the newcomer with surprising good grace, given his tendency toward lassitude and the puppy's toward perpetual motion. Josh wanted to wrestle constantly. Neither his play growls and mock attacks nor his nonstop nipping and chewing seemed to bother Gus very much; the latter was a deeply jowled and wrinkly fellow with an ample supply of loose flesh. Sometimes we would see the two of them racing downhill, the younger one's teeth fastened into Gus's cheek or neck, his puppy feet hardly touching the ground as they sped off. But when Gus's arthritis made it impossible for him to climb the stairs to sleep on the rug at the foot of our bed, Josh, who had happily shared that spot, retraced his steps to sleep beside him on the sheepskin rug in front of the woodstove.

We were down to one dog for several months after Gus died. Neither of us quite wanted to begin again with a new puppy. Maybe one dog was enough, we told each other. Josh was so easy to live with. He stayed faithfully on the property even when we drove off to do errands. He got along well with the horses and he coexisted with the sheep. He had been around through a couple of foalings so we knew he could be trusted around equine newborns as well.

At the end of April I went to New York City to a literary awards ceremony. An editor I knew only slightly was, according to the seating plan, scheduled to join our table. Since he was nowhere to be found, eventually the proceedings got under way without him. An hour later, he and his wife burst wild-eyed on the scene.

They had a harrowing tale to relate. Driving down the West Side Highway from Riverdale, they had caught sight of an emaciated-looking young dog dodging traffic, narrowly escaping sudden death several times under their horrified gaze as drivers swerved, their brakes screeching. Horns honked on all sides out of frustration. Stanley pulled the car over, leapt out, ripping his belt out of its belt loops as he ran, and took off in pursuit of the dog. At that point, the terrified creature hurdled the median divider and ran into the jaws of oncoming traffic. Somehow, Stanley managed to overtake him, downed him with a flying tackle, and collared him with the belt.

He and his wife, Jane, wrestled this apparition into the backseat of their station wagon. En route to the Poetry Society dinner at Gramercy Park, they stopped to buy some bottled water and a can of dog food and, using the widemouthed lid of a thermos, offered these alternately to their captive. Although quivering with apprehension, he was both hungry and thirsty. After that, he was willing to be patted and soothed and only whimpered briefly when they left him in the car.

When the speeches were over, several of us trooped down the block to where Stanley had providentially acquired a parking space. The pup was skeletal, all right, but he didn't shrink from the several pairs of hands that reached in to feel his head and neck. Stanley wasn't sure what he would do with him. He was afraid they wouldn't be able to socialize him with their aging male dog, but he hoped his vet could find a proper home.

I allowed as how we might try him in New Hampshire.

Stanley beamed.

The little audience assembled around the station wagon breathed its approval. I could feel myself being elevated to sainthood.

Hastily, I amended: "Of course, it depends on whether Victor agrees."

Everyone nodded solemnly. Those who knew my husband personally knew he was a soft touch. Hadn't he already taken in a couple of waif dogs and a series of abused horses? On the other hand, how many times can you go to the well before it runs dry?

When he hears *this* story, I said to myself, he won't be able to resist.

A week later, a newly inoculated, deloused, dewormed, bathed, and somewhat less disreputable-looking dog arrived with Stanley and Jane at our farm, along with a list of his immunizations, some feeding instructions, and thirty pounds of a very high-protein kibble. The New York vet had pronounced him dehydrated, malnourished, and suffering from exposure. He thought the dog was possibly a year old. Since he had virtually no toenails, the vet concluded that he had probably been out on the streets most of his life.

"Born behind a garbage can," Victor said, after introductions had taken place. "And nourished by one, from the looks of it."

It was true that the entire framework of the dog was still visible. You could see where each rib depended from the shelf of backbone. The head seemed strangely knobby, too, the face drawn almost into a grimace. And the dog's chest was tiny, in proportion to his body and leg length, most likely the result of his chronic malnutrition.

Positively portly by contrast, Josh was instantly agreeably disposed toward the newcomer. They rolled around amiably together, pretending war over the possession of a stick, then strutted around sharing it.

"Well, what do you think?" Stanley asked.

"It'll take quite a while to fatten him up," Victor said.

"Meanwhile, how about lunch?" I suggested neutrally. It looked as though the dog would stay.

A little controversy arose between husband and wife over the conferring of a name. Victor wanted to call the dog Bernstein, in honor of the composer of *West Side Story.* I wanted to name him Rilke, after the visionary German poet, who had also been sustained by angels.

I pointed out that Victor had named the barn cats Abra and Cadabra, after I had wanted to call them Emily and Lavinia.

"That was ten years ago."

"Well, he *is* mostly German Shepherd," Jane said. "And we *did* bring him along to a Poetry Society dinner."

No further protest was lodged, but I must confess that Rilke tried us sorely over the ensuing several months. An enthusiastic digger, he totally demolished my perennial bed, which used to butt up against a stone wall. Small things that lived in that wall were harried from their homes by Rilke.

House etiquette was unknown to him, as was the concept of "house." On the rare occasions that we left him behind, he had to be sequestered in the back hall because he demolished everything in sight in his outrage and terror. Happily, he is now housebroken, and he does not howl or act out when we leave him.

He must have learned his bird-stalking skills in quest of pigeons in Manhattan. Here in New Hampshire he crouches like a panther and advances stealthily on unsuspecting ground doves, a species that has grown fat and abundant hereabouts, crowding chickadees and nuthatches from the feeders to dine on black-oil sunflower seeds. He is so adept at catching mice and an occasional red squirrel that one wonders if he honed this skill on urban *Rattus rattus.*

Chipmunks, however, are just a hair too quick for him. So are the cats, with whom he seems to have an agreement. Some days they agree to be chased and some days they stand their ground, hissing. In the latter case, Rilke turns aside, pretending not to be interested. But snakes drive him wild. He stands above them baring his teeth hysterically, then makes little feints and jabs as they coil and hiss in bewilderment.

We have an abundance of garden and black snakes, several of which have always traveled freely into and out of the crawl space that extends under the back part of our house. In his zeal to get at one, Rilke excavated so frenetically under the foundation that he managed to rip away the phone line as well. "Can't imagine how this happened," said the repairman, installing a new one. We couldn't either, we said.

Given his fierce demeanor, I was worried how Rilke would behave with a new foal. Or with the sheep, for that matter; a little band of ewes comes to us every May when it is time to wean their lambs. To my surprise, he proved to be a model of decorum on both counts. He is equally trustworthy with small children, putting up with a lot of investigatory poking and grabbing.

On the downside, he cannot resist rolling in fresh manure or dead animals; apparently they smell the same to him. He leaps in any body of water, be it river, pond, or puddle, quenching his thirst as he fords the hazard. Muddy wallows are his favorites, but he quivers with terror when you tie him to the barn in order to give him a bath. An indefatigable explorer, he bounds over stone walls, races through scrub growth, flies across pastures, and returns matted with clumps of burrs, which have to be picked out while he squirms and carries on. He still, alas, chases pickup trucks unless you are on the site rattling the chain you are ready to throw at him. And an unchaperoned horse, allowed to walk down alone from the upper pasture to the paddock and thence into the barn, produces the same reaction.

Victor and Rilke have gone to dog school for nine sessions. The instructor—the chain was her idea—says there is nothing more she can teach him and that it will be another six months before he is dependable. Dependability means minding a command even when distracted, or when in the presence of other dogs, or especially when you don't want to.

You have to practice a lot to become dependable, so we have thirty-minute sit-stays and several down-ups. Josh, a graduate of the same course, went along on a few of Rilke's sessions, just for a refresher.

Rilke outweighs Josh now, and he often plays too rough. Whenever I see him wrestle Josh to the ground, grabbing him by his neck hairs, I think of Josh as a puppy tormenting Gus. By non-poets, this is called poetic justice. This poet calls it divine intervention by the Great Overdog, the one who placed him in Stanley's path and ultimately delivered him to us.

The New Girl

Margaret Cho

IT WAS PRETTY MUCH LIKE AN IMPULSE BUY, AS IF THE DOG were Tic Tacs or a lighter or one of those coupons offering to give the money to charity in exchange for your guilt and your cash. I responded to the e-mail describing the urgency of her situation, and in a flash she was here. At some point I had planned on getting a sister for Ralph, my four-and-a-half-year-old Shepherd mix, but her rescuer was so efficient that "at some point" became "right now." I didn't even have time to plan a neutral area where I could let the dogs get acquainted before taking them both home. The new girl arrived in a station wagon in the driveway, practically minutes after I had said "yes." She was faster than Domino's.

She didn't want to get out of the car at first. Ralph stood nearby on his leash, threatened and curious. He's a soft sort, doesn't get mad easily, but he was cross that day; his title of Lord of the Manor was about to be usurped. The nice lady rescuer carried the new girl out of the car. She had her tail between her legs and was hunched in a ball. She had been advertised as an Australian Shepherd mix; she didn't look at all like an Australian Shepherd, but she definitely looked like a mix. She was a short, skinny mutt, with short blond hair and a long white stripe down her muzzle. Her face was elegantly deerlike, when she wasn't growling at Ralph. I named her right then: Bronwyn Claire Fyfe Benowith-Cho. Bronwyn after a car I once owned, Claire and Fyfe, just because, and Benowith-Cho, my boyfriend Nick's mother's maiden name and my last name combined.

After an initial tussle, Bronwyn and Ralph didn't seem too perturbed with each other so I bid adieu to the nice lady rescuer and took my new family up to the house. Ralph looked at me with a look conveying what I can only interpret as betrayal. "Mummy. How could you?! I thought I was to be sole heir to the throne!" I reminded him that I had never promised him that he would inherit anything, and that there was no throne to begin with. He harrumphed and licked himself. Then Ralph proceeded to show Bronwyn all the things in the house that were his. "This is my ball! Don't play with it! That is my couch! Don't sit on it! That is my food bowl. That is my food bowl, too. Don't drink my water. You!!! Who are you?!!!"

I walked around them as Ralph continued his tour of "What's mine," picking up dusty toys he hadn't touched in months if she showed any interest in them. I picked up Bronwyn and sat her on my lap. She leaned her head down onto my chest so that she could pull in closer. Her body was warm and muscular and smelled dirty like street dog. She curled up in a tight circle as Ralph salivated with jealousy and tried to get on my lap, too. We three sat on the couch as the two battled it out to see who could get their head higher. Here was my new family.

Nick and I decided to get Bronwyn spayed and vaccinated straightaway, which I regretted as soon as she came back from the vet, dull-eyed and comatose. She laid her small blond body on Ralph's bed and didn't move for many hours. After an initial fit of entitlement, Ralph went and looked at his sister, his face a sorrowful map of genuine concern. He was worried about her! Either that or he was seriously mourning the loss of his bed. I was seriously mourning the loss of the upholstery on my couch, as the ailing Bronwyn, unable to get up and relieve herself in the backyard ("Those are my bushes!"), went all over the furniture instead. Seeing her so sick and confused made me forgive her instantly. I wondered how she must have felt.

Picked up off the street by a kindly stranger, suddenly thrust into a home with another dog who was intent on showing her that he was very comfortable being an only child, then just as suddenly sent off to the vet overnight to have her reproductive organs removed and her body shot up with all sorts of drugs. And then back to the confusing and scary new home, with a new mommy and daddy who seemed nice, but who knew? I wished there was a way to reassure her, to tell her that everything now was going to be okay. That she had landed in an extremely good place, and that time would erase all the sadness and pain she had already seen. I imagine that she had as many bad memories as she had scars on her body. Even though she was fairly young, she looked as if she had fought many battles, and lost more than once. She had a long scar that trailed down the side of her head, and telltale furless black lines all over her legs. I examined her as she lay in Ralph's bed. She didn't move at all, except for her tail, which still wagged furiously every time I approached. Ralph's bed was big enough for me and her to curl up in, so I held her and looked at her surgery scar, and made her a silent vow that if I could help it, it would be the last scar she'd ever get.

Bronwyn recovered quickly, and Ralph just decided to ignore her in hopes that she just might go away. Our initial attempts to engage her in play were unsuccessful. When offered a ball, Bronwyn would tilt her little Bambi face to one side as if she had no idea what it was. We soon realized, that in her brief and sad-up-until-now life, she had never played. We had to teach her how by showing immense interest in the ball, then tossing it back and forth between us, then offering it to her again. Ralph, a hopeless ball addict, was less than cooperative, stealing the ball and leaving us without a teaching implement. I began to worry that he might be seriously damaged by the sibling rivalry. I tried to give him more love and assurance that he was still my darling prince, just that now he might have to share his kingdom with a new princess, and that he would thank me later. Then I started to worry that Bronwyn would get a complex about not being fully accepted into her new home because I was making such a fuss over Ralph. All of a sudden, Nick started to whine about me paying more attention to the dogs than him. Pretty soon I was employing my hands, feet, lips, arms—everything, making sure that everyone got plenty of hugs and kisses and pats and rubs. I was a love machine, in full operation—24/7.

Bronwyn learned to play very quickly, and soon surpassed Ralph in the

"This is mine, but you can bite it for a second—NO—it's MINE!" game. They ran in fast circles around the yard, Ralph often giving up and standing confused as Bronwyn ran around him. She liked being outside much more than he did. He would go out, play a bit, do his business, then run back into the house to watch TV. Bronwyn would toss her toys up into the air and catch them, until she was so tired she'd start missing. Then she'd sunbathe sensuously on the doormat, brown eyes half closed, body hot from the rays, like a jet-set heiress on the white-sand beach in Ibiza. I'd come out and rub her warm fur as she turned herself over for more. I could see she was getting accustomed to the good life.

Ralph had given up his possessiveness over all the things in the house at dog level. Sharing did not come naturally to him, but I could see he was making an effort to do so. When I saw them both lying in his bed, rolled up into little dog doughnuts, I screamed because they looked so cute. They woke up and looked at me, annoyed, and went back to sleep with a sigh.

Bronwyn started to take on more and more dog responsibilities around the house. She initiated most of the play, nap times, pee and poo schedules. When she wanted to go, she'd fix Ralph in her "boss eyes" and walk over to the door. He'd follow soon after and then they'd both stare at me until I got the message.

Being so used to Nick and Ralph's male energy, it was interesting to have a girl around the house. Bronwyn stuck to me like glue, sitting quietly in the kitchen as I did my chores, lying patiently on the bathroom rug while I took a shower. She was like my daughter, intent on brushing up on her mommy skills. She made me want to be more feminine. I donned an apron and she shed her blond hair all over it.

I catch her staring at me with intense love and trust. When my eyes meet hers, her tail starts to wag excitedly, but she dares not move her body in fear of spoiling the moment. I look in her brown, limitless eyes, and I wonder what pain she has endured, the bad memories that make her cower whenever Nick and I raise our voices above a conversational level. When she snuggles close, with her muzzle in my neck, I wonder if I can erase that pain with my rigorous program of love and play.

I lie on my burgundy velvet couch, smelly with dog and hair everywhere, with Ralph and Bronwyn fighting for the curved space behind my legs or the soft pad of my belly, and I realize that I am happier than I have ever been.

Brave and Noble Is the Preschool Dog

Susan Straight

I NEVER HAD A DOG. I GREW UP IN A CAT HOUSEHOLD, WITH A mother who disliked dogs for their digging and mess and noise. I can't blame her, as we were five kids who had lizards, hamsters, parakeets, fish, and always, two or three cats.

But I wanted a dog so badly! I wanted a red Cocker Spaniel like Rusty, the fictional dog featured in novels I read again and again. I dreamed of a brave dog like Rusty, who swam into choppy ocean waves to rescue a boy, who sensed that a train was about to crash, who bounded into fields to find a lost girl. His coat was shiny and his eyes alert, and he was a hero.

At twelve, I brought home a stray while my parents were on vacation, knowing our elderly babysitter wouldn't notice. She didn't. My mother did, on her return, and so the dog went to live at my friend's house three streets away. I visited, but it wasn't the same.

When I married my childhood sweetheart, I knew he didn't want a dog, as he'd been raised with a black Cockapoo who hated everyone under twenty, and demonstrated it by biting them. We bought a house on a busy four-lane avenue, a former farmhouse with a big yard, and we had three kids.

Our first daughter was not a dog lover, as she'd been nipped on the hand by a boisterous Old English Sheepdog when she was two, and shortly afterward nipped on the face by an ill-tempered Sheltie down the block. Gaila likes rabbits. Our second daughter was not a dog lover, because she is obsessed with insects and wants to be an entomologist. Delphine collects bugs.

But our third daughter, Rosette, said "Dog" before she said "Daddy." She is a kindred spirit, as they say. Our neighbor, who baby-sat her twice a week when I went to work, got a yellow Labrador puppy named Chelsea days after Rosette was born, and they slept together on the bed, Rosette with her fist curled around Chelsea's felt-soft ear and her thumb in her mouth.

Her father and I divorced when she was only one, and Rosette began asking for a dog as soon as she could form sentences. When she was two, we took a trip to New York, just Rosette and I, and she met every dog in Gramercy Park, where we were staying. By the second day she was calling them by name, those city dogs out on their walks, and we had to eat in restaurants with sidewalk tables so we could visit her canine friends, who truly seemed to recognize the smell of her chubby crumb-laden hand.

I tried to prepare: I bought books about puppies and their care, about puppies walking through meadows and cavorting with other baby animals. Rosette had other ideas: "Yellow Labrador, Irish Setter, Border Collie, Basset Hound, Beagle." She got a dog breed book and we had to study their physical characteristics and temperaments. She was three then. In Prescott, Arizona, she identified King Charles Spaniels after an owner explained how rare the breed was, and she has remembered them since.

Having a child who loved dogs with this kind of passion was fascinating, but also intimidating. I knew we couldn't get a puppy, as people had warned that work and school would take us away for too long. Having cried for hours over lost or stray dogs on our avenue, Rosette wanted to adopt someone from the Humane Society. So in November of that year, we walked the gauntlet of cages and barking, and wary or pleading eyes.

Rosette went immediately to the shaggy black Spaniel named Teddy, who looked so depressed he barely ambled out to the chain-link. The big test was whether a dog could handle us as a family, so I'd brought all my girls and two of their small friends, along with one of our caged rabbits. The shelter assistant brought Teddy to us in the meeting area. He walked over to Rosette, licked her face, and sat beside her. He looked at the other girls as if to say, "Yeah, I see you." He looked at the rabbit as if to say, "Yeah, you're in a cage."

Teddy had been found in a neighboring city, with a slight limp and a bruised hip that indicated someone had been kicking him. He'd already been adopted once, but was returned by the childless couple who'd kept him in an apartment for up to ten hours at a time, because he urinated inside.

He peed once inside our house, the first day, but never again. He waited patiently for Rosette to let him outside, where she fed him, picked up his poop, and brushed him. Solemnly, she repeated to me, "I made a promise and I am keeping it."

Teddy is a classic shelter dog, in that he will never have had enough to eat. That first week, he ate a cake, plastic wrap and all, that had been left on the coffee table, and gobbled up a dropped Advil and a Flintstones multivitamin when I cleaned out my backpack. We stayed with him for hours, worried, while he waited for us to drop something else.

He wasn't a Cocker Spaniel, Rosette assured me, paging through one of her dog breed books until she found him. Teddy had shorter, ragged ears, a taller build, a longer nose. He was a Field Spaniel, Rosette said.

I studied him those first months, wondering about his bravery and nobility. Would he have the chance to save someone, like Rusty, my heroic red Cocker? When I lifted Rosette into the air and twirled her, he ran over and put a paw on her leg to make me put her down. If I tickled her, he wedged his head between us, never growling, but looking sternly at me, as if to say I should know better. Soon, when older sisters or friends were playing rough, Rosette would call, "Teddy!" and with applications of his stinky breath and head butts, he would make them leave her alone. Once, as an experiment, I tackled Gaila, who is my size, and tickled her. Teddy just watched, slightly bored.

Teddy's job was to save Rosette's spirit. She has dog love threading through her veins from some ancestor, dog love wound tightly around her heart like the branching arteries displayed in her encyclopedia. Unlike her sisters, she never really had a father who lived in our house. Teddy was hers alone. She slept in his dog bed, and he slept on her small fold-out couch in the living room. He walked her to preschool with me every day, and her class,

The Cute Kittens, mobbed him. He never barked or growled or even moved away. In his second week with us, Teddy sat in the middle of a circle of them, thirteen three-year-olds, and Rosette talked about him. Then he ate thirteen dog biscuits, to please everyone, and didn't throw up. He submitted to inspections and hard head pats and screaming. His eyes never left Rosette. I realized the extent of Teddy's nobility, and I was willing to accept his neediness.

Because now, four years later, he is a needy dog. He has no other dog friends, though we've tried repeatedly. Not even Chelsea, who he attacks along with her sister Hannah, another yellow Lab. Teddy will never accept another canine, even on the sidewalk for casual conversation, and he's injured himself repeatedly because his version of bravery makes him guard our fenced yard with blind ferocity. He has been bitten on the nose, while barking through the fence, by neighbors' dogs, and has hurt his leg chasing Chows and even Pit Bulls. Nearly every house in our neighborhood has at least two dogs, but Teddy will not even wag at them. Two dogs in my brother's tough pack, which runs in a nearby orange grove, like to visit us: We tried to acclimate Teddy to Soot and Charcoal on the front porch, which was fine until Rosette came banging out of the screen door to see them. Teddy promptly tried to take a chunk out of Soot's back leg.

Last summer, he destroyed a rear anterior cruciate ligament, chasing down passing dogs like an aging football player. I spent a thousand dollars on your good leg, I told him, when we took him for surgery. Two days in the animal hospital, along with anesthesia, left him altered, so anxious that he has never been the same since. His new ligament works fine, but he won't let me leave a room, blocking the doorway or the back of my chair with his body, in case he's abandoned again. His marked resemblance to Richard Nixon on an unhappy day has deepened. Teddy stares at me in the morning, jowly and melancholic because it's hot, or cold, or windy, or because I was asleep.

He hates it when we leave, and can't be left alone for even five minutes without trying to dig out or jump the fence. What with school and sports and errands, by the time we are done for the day, he is beside himself. And that's just when I usually have six or seven girls here for homework or basketball: Teddy sits under the basket, or sits on their papers, or tries to lie on my feet while I am at the stove, not a happy camper myself by that point in the afternoon.

I wanted a brave, independent dog who would keep out the marauding cats trying to kill the rabbits, who would bark at strange men, rather than inspecting them for Del Taco burritos and hot sauce. I realize we are not drowning in the ocean or lost in a field, but some Rusty-like nobility of demeanor would help, rather than the baleful and incredulous eyes that say to me, "You're trying to get to the cupboard for macaroni and cheese again, and I find that incredibly irritating when I am trying to get comfortable on your instep." When we tell him to go lie down, Teddy moves five inches, and his look combines glare and guilt in a way that's so presidential that I have to laugh.

A neighbor takes care of him when we go to work or on vacation, since Teddy is terminally anxious now. This summer Rosette turned seven, and on an East Coast trip she brought her dog breed book to identify new friends. She learned the intricacies of Sheltie breeding, studying the double merle; she walked a Jack Russell Terrier, and worried about the breathing of a black Lab with a lung tumor. But the only time she cried was when she missed Teddy. Not her father, or grandparents, or friends. Only her dog.

I have watched her, all these years. No one else feeds or walks Teddy, or picks up his poop, unless Rosette is sick. She doesn't always remember her homework, and plays no sports, preferring to amble around with her dog. I have had to learn patience from both of them, since Rosette is known as my Velcro child for her clinginess, and Teddy is called "the neediest dog on the planet" by our bemused neighbors, with their rough, independent German Shepherds and Rottweilers. But I realize, looking around at my house with its pack of girls, all female animals with hierarchies and assigned spaces and conflicting personalities, that Teddy picked the right place.

He stares at me now, while I write, daring me to move a muscle, draped across the doorway. I am not ashamed to admit that I am used to chaos and company, and when my kids are gone, I need someone else in the house. It helps that I'm accustomed to company that regards me censoriously if I am not doing something useful, like laundry, dishes, walking, dropping crumbs, or retrieving dog biscuits. This is the home of needy short animals, and Teddy fits in perfectly, bravely licking up stray puddles of toxic-blue Otter Pops, surviving the inexpert eye pokes associated with brushing by school friends who have never had a dog, and lying with one eye open under the mulberry tree where Rosette reads, waiting for her to come down so he can rescue her with his patience and devotion.

Blind Date

Stephen Kuusisto

I WALK BLINDFOLDED UP CAYUGA STREET IN DOWNTOWN Ithaca on a wet February morning. My cane sweeps the path, and my torso dips forward as if I'm wearing a bag of bird shot around my neck. But I move along safely and with reasonable effectiveness. Dave See and Mike Dillon follow behind but at some distance. I feel like Orpheus climbing out of Hades: I want to turn around and ask how it's going, but the rules are firm, and I walk with a plodding diligence, stepping in puddles, never quite knowing when to stop.

After the blindfold walk, Dave hands me a guide dog's harness. "I'm going to be your guide dog," he says. "My name is Juno."

I am to grasp the handle of the harness while Dave holds the front.

"I want you to lift the handle and say, 'Juno, forward!' and as we move, I want you to trust Juno's every step. Follow the harness. Put your trust in your dog guide."

Dave begins to pull, and I follow. He draws me around a pothole, and I follow. We arrive at a curb, and he stops, and I say, "Good dog!"

with a sweetened intonation that will prove important when I am paired with a real dog.

Trust is silent as the windmill. Life with a dog will begin my alchemical transformation in blindness, *la vita nuova.* The harness will unite us in confidence and guardianship. Working with Dave does not yet suggest this.

Back at my apartment he gives me a boot camp spiel about sacrifice, hard work, long hours, life with a roommate, the criticism of trainers, the possibility that I might not get a dog at all.

He explains the daily routine. Every morning I'll be awakened by a loudspeaker at six A.M. I must take the dog outside, then bring her in, feed her, and take her back out again. I'll have a half hour to shave and shower before breakfast. Immediately after the eggs and coffee I'll have an obedience class with my dog and a short lecture about dog handling. Then I'll board a bus for a day of field work—different traffic situations in the company of a trainer. My dog will already know what to do, and my job will be to learn how to work beside her. At the end of the day, the dog must be fed and walked again. Then there's dinner and an evening lecture. I'm to be in bed by ten P.M.—a good night's sleep is necessary. The whole process begins again the next day—and for twenty-five days after that.

Dave's descriptive challenge moves me to fortitude. I will be one of the ones to survive the canine kibbutz and emerge with a companion. I am absolutely convinced. Nothing can induce me to turn back now.

The next morning we gather in the courtyard to work with the trainers who guide us around the grounds. Each trainer has four students. Each holds a leather harness and plays the part of a guide dog. We practice commands for sitting the dogs, making them stay; we snap the training collar so the trainers can see how strong we are. Out in the kennels are dozens of fully trained guide dogs, waiting to be carefully chosen for each one of us.

Each successful team has a family behind it who actually raised the dog. Imagine loving an animal for over a year and then one morning you get up and put it into a crate and drive it to the airport and send it to the guide dog school. And as you're driving home past the fast food restaurants and shopping malls, you're crying. This dog has been everywhere with you: gone to work with you, gone to the high school football game.

Now what should you hope for?

You're sitting at a stoplight, the tears streaming down your cheeks.

You know there's a chance that the dog won't make it. Maybe this dog will come home again! Should you dare to hope for such a thing? Is it all right to think this—at least in private?

Imagine that your minivan still has a blanket on the floor. The car still has some prized dog hair and a faint, wet dog smell.

It's okay to hope the dog comes home. Isn't it?

Alas for you, there is a form of goodness that Dante described as "ardor." It's a spiritual practice, a gift to the world that is in turn a part of eternity.

Ardor.

If you're a blind man or woman, you may meet the people who raised your dog. You may form a bond, become a kind of extended family. Maybe not. Perhaps you might be shy, or your sense of maintaining a personal connection with your guide dog is necessarily a private thing. But no matter how you live, you have learned something about ardor.

There is no analogy to getting a guide dog. Holding the leather-and-metal harness and walking with Lynne Robertson, I feel as if my hands have been waiting for this—as if I've touched something central in the life of an ancestor. The sureness of the handle is like picking up the first chestnut all over again. I know Lynne is guiding me safely around the grounds. She's talking to me as we go.

"Your dog will also talk with you," she says as though she's reading my mind. "Really, the dog's body language and the information you'll receive from the position of the harness will be very important."

I sense that the Guiding Eyes training process is a ritual. First the novice commands an imaginary dog. Then we hold empty harnesses, like farmers who have sold their oxen. Finally after two days of observation, the trainers repair to a secret location to matchmake the students with their future dogs.

I tell Lynne that I need a dog who will be a cheerful frequent flyer—one who can handle either Manhattan or New Hampshire's woods.

I've taken the slow way to blindness, resisting it like a suspicious skater who fears the river. But no one here wastes any time explaining how they can't see, or how they can see a little. All the trainers are knowledgeable about the many types of blindness. Even the housekeeping staff has been through in-service training and has tried on occluding spectacles that replicate the varieties of vision loss. Everyone who works here has walked the building and grounds repeatedly under the conditions of blindness.

Imagine an institution that is really built on trust!

I drink Pepsi and talk long into the night with Hank. We both want to go places. We both have a planet hunger.

Because Hank had a sighted adolescence, he tells me about driving, wild nights on the back roads of North Carolina. Every now and then he lets out a confidential laugh, and I know he's remembering something hot. He's a native storyteller.

I tell him about life without driving, about trying to fit in and not succeeding.

We talk about Carolina.

We talk about motorcycles.

We get hardly any sleep.

It's dog day!

Hank is up at six A.M. as excited as a child on Christmas morning—he's talking on the phone, checking out the weather, doing a wild inventory of life—absorbing whatever happens to be at hand. It's been snowing hard; now it's sleeting. A plane has skidded off the runway at LaGuardia—twenty-four people were injured. Hank guesses we won't be going to town today. Dogs are on the horizon. It's dog day. Hank is like Eisenhower before the Normandy invasion—every nuance of weather is central.

Dog day. Showers and water pipes and doors slamming all over the building long before the regulation wake-up call.

The trainers assemble us, and one by one we're told the name and gender of our dog. I'm told that my dog is Corky, a female yellow Labrador Retriever. Then we're sent back to our rooms, each of us filled with suspense, each wondering about the new life to come, a life where the circle of blindness will be entered by a smart and reliable animal. How large will my dog be? Will she like me? How long will the bonding take? Can I trust my life to this heretofore imaginary creature?

The training staff knows each dog as an individual. Every dog has characteristics that will make a good match with a student.

Some dogs are fast, others slow. Some are temperamentally suited for working in the city, while others might do well in urban situations as occasional tourists but really shine in small-town settings. Guiding Eyes has dogs that are especially suited for working with human partners who have multiple disabilities. These dogs are taught to compensate for balance problems, for example, by adjusting their gait. Some dogs are trained to help people who are blind and deaf—they have a good command of hand signals. The entire kennel is full of guide dogs who individually possess special skills.

Waiting for the dog call is unlike any experience I've ever known. I find myself alone in my room revisiting periods of my life. I'm on the esplanade in Helsinki bumping into strangers, though I'm not drunk. I'm climbing up a flight of stairs in the New York subway system. Am I with my sister? Or alone? I'm entering a harbor in Greece, and Bettina is exulting about the temple on the hillside, and the sunset, and I see none of it. I want to leave images like these behind. These last moments, predog, defy description. I know that in the next few hours my life will be forever changed.

Suddenly the loudspeaker crackles, and my name is called. Lynne Robertson brings me into a special lounge with curtained doors at the far end. I sit in a straight-backed chair, and Rick Connell, the supervising trainer, hands me a brand-new leash.

"When Corky comes in, she's going to be very excited, and she'll probably jump all over you. Just take a little time to be your silly self with her. After you've had a few minutes, you can put the leash on and heel her back to your room." Lynne Robertson, the trainer who will work with me, tells me to call, "Corky."

There's a breeze from the far end of the room. The sliding doors open, and I can hear the curtains billowing. When I call Corky's name, my voice catches. I have to call her twice. I hear a sound like the snorting of a horse, and the musical dog tags, and then she's on top of me, her paws on my knees, her immense head straight in my face. I'm unprepared for the speed of it. This dog is kissing me. Her tail is banging like a rope. Tears are literally running down my face. She's a twenty-five-thousand-dollar dog, intelligent and superbly trained. But she's been kept in a kennel in advance of our meeting; her own loneliness has been honed.

I have the sensation that Corky is genuinely observing me, but the gaze is more encompassing than that of a pet dog. She seems to be absorbing me.

Janet Surman, a trainer, says suddenly, "Corky's in love."

I snap on Corky's leash, and we walk together for the first time back to our room.

It's the definitive blind date!

Corky is absolutely wild with excitement, and at eighty pounds, she's powerful. I think suddenly that I've been given a fake dog, or that Corky is in fact so astute that she's reflecting my own nervousness. Now she's standing over me nibbling my nose. Then she puts her front paws on my shoulders and starts on the rest of my face. Her tail knocks things off a chair.

Words are loose inside me, the lines from Wallace Stevens: "The angel flew round in the garden/The garden flew round with the clouds . . ."

Corky and I are romping like William Blake's emancipated chimney sweeps, freed from their soot and sporting in the air.

Soon I lie down beside her on the floor and begin talking.

"I tell you what, Cork: Let's you and me take care of each other. Let's go places! How do you like that idea?"

Tail wag.

"We'll use our common head!"

Tail wag.

"Your ears are so soft, they have no analogy."

"Hey, Cork: I bet you like to swim. We're going to New Hampshire in two months."

The tail.

By now my voice is a running wave.

This really is a date. We're learning about each other. We go outside, and I find that unlike the other guide dogs, Corky needs cajoling, even some signing from me, before she'll pee. The other guide dogs fidget and attempt to socialize with each other, but Corky is perfectly still. She's ready for this job.

On our first night together she demonstrates another part of her personality. Unlike Hank's dog, who sleeps contentedly through the night, Corky tries repeatedly to climb in bed with me. This is not permissible, according to the training rules, and I hiss at her in the dark. "Get down!"

She ignores me and wags her tail.

At four A.M. I begin to worry that the dog may be too goofy for this job.

The next morning in White Plains, Corky pulls me back from a Jeep that is cutting the curb.

She moves straight back. With strength.

Two pedestrians applaud. One says she'd like to get a guide dog, too. I laugh. But I can taste my lungs, as if I've been running in Pamplona.

For the first time I feel the sunken lanes under my feet.

The street is more my own. I belong here.

I'm walking without the fight-or-flee gunslinger crouch that has been the lifelong measure of blindness.

I'm not frightened by the general onslaught of sensation.

The harness is a transmitter, the dog is confident.

At every curb we come to a reliable and firm stop. I cannot fall.

At Guiding Eyes the operative phrase is, "A little stubbornness is a good thing in a guide dog!" When I think of this, I'll always be standing with Kathy Zubrycki, a senior trainer, on a cold March morning in White Plains, New York. We are with Corky at the sheer edge of a railroad platform. There's a ten-foot drop to the tracks below.

Kathy is telling me how Corky will not let me walk off the platform, and I listen in a bone-chilling wind with my collar turned up and my left hand on the harness. Behind us a train roars past on its way to New York City.

"Go on," says Kathy, "tell her to go forward."

"I think I'll just wait for the train to get here. I feel like going to Poughkeepsie!"

"Go on now. Corky isn't going to let anything happen to you, and neither am I."

I tell her that I believe that the dog will prevent me from walking off the platform, that I believe Corky is as good as her noble reputation, that she, Kathy Zubrycki, has a wonderful voice, a beautiful voice. I am babbling like Woody Allen.

Inwardly I'm thinking, What if the dog belongs to a suicide cult?

Then I laugh and exhort Corky to go forward.

She yanks me backward, turns, walks me in the opposite direction until we are safely away from the tracks.

Faith moves from belief into conviction, then to certainty.

We are a self-confirmed powerhouse, we two.

At age thirty-nine I learn to walk upright.

With the help of classmates and the trainers, I am choosing to be blind in a forceful way. I even begin to enjoy my mistakes.

One night when my sister is visiting the school, I walk into a screen door. Janet Surman sees this and says, "You looked really good coming through that screen!"

I know it's true!

Nothing like this has ever happened to me.

I am among sighted people who respect blindness.

There isn't an ounce of the patronizing or the sentimental in this. They work you hard when you're in residence, and they admire your breakthroughs: I am evaluated as a guide dog team. We work on and off the subways near Lincoln Center.

On a midtown bus the driver actually asks me where I want to get off.

We walk through a complicated and noisy construction site. Corky is absolutely in focus, in harness, in tandem, in control.

She's not afraid of the jackhammer.

She rides on escalators like Marlene Dietrich, all poise, greeting her public.

Back at Guiding Eyes she distinguishes herself by passing the famous "jelly doughnut test." The trainers have placed doughnuts and slices of pepperoni pizza around the training center. As we walk through the hallways, she pays them no attention and even guides me around them!

I suspect this dog reads the encyclopedia in her spare time.

At Pace University she circles around a tethered goat, leads me past a flock of loud geese. She stops at the top of a flight of stairs, even though a donkey is braying just behind an adjacent fence.

She takes me carefully through a Japanese garden.

We walk through an arbor where a hundred birds are singing.

We belong in this territory, she seems to say, and my own joints loosen. We slip through the unfamiliar with balance. Entanglements of harsh light do not slow us.

We work together through a revolving door into a mall.

All the while we're followed by Lynne or Janet, who applaud our successes and warn us of problems.

"Don't let her pull you that hard," Janet says. "Use the 'steady' command."

She shows me how to move the harness forward and back as a signal to slow the pace.

Corky slows. She's suddenly distracted by a parakeet in a pet store window!

"Tell her to 'hop up'!"

And now Corky refocuses, turns back to work.

Why didn't I yield to this earlier? Why did I take so long?

It doesn't matter. I'm doing it now.

We're moving fast!

Dave See was right. This partnership requires discipline and precision. The payoff is self-reliance and faith.

In a cavernous, shadowy department store I'm moving swiftly through abutments of stacked perfumes.

We pass what must be a line of women's coats. To me, they seem like a herd of white deer, a chorus line of dancing egrets. I don't know what the hell they are, but while I'm wondering about it, Corky is taking me around a huge wreath on a tripod that is precisely in the middle of the aisle.

I may be moving in fog, but nothing is going to puncture my life vest. I'm sailing through Macy's!

We shamble near the television sets, and I can hear a football game in progress. The salesman comes forward and admires the dog. Then he shares his game narrative with me. As he talks about the Dolphins, I discover that I'm not on my private adolescent raft. My new boat holds playfully to the river. The other boats signal me with their steam whistles.

Theodore Roethke wrote: "My eyes extend beyond the farthest bloom of the waves;/I lose and find myself in the long water;/I am gathered together once more;/I embrace the world."

On Sunday, March 27, 1994, I board a USAir flight from LaGuardia Airport in New York City to Ithaca, with Corky at my side. Lynne Robertson, who has accompanied us on every day of training and watched us grow into a safe, working twosome, comes with us to the boarding gate. "Okay, Corkster," Lynne says, "you look after this guy."

And then I'm walking down the gangway with Ms. Corky in the lead, and we enter the cabin of the plane. And our new life, which will be spent entirely together, has begun.

For the foreseeable future, Corky and I will be supported by artists' fellowships. Within months of our graduation from Guiding Eyes, we take up residency at the MacDowell Colony for the Arts in Peterborough, New Hampshire. Corky lies next to me on the braided rug of our forest cabin, and soon we're making noises together, visceral tunes, bone music, rubbing our backs, each of us growling. It's good, the dog and man making sounds together, and the exhausted parts fall away.

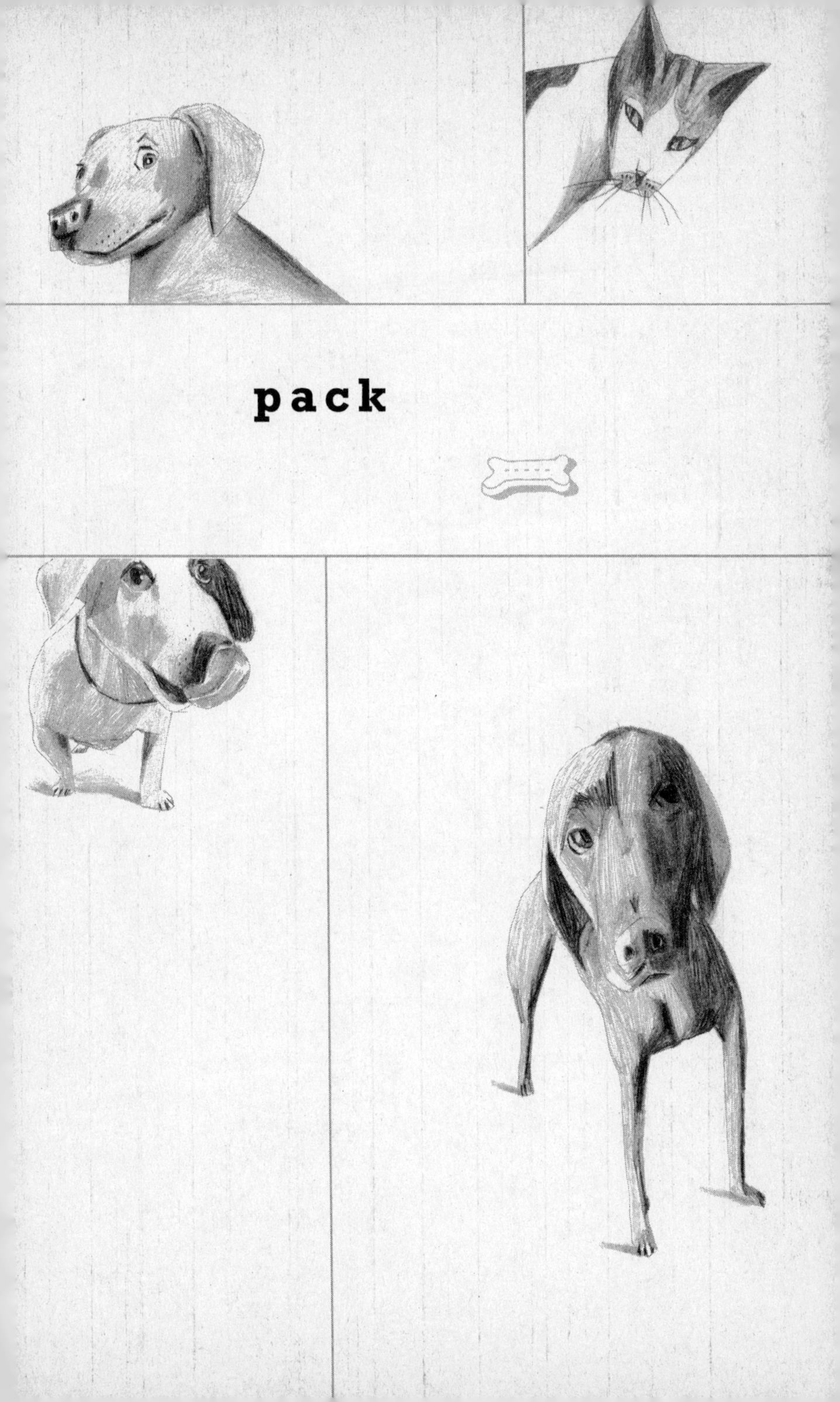

pack

A Woman's Best Friend

Erica Jong

MAN'S BEST FRIEND IS ALSO A WOMAN'S. A STRONG WOMAN CAN accomplish anything with a loyal dog at her side. Men may come and go, but dogs walk (and sniff) on forever. Like men, dogs think with their noses. Unlike men, dogs are fiercely loyal. I could tell you the story of my life through the dogs I have loved. I could tell you the story of the losses in my life through their deaths. Dogs come into our lives to teach us about love and loyalty. They depart to teach us about loss. We try to replace them but never quite succeed. A new dog never replaces an old dog; it merely expands the heart. If you have loved many dogs, your heart is very big.

Did I say "merely"? What dogs teach us is hardly mere. They teach us that if you love a creature, you can pick up its shit and not mind. They teach us that nothing is disgusting in love—neither smells nor spills. They teach us that all bodily effluvia are as sacred to God as prayers.

Where to begin this narrative of dogs I have loved? Shall I begin with

Tangerine, the black Cocker Spaniel that came into my life the summer I was thirteen when I lived in Lenox, Massachusetts? Or shall I begin with Jacques, the black Poodle who joined our family on Central Park West when I was sixteen? These were family dogs, shared with sisters, yelled at by my mother (never a dog person), so in a way they don't count.

The first dog I adopted on my own was a Bichon Frise called Poochkin, named after Aleksandr Pushkin, my grandfather's favorite poet. I bought him at a pet store on the Upper East Side (before I was enlightened about the horrors of puppy mills). I was thirty and fighting my desire for a baby when I fell in love with Poochkin. He was a baby surrogate for a while and then became the inspiration for pregnancy. (I so babied that dog that I was more than ready to baby a baby.) My then-husband and I not only slept with Poochkin, we bathed with him, brushed him, and jointly blew his curly coat dry (I worked the brush and Jon worked the dryer).

When we moved to Connecticut, Poochkin became a country dog, knocking up the neighbor's bitch (a Maltese), marking his territory aggressively, and masturbating with the Marimekko pillows. He ran wild in the Connecticut woods, attracting ticks and brambles—until he finally met a terrible end under the wheels of a Jeep driven by my daughter's nanny while my daughter was strapped in her car seat in the back. The nanny was in love with the carpenter who was building a new study for me. In her romantic delirium, she backed out of the driveway, and over the dog. I remember the howls of pain as I rushed Poochkin to the vet, my clothes covered with his blood, my heart as crushed as his. Not long ago I saw a Sally Jessy Raphael segment called "I Ran Over My Own Granddaughter" and I thought of Poochkin. I felt as guilty as those unhappy grandmothers did, although I wasn't even driving the car that killed Poochkin.

Poochkin died on the vet's operating table. I still keep an urn with his ashes in my study in Connecticut. Poochkin's dog collar and tags are draped casually around the urn's marble neck. On rainy nights I seem to hear him scratching at the back door to be let in.

During the days of Poochkin we also adopted a mutt from the pound, a big sorrowful-eyed red Raggedy Ann of a dog. Her pound name was Buffy, but we anointed her Virginia Woof. She persisted in answering to Buffy. She came to us with worms, dysentery, and fleas. We nursed her back to health and in a month or two she became an ideal companion. Someone had trained her carefully and soon she reverted to that discipline.

When my daughter Molly was born, Buffy used to guard me while I nursed the baby, howling at Poochkin maternally if he tried to jump on me seeking a nipple for himself. Buffy was a female; she understood that the baby came first. Poochkin had a male's narcissism: he humped pillows while I nursed the baby. He was not pleased that the pack leader (me) no longer gave him pride of place. He was like a childish husband having a fling to spite the new dyad of mother and baby. Every pillow became stiff.

Not long after Poochkin's death, my marriage fell apart. Jon got Buffy in the divorce. The baby was to be shared, but I lost Buffy to my ex. It was clear I needed a new dog. I went to a Bichon breeder in Connecticut and adopted a Bichon bitch. Emily Doggenson had such great bloodlines and such a brilliant future in the ring that the breeder would sell her to me only if I agreed to show her. Naive as I was about strange Connecticut customs like breeding and showing dogs, I went along with this folly.

I soon learned that having a show dog is like having a kid in boarding school. You are constantly required to send money and equipment, but you rarely see your offspring. When she comes home she usually needs grooming and she claims not to know who you are. She wants to parade around the kitchen and be applauded. She doesn't want to mess her coiffure by wrestling with you on the floor or muck up her smile fetching sticks. She is, in short, a snob. Superstardom has ruined her. All the ribbons she's won have gone to her head. And the breeder wants to whelp her and take the pick of the litter. By then I was so sick of the show-dog mentality that I happily gave the breeder the pick of the litter and took the runt. This was Poochini, olive-eyed, gentle, as sweet as her mother was stuck up. Poochini and I bonded at once. That became a problem.

Emily Doggenson began to abuse Poochini. She chewed on Poochini's tail. She humped her mercilessly to show dominance. She became the Mommie Dearest of dogs. She acted as if this darling litter-runt was a disgrace to her noble bloodlines. I kept Poochini and gave Emily back to the breeder (who was jubilant to have her champion returned to the kennel).

For a while all was well in Dogdom. Poochini arrived when my daughter was four and shepherded me through many relationships, many moves between New York and Connecticut, many summers in Venice. Poochini was amiable when I remarried; she adopted Ken faster than my daughter did and even remained good-humored when we rescued Basil Bastet, a green-eyed gray kitten from the Westport pound. Poochini was patient when we fell hopelessly in love with Basil. She even forgave Basil's unfortunate tendency to throw up on her in the car.

Poochini was a canine model of sobriety. She accepted the things she could not change. As she grew older, she became more philosophical. When Basil succumbed to cancer at six (after many months of chemotherapy), Poochini accepted, with equanimity, Latte and Espresso, the two kittens we adopted from Bide-A-Wee. By then Poochini was winding down. She had chased Basil around the house only to curl up and sleep with her, but Latte and Espresso couldn't rouse her much. Poochini had two knees replaced, plastic surgery on her moles, and she was heading for cataract removal. Increasingly, she began to resemble a stuffed animal—a stuffed animal that leaked. But she represented a whole phase of my life. Even when she impersonated an inanimate object, I could read complex emotions in her smallest sigh or snore. Even when she peed all over the Oriental rugs, I made excuses for her.

When she was seventeen and her bodily systems were failing, I continued to mop up after her rather than question her quality of life. Even after the vet and I reached the decision that if she couldn't eat, couldn't walk, and had more and more trouble breathing, she would have to be put down, I hesitated, waiting for her to recover. And she did come back to life many times. She took heart pills, arthritis pills, and thyroid pills, but still I could not bear to make the arrogant decision to deprive her of what little shreds of her life remained. Finally, a day came when she lay in her own pee and couldn't get up. We cried while the vet attached the pink plastic butterfly to her vein. We cried as the poison went in and she trustingly took the dose. Her eyes remained open. A terrible shudder shook her body. A whole chapter in my life closed.

That was six months ago and I still haven't been able to commit to a new dog. The cats have gleefully taken over the house, chasing each other and my daughter's visiting dog, Godzooki, a soulful-eyed black-and-white Cocker Spaniel puppy. Godzooki is loving and full of life, but I don't want to become attached to her.

I visit Web sites devoted to Poodle rescue, Greyhound rescue, Spaniel rescue, but Poochini's memory haunts me. I dream of Poochini. I dream that she is alive and healthy, waiting for us in Venice, on the *fondamento* in front of Harry's Dolce, near the crumbling palazzo we used to rent on Giudecca.

With her are my grandparents, my aunt Kitty, my friend Grace—all my beloved dead. Buffy is there, too. And Basil the cat. They are simply waiting for my arrival. In my dreams, we are all reunited in the City of Shades.

I can't bear to think of another Bichon. This time I want a big dog, a hunting animal to keep me safe when my daughter embarks on her own life. But something always stops me. My husband says, "Let's get a boy dog this time—a Labrador or a Sheepdog." My daughter tells me my life is incomplete without a Greyhound—or two—saved from the racetrack.

Then, an amazing thing happens. My daughter breaks up with her old boyfriend and gets involved with a new boyfriend who has an allergy to dog hair. Suddenly I am taking Godzooki to the country on weekends, and weekends are stretching into three and four days and sometimes even weeks. Godzooki is looking up at me as if I am her pack leader. She sits when I say "Sit." She retrieves her leash when I say "Out." She anointeth my head with saliva.

She may be my granddog, but she is acting more and more like *my* dog. My daughter's love life may have brought her to me, but Godzooki is here to stay. The cats seem to know this and they have stopped hissing at her. When she chases them around the apartment, they only pretend to be scared. I have even caught Latte going right up to her and sniffing. I have glimpsed Espresso rolling over to have her belly rubbed in a very Cocker-Spanielish way. So, I am researching Cocker Spaniels now and I am biding my time. Either Godzooki is the first of a matched set or she will crawl into that hollow place in my heart left by Poochini. The hollow place has grown bigger with each dog I've loved. I am probably destined to spend my twilight years with a pack of dogs and a houseful of cats. Worse ends can be imagined.

"We have been here so short a time/and we pretend we have invented memory," W. S. Merwin writes in his poem "Elders," speaking of human hubris among the animals. We humans like to flatter ourselves that we are smarter than the animals with which we share our lives. But really we love them for their wisdom, which is born of innocence. Dogs have no guile. Even vicious dogs such as Dobermans and Pit Bulls have no guile. They don't profess to love your work and then attack it. They don't lick you, then bite to draw blood. In a world of hypocrisy and betrayal, dogs are direct. They never lie.

They think with their noses, and the nose is the most primitive and infallible organ. If we could all live by our sense of smell, our lives would be much simpler. Other organs—eyes, genitals—betray, but the nose never lies. Dogs have infallible bullshit detectors. Moreover, they heed them as humans never do. We love dogs because they show us how to live with utmost simplicity: Rejoice and kick up your heels after a good shit. Love the one who feeds you. Curl up with the one who strokes your belly. Cherish a good master and lick him into enduring servitude. Celebrate life. Praise God. Find your way home no matter how long it takes. Watch out for the coyotes in the woods. Sniff every corner of the room before you decide to stay there. Turn around three times and create a magic circle before you settle down to dreaming. Decide to trust someone totally before you die.

These are some of the things I have learned from the dogs in my life. Cats teach other lessons—lessons about keeping your own counsel, cherishing your independence, and giving love without surrendering one's self. Dogs seem more slobbery and slavish. But it is we who become their slaves. As a species, humans are slow to trust. Perhaps that's because we have disregarded our noses for so many millennia. The nose is the only organ that tells it true. By living with dogs, we reclaim the feral in ourselves. We may seek to civilize them, but in truth they help us to reclaim the wildness in ourselves. They remind us that in ancient days we had much wisdom that we have since sadly abandoned: the wisdom of touch, the wisdom of smell, the wisdom of the senses.

These days I divide my weeks between Connecticut and Manhattan. When I want to work with the peace that comes only from long days alone, without the dynamo of the city whirring in my ears, I go to Connecticut, pray for snow, and retreat to my studio on stilts to work on my novel. That is when I simply cannot do without a dog.

Godzooki is becoming an exemplary muse. I feel safe in the country without human companions as long as she is there to be my early warning system. I rely on the fact that her nose and ears are sharper than mine are. I know she will bark long before the doorbell rings and keep me apprised of who is coming down my driveway—whether deer or delivery truck.

She has an I-thou relationship with every tree on my property so she constantly reminds me of how precious and singular each one is. The birches bend for her. The hemlocks drop their weighty armfuls of snow on her small head. Circling each one, she kicks up her heels like a creature that knows that God is good. She delights in the morning, greets noon by scratching at the door to go out, and becomes especially wary when the sun goes down. She is the wild side of me, expressing it without words. Somehow, she makes my playing with words more possible and more fulfilling. She and I have a perfect understanding about life. Language is good but language is not all there is. By sharing her domain of smells and sounds, I become more aware of the secret life that leads us.

"Every creature is a word of God," said Meister Eckehart, a fourteenth-century German mystical theologian. Listening to the animals, we hear the secrets of the universe.

Neighbors

Michael Paterniti

THE WEST END CEMETERY IS FULL OF OLD DEAD SEA CAPTAINS and soldiers from the War of 1812, kids who died of cholera, and wives who, after six or eight or ten children, just gave up. There are rich people under monuments, the Longfellow family in a vault, and paupers without so much as a wooden marker. No one's been buried here since the middle of this century, and so the place has fallen into disrepair. You see a lot of the marble and shell headstones in puzzle pieces on the ground or standing at crooked attention. About ten years ago the cemetery was a popular hangout for prostitutes and junkies—but now it's just dogs and their owners.

When I first moved to town a couple years ago with my girlfriend, Sara, we walked our dog in the cemetery. There was this guy there named Jeff, a big brawny American Indian, from the Duckwater tribe I think, who sort of qualified as my first friend in Portland. He told me how he grew up in Nevada and was adopted by white parents and then raised in a little redneck town where people really didn't like Indians. He'd moved around a lot and I pictured him as I was now, the stranger in a strange place. He walked with me in the cemetery, sometimes twice a day, whatever the weather. Or rather, we were both being walked by our dogs. His was a wolf mix named Keana, with a vacant, slightly menacing glint in her eye, who liked to rough up young puppies. And mine is a simple mutt named Trout, whose passion for chasing squirrels follows her lifetime commitment to rolling in poop.

It seemed like Jeff was always at the cemetery, sometimes up to eight hours in a row. He said he worked at night, supposedly for a local scuba-diving outfit, and that's why he had so much free time during the day. He told stories, endless stories, about his high school football exploits and the blown-out knee that ended his college career at safety. He talked about fishing, how he gill-netted in the rivers of southeast Alaska and then how he and his girlfriend had bought a house and now they weren't together anymore, and she had the house and he was here, a country away, walking his dog with people like me. He didn't seem angry at all. No, in fact, he seemed happy. Like every day he was as happy as he'd been the day before. And because of it he was good at drawing people out, at connecting the various factions inside the cemetery so that everyone stood around, nodding dumbly, listening to Jeff, our oblivious mayor, holding forth on Keana's new collar or perfect shampoo, while Keana took her pound of flesh out of some hapless pup.

This is not the way things normally work in the cemetery. The mere fact that I knew Jeff's name was unusual. Usually people didn't interact that much. Instead, we knew each other by handles. There was Dalmatian Man, father of three speckled dogs, one to whom he spoke in sign language. There was Greyhound Lady, regally walking her trio of Greyhounds until the day that Lightning, her beloved, dove through a plate-glass window during a thunderstorm and died. There was the man who walks and reads, and Frisbee Dude, and the Lawn Chair Family: an old father and his fifty-something son who daily set up their folding chairs near the cemetery gate. And the Pickup Artist, around whom no one was safe. And there was Crazy Shouting Man, owner of three ragtag mutts and an elder statesman of the cemetery, who, when I finally talked to him, wasn't Crazy Shouting Man at all. His name was Al, who said, "There are loads of people up there that I see all the time, some of them I've been seeing for years and I don't know their name. I recognize them and they recognize me, we talk about all sorts of things, and it just never really occurs to you to ask their name because you know their dog's name.

"As a matter of fact, I've always had these funny occasions where you run into people that you talk to a lot at the cemetery—you meet them somewhere . . . we were down at Granny Killam's when it was open one night and this woman came over and said, 'Al, how are you? How's the dogs? How's all this?' and I was with a bunch of friends and I thought, And this is . . . , and I realized I had no idea, it wasn't that I had forgotten her name, it was that I'd never known her name. I knew her dog . . . I mean, I had no idea. And, this was not somebody that I just knew very casually, this was somebody that I probably walked with three or four mornings a week. But you always find you know a lot more dogs than you know people, which, I think, says something about who's worth knowing anyway."

Even today what strikes me as amazing about the cemetery is that there are people here, people who show up twice a day and see other people here twice a day for years and many of them just don't know each other's real name, let alone what the other does for a living, or dreams of at night, or loves or hates. They just know each other's dogs' names. So when they refer to one another, they might say, "Circe's mom said Milk-Bones are full of preservatives, which is why she cooks her own." Or when they bump into each other downtown Christmas shopping, they'll say, "Ellroy's mom!" and then when nothing's left to say, say, "Uh, how goes it?"

Was this intimacy or a complete lack of intimacy? Sometimes it felt like both at once. You had the warmth of intimacy and the comfort of hiding behind your dog. And yet every day you saw people at their most naked, talking baby-talk to their hounds, kneeling to pick up poop. I asked my friend Julie, Reuben's mother, about this.

"I think I really get a sort of window into people's . . . well, into people's souls. You watch people very contentedly walking around, throwing the ball, interacting with their dogs or totally ignoring their dogs, and going at their own pace and every once in a while yelling for their dog and . . ."

Here's Al again: "I mean, I really judge people by how they behave toward their dog. When I see people hit a dog, I'm really sort of appalled and amazed that you would do that.

"I mean, I know who really, really likes their dogs and who doesn't. I know people who've got trophy dogs and people who've got the scruffiest, ugliest dog, but they really, really love that dog."

I think it was the love part that kept me going back to the cemetery. And then it became my social hour, my escape, where, more often than not, I'd find Jeff and Keana. The minute Jeff realized I was a writer he went to the library and over the course of a week read everything I'd ever written. And then, to my horror, wanted to talk about it. And he did this kind of thing with others, too.

When the leaves began to change during my first October in the West End cemetery, Jeff was already talking about a Christmas card he was planning—a photograph of Keana and himself. He brought it up obsessively, about how Keana was going to have a haircut and shampoo and have her nails clipped, and how he had arranged for a photographer, and how they were scouting locations. There were ups and downs in the saga as it played out over weeks—a good location that might not work out the day of the shoot if a nor'easter hit, the need to time everything just perfectly so that Keana would leave the beauty parlor and then immediately sit for her picture before she could come back to the cemetery and get muddy.

In retrospect there were little clues even then that something strange was going on with Jeff. While he said he owned a truck, I saw him only at bus stops around town. And the scuba-diving . . . later when I called various outfits in Portland, no one had ever heard of him. In the end, he had the photograph taken at Sears, he and Keana in the stiff, unsmiling pose of a Civil War–era husband and wife, he in his familiar blue sweatshirt hulking behind Keana, who was perfectly coifed. He was beaming when he handed the Christmas card to me, literally beaming.

After Christmas I left the country for several weeks and when I came back, some time after a massive ice storm, Jeff was nowhere to be found. The cemetery glittered with glazed headstones. It took days to unravel the story because people didn't seem to want to talk about it . . . didn't seem to want to talk about anything. Everyone just bundled into themselves, and Jeff . . . he was a very touchy subject, one that suddenly made us all feel defensive. What I learned was this: He'd had health problems, an infection of some kind. He went to the hospital at the same time that he was apparently forced out of his apartment. Money was tight. He'd asked someone from the cemetery to put him up, another line crossed. But that hadn't worked out. Keana was taken to a kennel by Megan, Matty's mom. And now she was calling the kennel regularly to see if Jeff had picked her up, but he hadn't. Week after week she called until it was clear that Jeff couldn't or wouldn't pick up Keana, that he was gone. That's when Keana was adopted by someone else.

Here's Megan: "You start talking about this stuff with somebody and then you realize, I didn't even know this person . . . like with Jeff, I mean, it was like you knew everything about his life but in the end how much of that was actually true? And, you know, you didn't even know this person . . . it was like August to December and he was gone. But it seemed like forever."

There were completely unsubstantiated rumors that he'd robbed a bank. Someone knew someone whose cousin had seen his photo on a Boston newscast. Maybe. But then most people were quick to accept this as fact. In a weird way, I wonder if we felt betrayed. Betrayed because Jeff had broken the simple rules of the cemetery. He'd become too intimate. Now he was gone and it was hard to say hi, let alone catch someone else's eye. During those dark winter months the cemetery became a kind of haunted, trustless place. In one of the endless conversations we had about him later, some people worried that he knew where we lived . . . someone threatened to track him down. But what for? So that he might never again bamboozle other hapless dog owners in other seaside towns into chatting about doggy shampoo?

Sara and I kept the Christmas card on our refrigerator right up until a couple of months ago, actually, when it quietly fell to a new rotation of refrigerator photos. We kept it there in hopes, I think, that he would come back and explain where he'd been, for I was pretty certain that he couldn't have robbed a bank. And if he had, I told myself, maybe it was because he had to. Maybe he'd been inches from a life he imagined for himself, with a dog that gave unconditional love, with friends he was guaranteed to see every day and he'd had a couple of bad breaks—got sick, ran out of money, lost his dog, and then panicked.

Now time has passed. People come and go and every six months the galaxy inside these gates breaks apart and reconfigures. Dogs die, people leave for nursing homes, others move, more arrive, and every day, today even, people are here walking in spectral circles like they're in Mecca. Circling the Kaaba. In general I'd say things are back to the way they were—intimate but not intimate. We stand around in dumbfounded joy with ten, twenty, thirty other gaping grown adults, reveling in the simplicity of stupidly entertaining dog play. Dalmatian Man still flashes sign language at his deaf Dalmatian, the Pickup Artist still works his magic, the Lawn Chair Family still sets up by the cemetery gate each day, covering their legs with wool blankets.

Fact is, even without somebody like Jeff pulling people together, if you stand on a corner with a bunch of strangers, eventually something happens that brings you together. Sometimes something small. The other night I went to the cemetery at sunset. There were the same broken headstones, the same sea captains and paupers, and there were all these living people, too, who only know me as Trout's dad, or as the guy who stupidly named his dog Trout, or however they see me. The dogs were playing hard, racing in circles, not wanting any of it to end, and a gigantic moon came up, came up tangerine. It was the kind of moon that stills everything, and we stood in a circle watching it rise. For a minute or two we just stood there glowing orange; the dogs didn't exist at all.

Play Dogs of the New West

Jon Billman

MY COW DOG, DAISY, AND I ARE GOING TO WORK. WE'RE EATING goldfish crackers—two for me, one for you—in my pickup truck and howling Buck Owens and Merle Haggard ballads off the tape deck, when we come across a broken pickup thirty-nine miles down forty miles of bad road. Old blue-and-rust Chevy. Open hood, pair of boots sticking out from underneath. Four tires bald as apples, three with air. I roll down the window and I can smell that they haven't had a shower for weeks.

South Dakota plates, they may be horse thieves, but friendly enough. The guy under the truck doesn't say much while the upright waddie speaks through the two front teeth he has left. "We've got a hundred twenty head a beef up Crystal Creek. Forty horses. Some not worth a bullet, but some's okay. Most ain't broke." He leans over to inspect for progress. "Been out for a month. Going into town for a shower and a couple beers."

"Got what you need?" I say.

"We ain't got nothing but a screw jack and no handle."

This waddie regards me as a yuppie and not to be relied on. I'm wearing a sun visor, the kind an amateur tennis player might wear. Hiking shorts, and some après-ski slip-ons popular with the lodge set, which isn't very smart considering the air force of mosquitoes and rocky tire-changing terrain. Sporting a coffee-stained T-shirt that reads something about a ski company. These punchers take me for the tourist I am, but this tourist has a jack. "I've got a bottle jack," I tell him. I pull over and rustle for the jack under the jump seat. Then I piece the handle together and reach it to the one under the truck. The jack is, embarrassingly, almost brand-new, though I have replaced a few tires on this very road. My tires happen to be brand-new as well, compliments of the Firestone recall. My truck is a little Japanese outfit that is never asked to haul anything more than a mountain bike or a canoe. These hands know my income doesn't come from cows and they may suspect a trust fund, which isn't accurate.

Daisy stays in the safety of the truck cab. A guy on horseback gaits by, checking cattle, two rangy Border Collies tailing behind, running in and out of the sagebrush. Daisy barks at them through the window. What a sissy, the ranch dogs must think. She can't even ride in the back of a truck, has to stay up front with the organic dog cookies and air-conditioning. Cow dogs, I think, have the most expressive eyes of any breed, and I see it in her brown pair—she hankers for the working cow-dog life.

Make it me, Daisy's whines say. Her bat ears perk up, those eyes go wide. I want to be a cowgirl, I want to cut calves and keep coyotes at bay. I was wired to be in the front row at brandings and sheep dockings. I can surf a two-story rick of hay. For her it is an atavistic need. I had unrequited dreams, too: I always wanted to be a pro ball player but wasn't nearly good enough. So I try to explain to Daisy that she is with me, and a play dog, because she wasn't very good at working cows. They docked her tail, turned her out, and she didn't perform up to snuff, flunked the tryout, was cut from the squad. I'm pretty sure she'd been abused; she still doesn't like tall men in cowboy hats. Most of the ranchers I know don't keep pets.

Dogs and wolves, researchers believe, diverged from a common ancestor around 135,000 years ago, domesticated 100,000 years ago. For the past thousand years, breeding has focused canines to perform specific work. In Wyoming, where we live, work means working cattle. Ain't much use for a dog who don't work cattle. (As I write this, a pickup truck with hay stacked two stories high rolls by, a pair of Blue Heelers surfing on top, guarding the stuff that's worth more than gold in this, the third year of severe drought.) Daisy, and a passel of doggies just like her, doesn't work cattle. She's a dog of the New West, accustomed to mountain bike trail drives instead of cattle drives, wool ski hats instead of herds of sheep. She's at home with her canine friends on the deck at the brew pub, or with me, angling for trout.

But that makes me wonder—what happens to a Cattle Dog that doesn't work cattle? How does such a dog evolve?

Will this branch of Kelpie evolve into the Rocky Mountain Trout Dog? She'd need a Labrador's fat for that, perhaps. Might Border Collies turn into North American Mountain Bike Dogs? Too longhaired, I think. Best to go with the cur that does it all, I think. Spring that pup from the pound and grab your skis.

Ranch dogs can smell a city mouse a country mile away; real ranch dogs would love to kick Daisy's ass. You see it when we drive by and they notice her, Little Miss Gourmet Kibble in her sissy Japanese truck. You there, with your Day-Glo yuppie bird-dog collar. Is that a *Frisbee* your owner has? What a sissy. Where you from—Pennsylvania? You going home to get your teeth brushed?

In fact, she is.

Bet you live in town, too.

We do.

I knew what it would mean when we picked her up at the pound. On trail runs above Kemmerer, she would run herd on pronghorn antelope, which is something like trying to herd those proverbial cats, though she would at least get them headed in any direction they wanted to go. I know she was thinking that this is why we were up there—why would anyone run all the way up Oyster Ridge just to unwind and think good thoughts?

Two years ago in Sublette County I had a working cowboy compliment my dog. "That's a good-looking Kelpie," he said. Thanks. "She work cattle?" Naw. "Break out the Frisbee, eh."

How did he know?

Real cow dogs are one-person animals and will go to most lengths to guard the truck and the string, including taking a hunk out of your calf if need be. They have a vital job to do and they're going to do it, Mister, so don't give them headaches. Real cow dogs don't get to play; they go to work 24/7 so others can play.

With people Daisy will act demure, blink her eyes, roll on her back, jump on you inappropriately, lick your face. With other dogs, females, Daisy is a punk. Our ski friends won't let her play with Addie, their babied Border Collie, nor Sadie, another Border Collie who downright hates Daisy and would like to kill her and has tried. More than once her owner, Marcia, and I have had to dive into the middle of a dogfight, skis still on our feet, then head back home and patch up our respective dogs over beers.

Daisy heels our neighbor's big yellow snow blower, snapping at the chain-wrapped tires. She runs herd on mountain bikers, but males only, which, I think, most closely resemble slow-moving beeves.

She tried herding Shriners in the Jackson Hole July Fourth parade, but my wife, Hilary, put the kibosh on this in short order.

Daisy doesn't truck with most men under cowboy hats, a handicap for canines in the cattle industry, but it works for her new career as "ski dog." Last spring Daisy and I were skiing Beaver Mountain and came upon two snowmobiles, yellow and black, beastly colors, nature's danger flag. Daisy heeled them—yip, yip, getalong you beasts! The riders, overweight folk, as snowmobilers often are, lifted their face shields and laughed, though sheepishly, like, that's real cute, but what's wrong with your dog, Mister? Her vet, Dr. Bob, called her a ski dog on her first checkup when his assistant asked what kind of dog she was. Dr. Bob is a cowboy and was tickled that this fine specimen landed on her feet, but a bit disappointed, I think, that she'd be frittering away her days running through nose-deep powder, eating dust behind the mountain bike, and swimming through holes in the river that moments before housed fine trout. In another four hundred years will cur genes program dogs to instinctively make dollar signs in the snow, dissecting my *S* turns with a straight line down the fall line? New breeds may even emerge—the Tetonic Telemarking dog—with genomes far more diverse than the inbred purebred pedigreed glamour dogs we have today.

Back to work. Today Daisy and I are headed to a couple of line cabins up the Gros Ventre River and the end of the line. My friend Tim Sandlin rents these cabins from a former governor of Wyoming. Tim is a fine novelist and

I remember when I was just a kid, admiring the hell out of Tim's books and the fact that his author photo showed him in front of such a rustic, romantic cabin. His outhouse here has cult status in the world of contemporary letters.

Tim paid his dues in order to live here; he lived in a teepee and washed dishes at the Lame Duck for years until he could finally afford to buy a place. Tim's is the biggest heart in all of Teton County and he allows us—me, Daisy, Hilary—to use these cabins whenever we please (just be sure to close the gate). This week, however, many people with the dubious occupation title of "writer" will show up.

Daisy and I will commute the hour each way into town in the morning for the dreaded writer's conference, and back each afternoon to watch the stars, contemplate our place in the world, and listen to the coyotes. Tim, the founder of this conference, is in charge, and he allows his B-team writers to stay out here while everyone else, the A-team, is off wining and dining. There are writers who have been on *Oprah*. I have never seen the *Oprah* show, so I was banished to the line shacks. Fine by me and Daisy. These conferences are exhausting and don't pay squat unless you're a "star," but we do them because Tim asked and we get to stay in this amazing place and there are good bars and restaurants in town and we can catch up with our drinking and eating. Daisy's main job here at the conference is to not, under any circumstances, heel any Pulitzer Prize winners.

Daisy loves this place. Last time we were here—last fall—there was a wonderful dead cow, bloated to twice normal size, in the front "yard" of the cabins, mostly bunchgrass and rabbitbrush, so close I could spit and bounce a sunflower seed hull off its belly. Daisy went straight for the hocks. The smell was insufferable for us, divine to Daisy. She barked, git up cow, you're hitting the trail—git up! Remember, a thousand years of genetic programming informs her it's her job.

One morning some hands rumbled up in an old four-wheel-drive pickup. They chained the dead cow's legs to the bumper of the truck and drove off. Opposing wheels dug into the dirt and then—pop—off came the beeve's front legs. Dead cow juice flew into the air. Daisy was beside herself, inside the cabin, trying to shoot through the fly screen using her head as a battering ram. All her circuits were telling her to go, full throttle, that there was bovine business being done, carnivorous possibilities, and she was part of the larger plan, if only to cover herself in dead cow and take some of it back to town to share the tale with buddies.

The temperature rose and the cow bloated even more. Or seemed to anyway if you count the smell's effects on my imagination. The hands came back in the afternoon, full-on sun, with a come-along and winched the carcass into the back of a truck. Took it down toward the river and dumped it for the coyotes and buzzards.

I let Daisy out of the truck and she makes a beeline to the grave, which is a stone's throw from the Gros Ventre River. Daisy rolls on her back, trying to absorb any dead-cow scent that might still be there. Then we fish.

Later Daisy and I eat chicken. It's our meal together. Hilary is not here—we have grease up to our elbows. We giggle and chew, belch and fart. I even give the love of my life a thimbleful of beer to wash down the bird. Hilary calls these trips "stealing away with my girlfriend." And in a way, it's true, given the way Daisy first flirted with me at the pound. We named her Daisy after Daisy Fuentes. But I tell everyone at these writer's conferences that she's named after Daisy Buchanan, the great love of Jay Gatsby. We leave the bones for the magpies. Daisy has chicken farts. Tomorrow there will be a party of writers here. And dogs.

Todd, a geriatric Corgi, got his collar hung in the willows of the creek we named Daisy Creek because no one else had taken the initiative to name it something else. Steve, local seller of fine books, jumped in like a Marine—*"Semper Fi!"*—and untangled the old dog very shortly before he would have drowned. A toast to Steve! Roxy is here, Tim and Carol's Australian who doesn't give eight eggs for Daisy's juvenile antics. Bluebell the cowpie-eating Poodle. Oakley, the rich kid–pampered Golden Retriever puppy named after the expensive sunglasses; Daisy would periodically roll Oakley for measure, letting him know who was in charge of this camp. And Daisy's favorite, Abbey, a cow dog/Labrador puppy that could be Daisy's sister, only with her long black tail intact. She is a ski/trail running dog from the Driggs, Idaho, pound. The two of them, a brace of bat-eared hellcat, ripped through the crowd and barbecued beans, upending bottles of beer and knocking over children in a less graceful canine impression of a Shriner's circus. As I watched this posse of New West dogs I realized that these nonworking "working dogs" (as they are called at Westminster) did not lose their sand after we stole them away from the ranches that are becoming fewer by the year; they very easily turned into "play dogs," a class not yet recognized by the kennel clubs. Perhaps I'm biased, but I'll argue that play dogs with cow-dog blood in them—Heelers, Shepherds, Kelpies, Collies—play harder than the ubiquitous Huskies, Labs, and lap dogs.

This lasted three beers long, when the dogs both collapsed, Abbey having to be carried to the car by her owner, Carrie, a Jackson Hole outdoor athlete and purveyor of bagels. None of the dogs harassed the Pulitzer Prize winner. Count it a good night and a job well done.

Daisy and I don't use the outhouse to whiz. I pee in the weeds. Beside me, Daisy pees in the weeds. Peeing, we look at each other in the light of the quarter moon. There is an understanding: We are lucky to be here, under the stars, at elevation, with the birds and bats and mosquitoes. I am not a baseball player. You are not sorting cattle on a working ranch. We are lucky just to be here, peeing in the weeds. Tomorrow we'll go fishing.

The Dog Is a Ham

Louise Bernikow

THE BACKSTORY, IN TWO SENTENCES: WHAT LOOKED LIKE A drowned muskrat on the backseat of a police car in a Manhattan park was in actuality an abandoned, gimpy brindled Boxer who moved in and transformed my life. A book was inevitable and when it was published, *Bark If You Love Me* had a promotional tour.

"You're really going to love this," I promised the dog, "starting with the plane, but first you have to practice getting into your little house." His name was now Libro. Amber eyes enlarged and nostrils flared, Libro contemplated the crate, borrowed from his well-traveled Portuguese sweetheart, Matteo. Blanket inside, for familiarity. Treat inside, for inducement. He minded having the door closed, but eventually, we managed.

Bark was my eighth book. I knew how to check that there actually were books to sign and sell wherever we went, talk in sound bites, repeat the sound bites, get the book's title into every sentence, pack a solid-color, mix-and-match wardrobe, intensify eyeliner for television, and take it like a woman when only three people showed up for a bookstore signing. I explained all this to Libro, whose new Italian leather leash, I told him, was a "dress-up leash," and not to be chewed on, as dress-up clothes were not be slobbered on and made-up faces were not to be smothered with kisses. Fame comes with a price. I'd bought a dog-paw rubber stamp—generic, to be sure, but more experienced folk had nixed my plan to have him dip his actual paw onto a pad and sign books himself. Toxic, they said. Attention span problems, too.

"Smile all the time. Wag your tail. Don't worry if they get your name wrong—we know it's not the astrological sign Libra, but let it go if people insist on telling you they too were born in October, okay? Don't correct them, no matter how dumb the comments are. Most people who interview us won't have read the book. Just be yourself. No barking. No peeing. No shoplifting."

Actually, the shoplifting—at a Borders store north of New York City—had amused the audience, which, miraculously, numbered more than three. We'd assumed our positions—I at the lectern, book open; Libro flat on the floor, water bowl nearby. (He had a few requirements, after all.) Halfway through page ten—where I tell him I've never even spoken to a dog before and haven't a clue how to manage if he really wants to live with me—Libro rose languidly and started to wander away. The store manager met my alarmed eyebrows with a permissive wave. I read on. Libro disappeared down an aisle. At the top of page fifteen, he returned—with a stuffed toy in his mouth! A black-and-white, six-legged thing that I took to be an octopus, but turned out to be a lemur. He trotted up and offered me the toy for a game of tug. The audience roared.

What a showman. But then, I knew that already. We'd begun our promotions at the top of the media food chain, with an A&E television network interview. Spiffy, clever Parker Ladd, the producer, sat us in side-by-side wing-back armchairs. Libro acted as though he'd seen bright lights, cable wires, cameras, interviewers, and producers all his young life. The camera moved in on me: "I'd have to say he opened my heart. . . ." Sappy, I know, and exactly the kind of treacle I disdain, but true. Libro looked over, moved to the edge of his chair, leaned over, rested his head on my shoulder, and let out the most audible, perfect, TV-moment sigh. Uncoached. Honest.

Fresh from that triumph, we packed for California. My bag: wardrobe, makeup, vitamins. His bag: leash, treats, vitamins. As suggested by Matteo's human travelers, I plastered the crate with neon-inked signs about who Libro was flying with—lest he be put on a plane to Kalamazoo and picked up by a drug lord—and then disassembled it for easier transport. As suggested by his vet, I fed him a tranquilizer at the airport, while a porter reassembled the crate and I did my millionth silent homage to single mothers for all they juggle. I was relying on the kindness of strangers and very large tips. Libro got into his little house willingly, if a little suspiciously, and I hounded every airline employee about his safety until I wished I had a tranquilizer for myself.

He staggered out of the crate in the San Francisco airport like a dog on an acid trip, eyes rolling, legs shaking. I threw my arms around him. He peed. I cried. He'd peed on someone's suitcase. I summoned two porters and escaped, cradling him on my lap during the ride into the city, where we collapsed together on the bed in our "dog friendly" hotel room. Luckily, I'd insisted on a day's recovery time before hitting the hustle. (Publishers are far more indulgent about "special needs" for a dog on tour than for a mere human author.) We wandered the city, Libro dubious about unfamiliar-smelling curbsides and lampposts, and then we bedded down, only to be assaulted by clattering dishes in the hotel's kitchen across the corridor. Could we please move somewhere quieter? The manager said we occupied the only "dog friendly" area of the hotel. One of the things I know about publicity tours, I told Libro, is that you can't let glitches bother you. Whatever happens is okay. He lifted his heavy head from the pillow, licked my face, and closed his eyes. He already knew.

Off we went in the morning, neither of us nervous, one of us covering the rental car's rear window with slobber as we crossed the Bay Bridge. In Berkeley, the Pacifica radio interviewer read a section of the book on the air and asked informed questions. Libro, on my lap, snoozed. Lunch with a magazine editor. Signing at a pet boutique, where the rumored three people showed. Sitting outside the shop with Libro attracting admirers did not convert to sales, but there were many biscuits on hand, pleasing one of us. Another reading, a bigger crowd, including a man who'd heard me on the radio that morning and wanted to come home to New York with us. Libro looked diffident, so I knew the guy was probably not a serial killer. Still, I shuddered. An open heart is a dangerous thing. None of my feminist friends came, no devotees of my earlier books, none of which even mentioned dogs. We live in divided and distinguished worlds, indeed. The stamp of Libro's paw charmed some buyers and when they asked if it was really HIS paw, I lied.

Sentimental interlude. An old flame, more like a former bonfire, had settled in San Francisco after hightailing it from New York, pre-Libro. Some years had passed. Meeting seemed reasonable. I told Libro nothing, being curious to observe his gut reaction, which I trust far more than I do my own. We drove over for a visit. Peter looked the same, was sweet to Libro, who was generically sweet in response. We trundled off to a magnificent beach, where the males frolicked athletically and I sunk into a picture-postcard bird's-eye view of the scene—surf, sky, sunshine, man, woman, dog—which made me sad. I'm still a sucker for happy family propaganda. How do couples living with dogs ever split up? Luckily, Libro's custody was unshared and I suspect one reason he so mysteriously chose me to live with was that he knew it would be, "Just you and me, kiddo," as I'd said.

As Libro does when, for example, I accidently drop a can on his head, I shook the Peter pain off. Later, driving away, I noticed the pup wasn't looking back.

"Whaddya think?"

Nice guy, but I wouldn't want to live with him.

The next day, we headed south along the coast, approximating a dream come true. That fateful day in New York, when Libro unaccountably made himself part of my life, I'd had an unspoken secret and a vision. The secret was, I'll keep you if you pay for yourself, which sounds hard-hearted, but remember, I'd never known a dog before and I was a single woman writer, somewhat phobic about dependents. The vision was, I see you riding down the Pacific Coast Highway in the backseat of a convertible, wearing Armani sunglasses. Libro *had* paid for himself, standing under the desk or nestling his head in my lap as I wrote the book that got the trip that tested my ability to condense our story into sound bites. Now we actually *were* driving down the Pacific Coast Highway. I'd scotched the convertible idea, fearing storms or rollovers. He'd scotched the sunglasses, along with any other accessory—bandanna, straw hat, Halloween costume—I'd dreamed up. He hated them. He'd gone to a Halloween party as a nudist.

We rolled into Menlo Park, where the local independent bookstore had gotten it exactly right—a whole window devoted to us (huge photograph, many books) and a reading to which customers could bring their dogs. As we say in Spanish, *"Eso es vivir."* Now, that's living! And that's good business, too. The store was packed. A woman who rescued Greyhounds sat right in front. Libro, who generally growls at high-strung hounds, was on good public behavior. A Bernese Mountain Dog flopped in the rear, several Shepherds sat politely, some white puffy dogs snuggled on people's laps, and a scattering of mutts sprawled all over the floor.

"Abajo," I said, and Libro lay down at my feet, looking smugly out at the audience. Showing off his bilingual ability had become part of our road *schtick.* I began to read. Libro snored slightly. I came to the part where I named him "Libro"—*"no toca los libros,"* I'd said as he surveyed the place that would become home—don't touch the books. When I read the line, *"no toca los libros,"* he stood up. Maybe he thought I was calling his name to draw him back from dreamland, but it sure as hell looked as though he was taking a bow. The humans giggled, but the dogs began to bark. The Greyhound barked first, then the dogs in the row behind, squeaky barks, squawky barks, basso barks, all the way back to the Bernese and around the room in a wave.

I panicked, but the wave subsided as soon as Libro, on my instruction, lay down again. So I went on. But every time "Libro" occurred on the page, he stood and the wave started up. I got used to it.

"Abajo," I said. The chorus of barks became a murmur and an occasional yelp.

The store sold every copy they had. One customer even followed us to the rental car, where I had a few extras stored in the trunk.

"Attaboy," I said, as we drove off in a cloud of success, heading farther south. "Good dog."

Recreational interlude. An empty, wide beach, mid-afternoon on a clear, sunny day and a pumpernickel-colored New York City dog racing around. Suddenly, in the sky—a bird, a plane, a . . . ? A man with wings. I knew that, but Libro didn't and as the man drifted downward, then plunked onto the sand, I held the growling canine by his collar and tried to explain.

"Will you let my dog smell you so he knows you're human?" I called out.

Reassured, Libro and I and the human trotted over a hill and up the beach, where a hang-gliding school was established. The young man running it—after a quick game of welcoming tug with Libro—told me that when the humans are in the sky, Icarus-like, the birds play with them. I looked up and sure enough, games of "dare" and "chicken" were being conducted, interspecially—high above our heads. For an instant, I actually saw all of nature in tune—ocean, sky, birds, humans, and dog. Like I said, living with Libro has changed me. Try putting that into a sound bite that doesn't end up on the cutting-room floor.

In Carmel, "dog friendly" is an understatement at the red-tile–roofed, white-stucco hotel partly owned by Doris Day, where canines get menus, bowls, and beds. And an invitation to a reading in the vast living room, where we set up in front of a wall-to-wall flagstone fireplace. Locals, drawn by a story in the local newspaper, trickled in. Hotel guests arrived. The four-legged guests climbed onto the chintz furniture and settled down, while their well-dressed human companions took to the floor. Libro remained in position this time. Nearly every person bought a book. While I was signing and stamping, I chitchatted, as one always does.

"Do you have a dog?" I said to a thin elderly man on arm crutches, with a hearing aid in each ear. He had arrived unaccompanied.

"No," he said, "but I'm in love with a dog." He proceeded to tell me about the black Lab next door who came to visit him every day. Tears formed at the edges of his eyes.

In the pre-Libro days, this was exactly the kind of blather that made me roll my eyes, if not think of calling the psych medics. Now I merely touched the man's arm sympathetically and added some slurpy kisses to the inscription in his book. I'm ruined.

We went home after Carmel, Libro traveling in his little house without fuss or medication and arriving in New York without incident. We did a lot more East Coast promotion, including a television show where the host warned me not to let Libro turn his back to the camera, which would then capture his asshole for the whole world to see, and a bookstore signing in New England, where the store's owners had "lost" their Boxer and wanted to play with Libro much more than they wanted to sell books. I kept checking Libro for signs of burnout, but there were none. Each time he jumped into the backseat of the rental car as eagerly as the first time. He entered every radio station, hotel, or bookstore tail up, ears flapping, nose on overdrive, as though something magnificent waited for him there. If there were three people waiting or a hundred, a crowded studio or a setup with one camera in a hotel room—as long as there was attention, plus water, biscuits, and me, he seemed happy. He never met a fan he didn't like.

And it paid off. We have a small nest egg for old age. And in the dead of winter, when days are short and lonely, when it's just him and me and new words falling slowly onto a new page, without a spotlight or applause, I can look deep into those amber eyes and say, "Hey, kiddo, do you remember California?"

Why We Don't Play Chess

George Singleton

OVER THE LAST ELEVEN YEARS A VARIETY OF STRAY DOGS HAVE moved in with Glenda and me, out here in the country, in the middle of nowhere South Carolina. Between twenty and fifty miles away is a long string of new suburbia, along Interstate 85, and I can only surmise that those hammerheads living out that way bring their unwanted animals and dump them nearby. Across from our house stands about five hundred acres of tree farm, and at night we can hear dogs running, yelping, howling, and usually finding our driveway soon thereafter. At this moment we have ten dogs, all mixed breeds. Fourteen-year-old Nutmeg had to be put down last month, and is buried in the fenced-in backyard beside Kelly, Lucy, and a good half dozen unknown and nameless dogs found dead in our front yard, where *other* hammerheads—those who drive 60 miles an hour down two-lane Hester Store Road each morning in order to work at the new factories along I-85—didn't stop after hitting what tree-farm dogs hadn't made it to home base, i.e., here.

I should mention that we haven't kept every dog that came along, either. My mother has an ex-feral dog named Maggie. Various friends, neighbors, and veterinarians have taken over dogs. And I've gone out more than a few times to find some nonblinking and skittish cur, called her toward me, then had her barrel back into the tree farm.

Oh, it's an exciting life. It keeps us busy, for one, and when Glenda and I have to take off for one reason or another I like to think that we're offering a valuable lesson to our dog-sitters in a variety of ways. Keeping our dogs teaches patience. It teaches our young dog-sitters—usually students or ex-students—dog psychology. And for anyone who says the younger generation never exercises their collective minds, let me say that my feeding instructions, at the very least, have more possible plot twists than one of those old, old chess matches played between Russian grand masters.

My dog River, aged eleven and coyote-looking, can eat in any room in the house. But she must eat alone. River's the queen of the entire operation, an alpha dog inside or out. She has never attacked one of the other dogs, nor has she bitten one. But she bares her teeth and lets out growls similar to bad bedsprings, over and over. She looks peripherally, always. If another dog doesn't finish his or her meal, River will forever gladly stick her head in the bowl and eat. Then she'll get sick later on in the night.

Joan kind of looks like a yellow Lab, and she's the alpha dog outside when River's not present. Joan rarely comes inside, as a matter of fact, and stays in a 20 × 40-foot chain-link pen, which leads into a mostly empty 12 × 20-foot storage shed. Joan shares this facility with Hershey, a brown Weimaraner-looking dog who can leap over the chain-link fence. So he's on a long lead, tied to the trunk of a peach tree. Hershey can still leap over the fence, and come out into the yard about another fifteen feet. And he does so in order to eat, seeing as Joan will bully him and take his food. If let loose and unsupervised, Hershey digs holes the size of bomb shelters.

Inklet looks like a black Lab, and she spends most of her day in Glenda's clay studio, with Ann, who is mostly Pit Bull. Ann owns fused back legs, and hops. Between Joan, Hershey, Inklet, and Ann, you could count about a dozen teeth. All of them have a hankering for immature peaches that fall off the trees in the backyard, and over the years they have ground their teeth to little nubs.

Inklet eats slowly; Ann doesn't. The two can eat together, but Ann needs to go outside *beforehand* because she'll urinate in her bowl directly after eating, so that nobody else will touch her dining area. At least that's my theory. Hershey does the same thing, on the other side of the chain-link fence, right before jumping back to be with Joan when all of the inside dogs get let out, ready to corner poor Hershey, seeing as he seems to be the low dog.

Nick is fairly new, not a year old, a black, black, sleek mostly Pointer. He still eats like a wild dog. If he eats in the company of the other dogs, he'll bolt down his food, get an odd look on his face, regurgitate, and then make me walk back out of the room not feeling so well myself. So Nick needs to eat on the back patio, *only if* Hershey's done with his food.

It's important to know, too, that Glenda and I got tired of walking all of these dogs on leashes each morning, and she splurged to fence in an acre out back with a 6-foot-high cedar privacy fence, which surrounds the pen, the barn, the fenced-in raised-bed gardens (every one of our dogs thinks that tennis balls grow on tomato plants) and so on.

Charlie, who lived in our monkey grass one winter for a couple weeks before coming in, looks like a miniature Spaniel. He barely eats a cup of dog food a day. But he'll fight to the death if anyone comes near his bowl. Marty has an underbite that could get him a job as a soup ladle at any fancy French restaurant. The vet said he could be made up of about eight different dogs. Marty can eat with Charlie, *if and only if* their bowls are on opposite sides of the kitchen. Stella kind of looks like a miniature River, and she's been known to bare teeth and sink them in if another dog happens by. She can eat in the kitchen, too, if Glenda or I stand there; otherwise she eats in the hallway.

Dooley's about a hundred pounds of white-and-liver–freckled, manic, goofy off-bird dog. He showed up one winter morning, practically crawling across the front yard, as submissive as he could be. But he has the personality of an old drunk: If he's not telling the other dogs how much he loves them—inviting them over to share his bowl—then he's going for the jugular. Dooley *must* eat alone in what used to be a laundry room.

Stella, Marty, and Charlie cannot eat in my workroom because they're small, and the covered cat litter box is back here, and they think it's an hors d'oeuvre tray. Dooley can never eat outside because he'll see a carpenter bee and chase it forever. When any of the dogs are feeling puny and have lost their appetite for dry dog food—and we get them those special diet bags, for old dogs, dogs with bad joints, psychotic dogs—then we have to feed them a mixture of wet food and table scraps. For the most part our dogs are never finicky; a good ex-tree-farm–living stray dog will take dry food over field mice, snakes, and roadkill, I'm thinking.

If the dogs leave food in their bowls, though, it must be picked up soon thereafter, for Herb the cat—also a stray, and mostly a dog—has an appetite for their food. Or maybe he only wants them to think he's really boss.

If it's thundering, Dooley, Inklet, Ann, Joan, and Hershey won't eat at all, and need to be taken one at a time to a closed-door bathroom. If it's that Spring-Forward or Fall-Back Day and we change the clocks, it goofs up everybody involved. If it's dead winter, Glenda and I go through this routine in the morning and afternoon, though with half as much food.

On any given day, any one of our dogs—aged ten months to maybe twelve years old—could change his mind as to what he wants. At any time, I know, one of the dogs could become a bishop and move as diagonally as he wanted. Any one of the dogs could evolve into a rook, and move forward, backward, or sideways in regard to food distribution and place setting. These ex-strays are never pawns. They do not move forward one square at a time.

Clearly—if I had the time or wherewithal—if I played chess, half of my dogs would mistake the pieces or pawns for stylized peach pits. And they would gnaw and growl and check each other's distance, and wag their tails like men in a park, thinking ten moves ahead.

Sleeping with the Pack

Michael J. Rosen

OF ALL THE DOGS WE HAD AS CHILDREN, ONE, MY PARENTS TELL me, never left my side—at least, when he was home. Freckles, their first dog, a Cocker Spaniel, accompanied the mail carrier on his route through the entire neighborhood, meeting him each morning at the bus stop. Otherwise, Freckles slept beneath my crib or lay beside the stroller. Even more than my mother's breath or body's scents, even more than my grandfather's cologne on those nights he walked his colicky first grandson up and down the hallway, the scented molecules of the canine world were what my infant nose took in. Even if my pristine brain couldn't identify those scents any more than a person can discern the astrological stars under which a life begins, I was born into an atmosphere in which a dog star was a constant.

One of my early memories (this is 1960 or so): standing inside the hall closet petting the fur hem of my grandmother's coat. When we'd drive to some restaurant, I'd squish beside her in the backseat, gently, endlessly stroking her mink collar or fox cuff or whatever it was. What it was was *unnatural:* nothing like anything in the rough world I knew, nothing like what anyone else I knew wore. That pelt made my grandmother more animal-like—doglike, to be specific, since that's the only animal I'd ever petted, which brought her closer to me. As the poet Rilke suggests, animals and *not* adults are nearer kin to a child. On those car rides, I'd fall asleep beside my mother's mother, utterly pacified by that fur.

To this day, nothing releases me into a drowsy state faster than riding in a car or lying against a dog's fur.

Dog-care books preach about allowing the dog, as a key member of your social pack, to sleep near you—if not *on* the bed (various studies suggest that more than 40 percent of us share our beds with canines), then at least somewhere in the bedroom or within monitoring, sniffing distance. Such physical proximity is crucial for packs where the humans are gone much of the day. The long nocturnal stretch reinforces the security that pack identity provides.

At this house, both humans are fortunate to work from home most days, living as part of the pack both day and night—yet I still appreciate the notion that my dogs inhale my scent while I'm asleep. To my dogs, I must possess a distinct complex of odors, even though to my nose this individual aroma is as ineffable as the very idea of "home." (Home, in fact, is the very quality that our sleeping together stockpiles for those hours they're alone in the physical house without "home"—meaning, their two humans).

But beyond fulfilling that important pack need, this sleeping arrangement provides comforts more crucial than a perfectly clean comforter. There are few forces as strong as a sleeping dog's gravity: the pull to lie next to your own dog in bed or in a square of winter sunlight on the floor, to yield to that tug of drowsiness as you stroke the fur of a large dog dozing tranquilly. Even if my role is alpha male, I like this puppy mode, snuggling against a dog's curved back, pressing my chest against the heat-radiant fur, lolling an arm across the dog's rising and falling chest, and breathing more slowly, inhaling whatever cypress, clover, or musk smells merge in the coat. Aside from the walks we take together, the four of us burrowed in our bedroom den provides the headiest, most potent sense of our pack.

Though I've forgotten most of my short-lived time in medical school, I remember the words *hypnogogic* and *hypnopompic:* the state of going to sleep and the state of waking up. But knowing words for these bookends of dreams provides a handle, perhaps a legitimacy, to these two states that I most love to share with dogs. There are further reasons.

First, there is the heat I love, the dog's prewarming of a chilly bed through the covers, as well as the dog's own insulating warmth above the blankets.

There's the security of their watchfulness even in sleep. As subconsciously as they continue to scrutinize the nuances of each noise for anything that might warrant rousing into an alarm, I, too, on some unconscious level, must take in their guarding presence as I sleep. It's the same invisible trust we cede the motion detectors' superior knowledge.

And there's their sheer weight. Recently an acquaintance wrote about acquiring her first Papillon (she'd bred the substantial Portuguese Water Spaniel most of her life): "You really must get *another* dog, a small one, for backup, just for sleeping. You don't know what it's like to wake up with a dog in bed." I replied immediately: "Ah, but *you* don't know what it's like to fumble into consciousness thinking that you've lost the use of your lower extremities, trying to piece together dream fragments . . . *Was there an accident? What happened? I couldn't have* . . . before realizing that your ninety-pound dog and your seventy-five-pound dog are stretched on either side of your body, anchoring the covers across your legs the way the Lilliputians restrained Gulliver." Still, I love that security.

What's more, dogs rarely mind your joining them at rest. Nor do they often refuse the request to stop whatever else they might have been doing to join you for a rest. People aren't as accommodating; we're fidgety, physically and psychologically. Human naps are usually taken solo.

Finally, there is the sound of these three other breaths that I love—growing longer and more plangent as their sleeps deepen. Even the occasional snores and twitches are reassuring. And, perhaps best of all, I love to wake and find the bedroom windows fogged or even glazed with ice from the condensation of our four breaths, before beginning whatever breathless schedule the new day has brought.

Evolution? Or the Crown of Creation? (Has Dog Become Master?)

Carolyn Chute

Morning

Michael, my husband, is a human. This is important to remember.

And I am human. I am human. Remember this. The confusion is only temporary.

Wasn't there some significance to being human? We, the inventors of bombs and banks, eggbeaters and bridges, gifts and gift-giving, extortion, jetliners, pottery, roulette wheels, hammers, nails, nuke waste, paper bags, elastics (rubber bands), the Post Office and the CIA? And Cadillacs. And credentials. And butterfly nets and torture chambers. And especially *humans* invented *empires.*

Michael, my human, has sad green-gold-brown eyes and rarely smiles. He has a wonderful long tapered beard, black, though as I squint at him from across the dimly lit room, I see that, yes, the beard has lately become flagged down its center with gray. On his head a hat. A felt crusher like a lot of guys around here like to wear, the perfect hat for farming, for logging. From his father's side of the family, he has been graced with somewhat pointed ears.

He sits squarely on the seat of his rocking chair . . . no, he is hunch-shouldered. He looks bothered. Something on his mind.

The girls are on their pillows on other rockers, and one is under the table of springtime impatiens cuttings and the coffeemaker, there by the window . . . the east side of the house, the brightest side, though it is a dark steamy green May day, blurred and dotted on the many glass panes with rain.

The girls are heavily bearded, too. Margaret has a silvery freshet on the chin, though it seems like only weeks ago that she was young and significantly black, and had more of a sense of humor. Lately, she is a matron of rigid routines, staring crankily and expectantly at me wherever I may stand or sit, bend or scooch, kneel or crawl.

Noon

Though it is rainy, it is heating up inside and out. They all stare at me, waiting. The tongues of Helen, Margaret, Florence, and Betty ripple in and out in the gray, green, and sepia light; ribbons of scarlet are such tongues against their black and substantial apparitions. Michael's tongue stays in his mouth, however, though I know he must be hot, too, because he has taken off one of his work shirts. Hat remains.

I am making dinner. We call it "dinner" in Maine, not "lunch." I place their dinners on their plates and serve them. Then I go upstairs to work. I am a writer. I sit upstairs and pound keys. And every few minutes I stop and listen. It's quiet downstairs.

Late afternoon

I notice it has stopped raining, and I would like to get a load of laundry started and hung out. I leave my workroom and head out through the upstairs hall. In spite of many windows, it is dark in our home these days, thick and dim and Plutonic. Well, the sun is burning through, but the world situation and the shriveling and gasping of our income, as well as our "health issues" that come with age . . . ahem . . . *disease issues* is what they are . . . let's not resort to doublespeak . . . all this does not exactly cast any inner sunshine into these rooms.

Downstairs now, I see that Michael has vanished, probably outside bucksawing wood for next fall. But the girls are all on their pillows. They may have been dreaming a moment ago, but there is no sneaking past them. Their eyelids snap open and they rise to their feet, their black, black gleamy eyes fixed on me. This is, yes, stalking behavior. This is intended to strike fear in me, not because of the old meaning of stalking . . . the wolf thing . . . no, this is not about biting and ripping. This is worse. This is a *system.* This is a sleek, ingeniously unrumpled, perfect program. This is a household-sized Full Spectrum Dominance.

Evening

Michael and I go into our bedroom to have a private discussion without THEM. We are trying to figure out exactly when it all went wrong. When did it begin? Our eyes cautiously slide up toward the framed pictures of Toto, our *first.* He is wearing his bee suit, which he insisted on wearing even after that long-ago Halloween. He was not only our *first.* But he was at that time our *only.* It seemed cute then, even though *it* was creeping in, creeping into our lives, *it,* the thing which has now gotten hold of us, this potency, this salesmanship, this vampire force, this irresistible honeyed deadly attraction, our descent.

Morning

Their eyes guide me. Snacks. Then pills. Then walks. Then more snacks. They like my squeaky voice. My voice isn't normally squeaky (I'm a tall woman so my voice is *not* squeaky) but they like my voice to be squeaky, so squeaky it is. The squeakier I talk, the more I am rewarded with their praise, their tails wagging. No, not tails *wagging.* These are stubby tails (no, not docked. I said *stubby.* Stubby legs, stubby tails, HUGE necks, HUGE heads, broad chests. Large black rubbery noses. Beady forceful powerful *beautiful ohmygawd gorgeous* mean little eyes) . . . these stubby tails do not wag to reward my good behavior. Their tails quiver like the warning tails of rattlesnakes.

Now the rawhide things. Florence chews hers up fast. Betty chews slowly, then swallows it, then barks it back up. She has made it clear that I am to bark back at her. She barks, burps up the slimy thing, and I bark. She chews, swallows, then barks, burps. I bark. This can go on for forty-five minutes. If I don't follow procedure, she'll follow me around and jab the backs of my calves.

Late morning

I sit alone in the bathroom on the tub edge to get *away* from *them.* Michael has gone to town on errands. I am still trying to figure how it happened. Something inside me, right? Some old old old ancient human weakness . . . a flaw . . . a crack in the genetic coding . . . a raw red reflex . . . Guilt? . . . No. Love? . . . No. It's not exactly like anything else. I sigh.

I sneak out into the hall. I need to get upstairs to work on my book. I *must* get past them. I tiptoe.

Yes, they are all there, dreaming on their pillows. I am not breathing. I tiptoe almost to the middle of the room, not even a floor-creak underfoot, just their inner radar for where I am at all times. Their small glowing black eyes snap open. They simultaneously rise on their pillows. I almost weep. I reach for their "walkbox." This is a small box that holds their snacks, which they demand once they are outside beginning their walk.

Moments later

We are "walking." We live in the woods, so leashes are not necessary. And besides, the girls are not going to run afar. They are not deer chasers or moose chasers. They are diggers. They are *built* like badgers for *killing* badgers. What they do, if they *were* to do a badger, is each take a badger hole and guard it. Helen is our Alpha. Helen of Parsonsfield. Queen. Like the face "that launched a thousand ships." She starts to dig. She is a *powerful* digger and *means business.* There are about forty-six (expanded-by-Helen) chipmunk holes around our yard that the insurance man has never seen. If there were badgers down in these holes (instead of cocky sassy unruffable chipmunks), and if Helen keeps whittling away there on the situation, the badgers would come out of all the exit holes right into the natural steel-jaw traps built into the faces of Florence, Margaret, and Betty.

But there are no badgers in Maine. Chip and Dale as prizes just aren't worth the full regiment. The digging usually ends after twenty minutes.

In fact, after about seven or eight minutes of this, I get bored and want to just go back inside, up to my workroom to create ART. But if I fuss too soon, the four of them give me The Look. This is the greatest, most formidable weapon of all: The Sad Look. The Carolyn-you-are-a-mean-selfish-uncool-person look. And so our "walk," which is only a few feet from the house, moving ponderously from one set of holes to the next, lasts about an hour and a half.

After dinner

The human, Michael, whispers to me that he'd like to have a word in *private.* We sneak into the bathroom and close the door. He asks if I'd like to smooch. Smooching is not easy *in front of them,* even a quick in-passing smooch. They charge us (you know, like the cavalry) and whine and then they jab us in the calves and shins, trying to divert this special energy of ours into their issues.

A little smooching begins.

Instantly there are a couple of angry volleys upon the door. Just Betty at first.

We freeze.

But then we decide to go ahead with it. But it's tense for us as the banging, scratching, digging, whimpering, howling, and barking outside the door never stops, never stops, never ever ever stops.

Evening

Michael shows me one of his drawings he has been working on for a few nights. I like the colors and all his quirky details. He has always been an artist. As a kid, it was graffiti and doodles. Faces. Spirits. The apple cold storage, where he worked when I met him almost twenty-five years ago, still has the devil faces he painted up there with the black tarry room-sealer stuff.

Now he has art books. At first his pictures were of his life, like image journals. For instance, the one of himself and his friend Emil standing around a bonfire. The sky is pink. The trees are potent shades of green and blue, thistled in black. So many tiny lines, whole geographies and even flesh made entirely of brisk persnickety but nervous lines. See, this picture is clearly *two humans* enjoying a camping trip.

But now it is all changed. What is happening to us? Michael's drawings have phased into a cry for help, maybe. What do *you* think it is? There are men and women with paws. Black rubbery noses. No clothes. They are naturally and completely furry. Each wears an unreadable expression.

I close the art book. I look into Michael's eyes.

Another day

I study the photo of Toto by the refrigerator. No, not Toto in his bee suit. This one is Toto (remember, he was our *first)* wearing his Yale T-shirt. He collected them. Mostly from colleges we went to (Toto and Michael and I) so I could do a reading or lecture or teaching thing for my "career." A blue-and-white T-shirt was his Colby. Bowdoin was gray. Dartmouth was green. He had a gray UNH, a black USM (depicting a black bear), and many others. Toto was a gentleman. He tried to be like us (the humans).

If we wore Groucho Marx noses or pig noses with the grandson, Toto wore Groucho Marx and pig noses, too. When we flossed our teeth, he (with assistance) flossed his.

So cute.

It's all math. *One* of them and *two* of us = the human paradigm. But if it is *four* of them and only *two* of us = the woofy paradigm.

Another day

I am looking at the bills. *Scary.* A lot of *vet* bills. And with the cost of *everything in this world* going up and our income flat out near zero, we are trying not to spend. So mostly it is ricy foods and no doctor visits for Michael and me, even though I have acquired a painful limp, a sharp (almost electric) pain in my left ear, and four busted teeth; and how it is, I often stop breathing in the night. Add to that double vision. But as we all know, here in America, unless you are a high-up politician and the like, there's no free lunch.

Michael has an errand in town and I would like to go. Writing at my books and essays all the time, I don't see much of the world beyond the end of our dirt road.

"It's too hot to take the girls," Michael points out.

I look down at them, all four of them shoulder to shoulder around the door, ready to go.

I know if I go with Michael and leave them home, they will be *bored.* Or something. One of the reasons we decided on so many of them, rather than an *only,* was so there wouldn't be those times when off we go, leaving one poor little soul alone. But, as all of it has backfired, so has this part as well.

"I'll stay home with them," I announce. They happily bounce around me . . . or rather they *heavily* bounce around me badger-style.

The truck is parked close to the door. The windshield reflects the morning sun in spite of the late-May pollenish green cast. I stand on the granite door-rock for a sad good-bye with Michael. Instead of kissing good-bye, we touch noses. I can't remember when it was we actually *kissed* good-bye. But I know we used to.

Michael drives away.

The girls demand snacks. As I am passing the small bone-shaped cookies around, Florence drops hers. After some recent and expensive X rays on Florence's jaws, we found there is nothing wrong with her teeth. She just does not *prefer* this discount-type dog snack. So I go and rustle through the refrigerator for something that will make the grade.

Another day

Another day older and deeper in debt. Poor in finances but rich in friends, we get word that famous folksingers have offered to come to Maine to do benefits for us to help raise money for some of our pressing bills and especially for a few visits to "human doctors." One of the benefit performances is to be here at our house.

Michael and I race around sweeping and rearranging furniture. Most of the furniture is arranged for the girls, pillows and piles of rags. Cement-block steps to a pulled-together circle of rocking chairs ("Stairway to Helen") to accommodate stubby legs. No couch. No end tables. No pretty rugs. Florence's program of peeing on any furniture that looks too human has determined the decor since her arrival here eight years ago.

Seeing that we are obviously preparing for the arrival of outside humans, Betty positions herself by the door, ears wide open like two "dishes" of military radar. She has already ripped the hand open of a friend who sat in a chair here once to chat with Michael (which the insurance man also doesn't know about). Fortunately we usually don't entertain *here,* but hang out with our friends *out there* at political protests, direct actions, State House "raids," meetings, and Chautauquas.

Okay, so Betty is ready.

Carloads and truckloads of activist-type humans arrive with their video cameras, bags of food, chips, soda pop, veggie casseroles, Coney Island–style hot dogs, salads, breads. Some wear black bandannas and other anarchist apparel, some wear camo and bush hats. Then there're the ones with jeans, sweaters, and funny hats. Then the preppies, chinos, pale shirts, and cute shoes. All types and sizes of radical human.

Food is everywhere in bowls and bags, frying in pans. The musicians set up. A high-school-aged band sets up first, a wonderful addition to the folksingers. Humans from Vermont. Humans from Massachusetts. Humans from Washington State.

Betty is locked in the other room, chin on paws, eyes blazing, in her flabbergasted retaliationist mode.

Margaret and Florence circulate as fairly cool hostesses. Helen of Parsonsfield remains distant, eyes scanning the crowd of fifty or more humans, including really small humans, humans in the pup stage. They tend to drop food.

That night

The doorman passed us the money, three hundred bucks almost. Enough for a couple of doctor visits or half the interest on a month's house payment (house ransom, we call it). We are overwhelmed with gratitude. We hug the last humans to leave and watch them drive away.

The next morning

Before I call to make an appointment with the foot doc or ear doc or dentist . . . or maybe one of the other docs . . . there are so many ways to go, am trying to decide best where to start . . . the girls pressure me to take them out to "walk."

Only a few feet from the back porch, I see Margaret with her head moving funny. She is eating something. Crunching away. What is it? I open her jaws (remember, the girls have huge jaws). I feel around in there. Rocks! Margaret is eating rocks!

A few days later

We have driven many miles up into the higher mountains to a very special vet, one who does tooth surgery. Margaret enters the waiting room wearing her pink harness, so eye-dazzling against her broad black furry chest. She watches as I count out all the benefit money as down payment toward her dental work. Sure, if it had just been a couple of her incisors, that's one thing. But Margaret's only grinding teeth in the waaaayyyy back were the ones broken in half. And her favorite pastime is lounging on her pillows with her rawhide things. So here we are.

Moments later

I limp out to the truck and the sharp pain in my ear is beginning to flare up, and my double vision makes funny lines around the truck handle as I reach for it. I look back at the glass doors of the fancy vet dentist's office and blink back my awe of this universe.

Donna and Harry

Jon Katz

MY DOGS HEARD THE SOUNDS BEFORE I DID—SOMEONE CROONING a song, a dog baying intermittently in response. As we rounded a wooded corner at a park near our house, we came upon them: a woman sitting on a wooden bench, serenading a rust-colored Welsh Corgi with enormous eyes and even larger ears.

She was singing to the tune of "Rudolph the Red-Nosed Reindeer" and gazing at the dog, who was focused just as intently on her, head tilting. The lyrics were primitive, the story timeless:

Harry the Welsh Corgi
Had really big, big ears
They never did stop growing
Throughout the years
All of the other Corgis
Laughed at him and even jeered
They would tell poor Harry,
"Hey, man, your ears are queer."

And Harry—we supposed—was singing back, offering a joyous howl every third or fourth line. It was quite a duet.

The woman looked pale and

weary; her stomach was distended. Her brunette wig, too, suggested chemotherapy. But there was a big smile on her face.

The song, as it unfolded over several stanzas and we eavesdropped discreetly from behind a stand of trees, was the tale of a hapless Corgi ridiculed and rejected by his peers until Santa arrived to confer acceptance.

This Corgi did, in fact, have Dumbo-sized ears. They could have helicoptered him right into the sky if he could flap them fast enough.

The power of this intimate scene was mesmerizing, and it was a bit embarrassing to have stumbled upon it.

My dogs charged forward to greet Harry with the usual sniffing, circling, and investigating. The woman looked a bit mortified. "So am I imagining things?" I said, mostly to break the ice. "Or were you singing to your dog? I do it all the time."

She blushed, introducing herself—Donna—and struggling a bit to get up off the bench. I thought at first she was somewhere in her sixties; later she told me that she was in her late forties. But her balance was off and she moved slowly, with great fatigue.

"I admit it," she said, with a smile and a shrug. "I sing to Harry all the time. We sing to each other. It's silly, isn't it?"

We connected easily enough. With dog people, one thing generally leads to another. It didn't take long for us to trade stories.

She'd worked as an office manager for an insurance company north of Princeton for thirty years, but she was planning to retire soon. Yes, she was sick, and was working fewer hours than before. She'd undergone a series of debilitating surgeries and chemotherapy treatments for breast cancer; they'd left her swollen and, as she put it, "wrung out."

She lived alone now, in a nearby garden apartment complex, her husband having left a year after her diagnosis. She was a throwback in the rapidly yuppifying town, a working-class office worker who was being supplanted by the wealthy Boomers and Yuppies pouring in from New York City with their small kids.

"He isn't a bad guy, just not a strong guy," she said. "In a way, it was just as well. We were having problems before all this, to be honest, so it wasn't only about my being sick. And I think I would have ended up worrying about him all the time.

"So I went to a breeder I found on the Internet and got Harry when he was nine weeks old. He was definitely the runt of the litter, the odd one out. I fell in love with him from the minute I saw those big ears and big eyes."

Every time she mentioned his name, Harry's head swiveled, and he came running over for a pat and a smooch. Certain dogs just exude unrelenting sweetness; Harry was one of them. He and Donna kept the sort of continuous eye contact that trainers love so much. Harry kept so close an eye on her that she rarely had to utter commands. He simply went where she went. They nearly melted with affection whenever they looked at each other.

Few working dogs worked harder than Harry. Much of the work that dogs are being asked to do in contemporary America involves not guarding livestock or hunting birds, but tending to human beings and their emotional needs.

And Donna was in need. As she moved in and out of operating rooms, many of her friends had drifted away, too. She understood. "It was too hard for them," she said. "Between the divorce and the cancer, I think I had the mark of Cain on me. People just don't know what to do. It hurt at first, then I accepted it, and I decided to make my stand with Harry—the two of us. I know he isn't a person, and I don't treat him like one, but I couldn't have made a better choice." Harry wasn't about to drift away. He rarely even looked away.

She referred repeatedly to The Plan. She had a plan. Step one: Retire. Step two: Buy a small farmhouse in rural Pennsylvania. Step three: Make arrangements for Harry to live with her remaining close friend, Joan, who loved dogs. Step four: When it was time, die in her peaceful new home, with Harry by her bedside. With her pension, savings, and benefits, she'd have just enough to pull off The Plan. She didn't figure on being around more than a year or two, anyway. Some of her remaining money would be earmarked for Harry's lifelong care.

Over the next few months, I visited with Donna and Harry in her spartan apartment—in one of those nondescript brick complexes with a pseudo-aristocratic name. The apartment was orderly and comfortable, but spare: Donna had hung inexpensive framed posters of dogs and birds on the walls and scattered plants around the rooms, but there wasn't a lot of furniture; the sofas and chairs she had were functional and inexpensive.

Mornings, Donna and Harry went for a walk in the woods behind the complex. Then she went to work, when and for as long as she was able. Then home for an early dinner—a small salad, soup, and a sandwich for her, a can of Pedigree for Harry, followed by a few freeze-dried liver treats. As they were expensive—$4.99 for a can with about forty pieces—Harry got two or three a night, parceled out during the time between dinner and bedtime. The second she reached for the can, Harry was at her feet, eyes wide, tail wagging. He took each treat over to the far corner of the living room, where he devoured it as carefully and enthusiastically as if it were a hunk of red meat.

Donna didn't use rawhide or chewbones out of fear that Harry would choke on them. A pair of binoculars and a thick guide to birds that inhabit the Northeast sat on a coffee table. There was a thin layer of dust on both. The lime green wooden birdhouse by the bedroom window was unoccupied, the bins empty of food.

Then an after-dinner walk in the park, the last of the night. The TV would then go on, and while Donna watched, she tossed a hard rubber ball for Harry, who growlingly pursued it all over the apartment, racing from one room to another until he was worn out. By 9 P.M., an elaborate consumption of a half dozen pills and then bed.

Harry had a cedar bed in each room, but he slept in Donna's bed alongside the pillow. On hot nights, she would leave the patio door open, and he would sometimes sleep out there, and try to catch whatever breeze there might be.

The apartment had a fenced postage stamp of a patio where she and Harry could sit and take the sun. Technically, the place didn't permit dogs, but if owners didn't flaunt their existence and the dogs were cleaned up after, stayed quiet, and didn't bite anybody, nobody bothered them. Like almost all true dog lovers, Donna was unfailingly conscientious about cleaning up after her dog, hauling biodegradable clean-up bags around in the purple fanny pack she always carried outside. She didn't want to give anybody any reason to dislike or ban dogs.

When she felt down, or "teary," as she sometimes put it, Harry yelped, squirmed, and looked generally ridiculous with those huge ears, winning a smile or even a laugh. He could twinkle. He apparently had scant tolerance for moping or brooding; at their first sign, he was up nosing around, getting Donna moving or singing. Sometimes he just pressed against her for a long cuddle.

Truckloads of books and studies address the emotional lives of dogs, but it seems almost impossible to know much with any real certainty, even as people increasingly turn to them to fill the emotional gaps in their lives.

Sometimes, they seem to be emotional canvases on which people can paint whatever they need or want. They can never adjust the picture or point out where we might be wrong. We can only observe and guess about the origins and complexity of people's and dogs' sometimes profound attachments.

Any of our theories—and there are many—is as good and true as any other. The emotional bonds between people and their dogs remain private and powerful, often unhindered by contradiction or reality, free to grow and expand in ways outsiders can never fully grasp. But Harry seemed to understand that he had a task to perform, and he took his work seriously.

Whenever Donna reached down, Harry's head was under her hand. While she read, he dozed. When she breathed oddly or groaned in pain, he'd practically glue himself to her side.

He went along as she visited her various doctors, waiting eagerly in the car, staring at the last spot he'd seen her, squealing with joy when she returned, even as she struggled to deal with uncomfortable procedures, a growing array of medications and insurance forms, and a dismaying stream of bad news.

She lost much of her hair, gained weight as the result of some of the medications and procedures, and then rapidly lost it again, struggled to summon the energy to get through each day. Through this, Harry helped in every way he could; at times, he was the only thing that did.

Donna's friend Joan also came by regularly, working hard to build a relationship with Harry, bringing treats and toys and making a big fuss over him. He was obviously fond of her, as he was with almost everyone he met, but he stayed focused on Donna. Did he know something was wrong? Impossible to say. But he couldn't have worked any harder at watching over her.

"He means the world to me," she told me one day in the park. "It's hard for even my closest friends to talk to me about this, and my husband just cracked. Harry is my heart, he makes me smile, keeps me company, gets me off my butt." I was struck by how often I had heard people use this term, a person referring to a dog as their "heart" or their "lifetime dog." In certain contexts and situations, dogs are able to connect with the deepest part of a person, with their heart and soul. That was what had happened between Donna and Harry. Nobody could have a better, more devoted, or understanding companion.

Donna was a strong, good-hearted, resourceful, and inherently optimistic person. She never complained about her illness or expressed any bitterness toward the husband and friends who'd abandoned her. She relied on a dog to ward off loneliness, provide activity, support, and succor.

Was this a good thing? Was Harry being asked to do something that a dog can't possibly understand? But this was a question, not an argument. Stories about dogs like Harry are always told with warmth and wonder, but I am sometimes haunted by the idea that Donna should have had more people caring for her, not just a devoted Corgi. Harry couldn't talk to her about her illness or her death the way friends or relatives would. Yet Harry and Donna's relationship was pure, joyous, faithful, and comforting. In the absence of people, I hated to think of her without the big-eared Corgi. And it appeared to be Donna's choice as well as her fate.

"It's a simple relationship. What he does is make me feel loved, and what he also does is keep me concentrating on loving back," she explained one night. "I need that. I don't think dogs are a replacement for people. Yet sometimes they are, aren't they?"

Sometimes, for better or worse, dogs are a replacement for people. As the dog population grows, and as traditional opportunities for dogs to run, work, and play diminish—thanks partly to the growing numbers of dogs and the corresponding wave of lawsuits, leash laws, and other regulations—dogs and their roles are evolving. Scholar after scholar has pointed out that despite all our new information technology, we've become an increasingly disconnected society. It grows ever more difficult for people to meet and get to know one another.

The new work of dogs, increasingly, appears to bridge that gap and fill some of those holes. Sometimes that's a great thing, a role that works to everybody's advantage. Sometimes not. When people turn to dogs as a substitute for humans, or use them to take on, rework, and resolve deep and old issues in their lives, they may turn away from the notion of facing their problems.

And who, precisely, speaks for the dogs?

The millions of dogs who are ignored or poorly trained, mistreated and abandoned, left in shelters or who are acting out neurotically, destructively, and aggressively in private homes, suggest that dogs can't always meet the growing expectations people have for them.

But that can't be said of Harry. As Donna flags—I see her at home more than in the park these days—I've begun to doubt The Plan. She may never get to that farmhouse, and she seems to know it. Over time, references to The Plan diminished, then ceased.

But one thing is sure: When Donna dies, she will not be alone. Harry will be by her side, singing his own kind of song. She will leave this world feeling loved.

Living in Dog Years

Bill Vaughn

SPYING FROM MY HAMMOCK AS RADISH DRAGGED HOME THE spine of a winter-killed whitetail he'd scavenged in the forest, I realized that I had developed a bad case of professional jealousy. The truth is, my thirteen-year-old red Heeler was far better at what he did than I am at what I do. While I was missing the boat, buying high and selling low, choking on the anxieties that settle in with the night, yet feeling nothing in the morning except that cool remove, Radish joyously organized *his* days so that they passed before him like gleaming cans of Alpo on an endless conveyor belt. Because he was a monument to the simple life naturally lived, I decided to study him, to read him as if he were one of those get-ahead books, *Ten Habits of the Super Successful,* say, or *Twelve Steps to the New You.*

The next morning I wandered from the bedroom to find him sprawled on the living room couch with Clara, our little four-year-old Border Collie. On the other couch were three of their pals from the neighborhood, an expensive Corgi of the Cardigan variety named Mr. Rogers, an Australian Shepherd named Cricket, and a sweet-tempered Pit Bull named Big Head Todd. These high breeds sometimes spent the night whenever Radish allowed them through the dog door. They had about them the contemplative emotional weather of people who had just settled onto their beach blankets with a best-seller and a cold one. My wife, Kitty, ushered out the neighbors so the home dogs could eat their breakfasts of chicken and rice bran. And then our summer day began.

Radish trotted down the hill behind the house to the slough for a drink and the first of his many swims. Next stop was the corrals, where Kitty was feeding the horses. Radish made a beeline for Mokie, a mare Kitty's family has owned for all of the horse's thirty-five years. His obsession with this geriatric wonder was based on the fact that, because her teeth have been ground to stubs, much of the meal she chews dribbles from her mouth and falls to the ground. Next, after grazing on horse feed, Radish sampled a nice fresh horse turd, a delicacy no dog can seem to resist, rendering the phrase "shit-eating dog" redundant. Whether he liked the texture of it or he sought the undigested grain in this offal, he was so fond of a little taste every day that in the winter he smuggled in frozen hunks of it, dropping them on the hearth to thaw.

When he was finished at the corrals I followed as he headed across our front field, under the wood-rail fence, and out into the pastures of the ranch next door. When we first moved to this floodplain in western Montana, Radish counted on the fact that the rancher fed his cattle every morning with milled oats. Because oats come under the heading of what Radish does for a living, he made these feedlots a mandatory stop on his daily roam before the rancher went to an all-hay diet. But it wasn't the memory of porridge that drove Radish on, it was grooming. Or maybe *image enhancement* would better describe the streak of green cow shit that he smeared across his cape as he rolled on his back in the muck, his legs waving languidly in the sweet mountain air. He jumped to his feet with a satisfied grunt and turned to admire the glorious mess he'd made of himself.

I walked him back down to the slough and heaved a stick into the water. He went after it like a shot, throwing himself off the bank and hitting so hard his belly flop spooked a pair of pheasants, who exploded from the brush with a stream of cuss words and a furious flurry of wings. When Clara heard the ruckus she streaked from the house, down the hill, and flung herself in the water as well, in order to wrestle Radish for the stick. They swam around each other in circles, growling, a dog fixed to each end of the stick, until Radish let her have what she wanted. It was his nature to live and let live. He'd been in only two fights—a blue Heeler named Bingo tore his right ear, and a neighbor's calico named Wilma jumped on his back and rode him like a bronc.

We got Radish from a cattle rancher named Jerry Hamel, whose spread is on the Flathead Indian Reservation. Six years earlier we'd bought a mare from Hamel, and trusted his estimation of animals. But when we drove up to look at the pup he was so fat and his legs so short I decided this blob couldn't possibly be a Heeler—that speedy and quick-witted working breed that everyone in the West who traffics in quarter horses simply must own to complete his self-conscious ensemble.

But Jerry assured me that this bag of butter was indeed a Heeler; he was fat because he and his brother, Mouse, were the only pups in the litter. When we drove back to the rez a few weeks later, Radish and Shine, his momma, were playing in an irrigation ditch. Before he could waddle off I snatched him up. While I sat with him in the truck and Kitty chatted with Hamel I noticed that this new addition to our menagerie had no tail.

"Jerry!" I called, not knowing then that working dogs are often docked so there's nothing to get in the way of the work. "Where's his tail?"

"Ho, you know Indians," Hamel said. "We ate it."

When Radish was clean he rolled in the grass, then suddenly began barking furiously at a pair of red-tailed hawks, who looked down from their gyres to see if this nuisance might be something good to eat. His love-hate relationship with birds sprang from the dressing-down I gave him after he tried to eat a neighbor's chicken the very day in 1990 we moved from the city to the country. "Yer dawg done bit off Gary's butt hole," Gary's rednecked owner observed, cradling his damaged rooster, which would soon recover.

Maybe this kind of projectile barking was a compensation for his ebbing powers—his hindquarters, for example, had begun showing the emaciation that strikes the males of all mammals, plus he'd developed a heart murmur. Or maybe it was just a new tactic he was employing in his ceaseless harvest of the world. But friends, this dog could bark! When it happened unexpectedly indoors, your stunned eardrums hummed afterward from the force of it. In the autumns Radish sat under our Goodland apple tree and barked heavenward until fatigued, nerve-rattled fruit just gave up and dropped from the branch.

He went back to the slough for a beverage, and then grazed on the tender tops of the broadgrass that carpets the banks between the cattails. After joining Clara and Mr. Rogers for a chase game in the backyard, he went for a nap to a special spot under a mountain laurel in our walled garden. An hour later, with temperatures pushing ninety, he padded into my office and ordered me to take him swimming in the river.

The instant I grabbed an inner tube from the elm where the tubes are stored, the dogs bolted before me over an earthen dam blocking the slough, along a winding footbridge I'd built across a stream called Little Back Creek, and loped down the path through the forest under a canopy of cottonwoods to the river. Without waiting for me, Clara flung herself from the bank, with Radish close behind, and they began paddling furiously for the opposite shore. Although the channel here is only a hundred yards wide, the flood swept us downstream twice that distance before we could beach ourselves on Radish Island. The dogs shook themselves and raced down the gravel to a sandy lagoon on the tip of the island where a languid whirlpool keeps the sticks I throw in play.

Although he was bred to work cattle, Radish had never been fully trained to do anything. In the mid-1990s, after I decided to finish some unfinished tasks, including my college degree and the requirements to become an Eagle Scout, I recruited our veterinarian to administer the performance test for the Dog Care merit badge. When he asked me to put my animal through his paces, Radish crawled under the horse trailer after I ordered him to stay, began barking when I ordered him to sit, and peed on the vet's truck when I yelled at him to fetch a stick.

"I'm going to pass you," the vet said. "But only because you did good on the knowledge part. Maybe you should think about obedience school."

Too late for that, I thought, shaking his hand. Radish came and went as he pleased, slept on the furniture, drank from the toilets, climbed on the tables to look for butter, and yapped like a hyena when I licked my plate because that also came under the heading of what he did for a living. Some people were horrified that I was raising a hippie, but I admired the liberties he took. They are the canine equivalents of what I would do if I had more courage—the complete 352-day year I would devote to nothing except learning Welsh, building a still, making preparations to have a taxidermist freeze-dry my carcass on Getaway Day, and riding my horses from Caracas to Buenos Aires.

Uneducated as he was, however, Radish had always been a quick study. He immediately learned how to heel, how to use his dog door, and how to cajole what he wanted from horses without getting kicked. Because a parcel delivery driver gave him a biscuit ten years ago, he began leaping into all delivery vans the moment they pulled up to the house, and would lope down the lane to the neighbor's if a van stopped there instead of here. Since they knew that he would not exit their vehicles until he got a treat, the FedEx and UPS and Airborne Express drivers all began carrying biscuits when they came this way.

His vocabulary included twenty-three words. When you told him to fetch the ball, he would not fetch a stick. When you told him to get the box, he would savagely tear apart any of the cardboard boxes I threw in the yard. When you ordered him to get the Mousy, he brought forth a pink rubber toy he'd owned for three years, gnawing it only hard enough to make it squeak. And when you yelled *"Mouse!"* he knew that what you meant was not *his* mouse but mice at large. He killed scores of these vermin in the house and in the feed shed by quickly crushing their heads, but ate only one of them—the first one he killed, which made him nauseous.

While we strolled through the river grass to the head of the island, Radish disappeared, as he often did on these day trips, and didn't join us until Kitty and I were reading in bed late that night. He jumped up between us, forcing Clara to make room, and was asleep before I could say hello. I smelled his coat and rubbed it, trying to figure out where he'd been. Here was the faint astringency of the feral mint that grows in a briar patch not even the horses can penetrate. From his belly I plucked off a couple of beggar's lice that told me he'd visited a thicket where he once dined on a the remains of a fool's hen a fox had killed. And here on his hock was a dusting of wood ash that had clung there when he'd walked through a fire ring where we'd gathered in the snow around a Christmas bonfire.

But it wasn't till he farted with a burlesque blat that I knew he'd been on the trail of something dead to eat. Whatever it was—beaver, duck,

ing at my bandaged ankle and the crutches. "What happened to you?" she said.

That night I suggested we trade places because the doc said to keep my ankle elevated and quiet. Ever since we got married, I'd been sleeping between my wife and the bedroom door—sleeping that way through two apartments and one house. It's as if I'll be on hand to protect her from a burglar or something. I imagine all guys sleep this way, waiting for a crash in the night, for a big shape to fill up the doorway. I imagine women sleep tuned in to smaller sounds. Raccoons in the garbage cans or babies crying to be changed and fed. I think my wife still sleeps this way even though we won't be having any kids—unless a baby comes along for adoption before that agency decides we're too old. My wife, she got the room all ready—painted it, made curtains—but nothing's happened yet.

So we switched places that night for the first time, me with my foot bandaged and stiff, propped up on pillows like a beacon. My wife put my magazines and the remote for the TV beside me on her table, then she got into bed real careful.

In the dim light of our bed lamps the dog went crazy. He traveled back and forth and back and forth. He sleeps in the crook of my wife's knees, between her and the wall. But that night he couldn't find his place. He kept seeing me, probably smelling my fear that he'd pounce on my ankle.

"Maybe we should keep the dog out tonight," I said.

"Good idea," she said. She started getting out of bed real careful-like again, then suddenly the dog got smart. He let out a bark and jumped up and got himself settled in between us, this big dog, although it took a while for him to adjust to the warmer wall—me. We slept that way for almost a month. Ankles take a while to heal like everything else. Then one night my wife said, "Let's change back," and the same thing happened. Back and forth, back and forth.

Tonight, again, I'm feeling restless. When my wife comes in, she notices immediately.

"It's been a while," I say from her side of the bed. I am sitting up, sheets tucked tight beneath my arms.

She laughs. "He loves it." My wife is game. She puts on one of my old T-shirts and climbs in. I turn off the light. As we begin to listen, I grope for her hand beneath the sheet. I scratch her palm a little like I used to do. It's been a long time for other things too. She gives my hand a squeeze, then pats it. Then she lets it go. We wait for the dog.

Sure enough, pretty soon the dog comes along and back and forth, and back and forth. We are both tense, listening. The dog is getting older now and he's been showing signs of arthritis in his joints. So my wife begins to give him hints. She whispers his name. She pats the bed between us down behind her knees. I feel the bedspread flatten and puff, flatten and puff. Soon the dog heaves himself up with a bark and flops down in the space between us. Hair flies everywhere. He scratches. He slobbers and smells bad. He snores. He sleeps long after we get up, get dressed. Sometimes he whimpers in his sleep. I worry about the dog. I worry about us.

Citizen Canine

Charles Siebert

IT IS A DEFINITIVE SIGN THAT A CULTURE IS ENJOYING AN extended period of peace and prosperity when it is able to extend all of its creature comforts to its creatures. As a devoted dog owner, I've been particularly aware of this trend for some time. To wit: I heard an interview on the radio not long ago with a man who claims to have built a machine that translates barking into English. He said he'd already deciphered his dog's first full sentence. I ran to turn up my radio. This was, after all, a moment mankind has dreamt of since about the dawn of consciousness. "I want," a warbly, metallic voice began, "to go to Dairy Queen!" But even as we await that day when our dogs will be donning smoking jackets and herding us into parlors for a rousing interspecial exchange, it seems the language barrier is about the only one left anymore between the dog and its full-scale admittance into our frame of reference.

Most breeds have been pulled by us so far from their original purpose—be it to aid in the hunt or help keep the domestic herds in line—

that they've essentially been rendered retarded, four-legged renditions of us: shepherds of shifting moods (theirs and ours), exceptionally eager humpers of couch pillows in sky-borne apartments. Today's dogs have their own gyms and parks, and, in addition to the traditional grooming salon, they have dog spas. They have psychiatrists, especially the urban dog, prone to bouts of ennui so deep they'll stare for hours out apartment windows and occasionally off themselves by leaping from them. There are special dog photographers and dog schools and day-care centers, and for their owners' more extended leaves, there are both dog camps—advertising such features as "off-leash outings"—and dog hotels. A new one opened recently in Manhattan featuring a health spa, a massage parlor, and relaxing CD recordings.

When I was a boy in the early '60s, a pet store was where you went to get a pet. The pet's necessities you found at the supermarket, in the "Pet Supplies" section. Now, of course, we have the pet emporium, proffering everything from glow-in-the-dark collars and fetch balls to carrying cases and even shoes—one of the real sore points in the civilizing process of the dog being the effect of our winter sidewalk salt on their bare paws.

As for what to feed the modern dog, there is now a confounding assortment of foods, the varying ingredients and nutritional values of which I spend more time contemplating than I do that of my own diet. Every month or so, meanwhile, some new, improved concoction arrives with things like special digestive enzymes, and "Direct Fed Microbials," and yucca extracts that are said to reduce stool and urine odor; foods that, as the brochure for the most recent addition to my local purveyor's shelves boldly proclaims, "revolutionize the way [our] companion carnivores are fed."

Now, I love my companion carnivores and feel I've done my best to keep up with all the latest developments on their behalf, but sometimes, as I scour the emporium aisles for all the latest accessories, and pore over the various food ingredient labels, I hear my father's voice calling to me: "What are you doing? It's a damn dog. Throw it some Alpo and be done with it."

All of which makes the most recent development in the civilizing of the canine very ironic indeed. I first got wind of it a few months ago in the course of my daily dog walks in Brooklyn's Prospect Park, known to be one of the more cutting-edge canine-friendly greenswards of any city anywhere, boasting lenient off-lead laws, special, ground-level dog water fountains, and a very civic-minded society of dog walkers known as FIDO—Fellowship for the Interests of Dogs and their Owners. What all of this mostly amounts to is a bunch of us humans, standing around in little clutches, blabbing, like overly indulgent parents, all sorts of nonsense about our dogs and how and why they do the cute little things they do, while they dash all around us, trying to mount each other's head. It was during just such a session that I overheard a fellow dog owner telling another about how she had been "stalled with her traditional vet," and was now seeing a holistic veterinarian who has advised her that the majority of today's newfangled foods are, in fact, either slowly poisoning dogs with various chemical additives or unduly straining their digestive systems with super-balanced diets that try to cram everything a dog needs into each meal. "My dogs eat only raw meat now," the woman proudly declared as I skulked off, suddenly mortified by my two pampered and possibly poisoned pooches. "I mean they are, after all, dogs." Not long after this interlude, I was thumbing through my latest issue of *The Bark* and came upon an interview with a holistic veterinarian named Dr. Martin Goldstein. Dr. Goldstein seems a somewhat cautious advocate of the BARF diet (bones and raw food) but says that even for dogs being fed the most nutritious organic and homegrown foods, dietary supplements are still necessary, "to put back into balance what has been out of whack for so long. . . . We have," he says, "gone so far from nature that animals in domestication cannot do it alone anymore."

Of course, all of this has thrown me entirely out of whack about who my dogs even are anymore and how exactly I'm supposed to treat them. Chemical additives notwithstanding, my father's German Shepherd "Hoss" lived twelve years on Alpo and Gravy Train. My first dog, Lucy, a Dalmatian who died just over a year ago, lasted thirteen years on a variety of the best and latest of the premium-processed dry dog foods.

Still, until we get all the kinks worked out of that bark-translating machine, the ongoing argument over what's best for the dog will remain a trifle one-sided, and the prevailing wisdom now seems to be that no self-respecting dog can be considered truly advanced until it has been exposed to the same alternatives to our own advancements that we have.

I once lived in a world ruled by dogs. All day they roamed the streets and etched lawns of the two-story brick houses that surrounded my ground-floor apartment in a small working-class community on the outskirts of Houston, Texas, where I was a teaching-fellow in creative writing for three years. They kept watch over everyone and -thing in the neighborhood. If a strange car came along, they'd start at the bright fender and chase it right out of view. When I stepped out my door in the morning, they'd be there to check me out, passing by, noses up, like schools of hairy, sniffing fish. Often, a lone sentinel would be posted at the neighborhood's outskirts. I remember one in particular, a little white banshee that I somehow ran afoul of on my way to campus one Friday afternoon. He was sitting out in front of the cantina that I walked past each day, alongside the Union Pacific railroad tracks. The dog eyed every step of my approach and, when I'd gotten a good thirty feet past him, crept up and sank his little scissor teeth into the back of my leg about calf-high. I tried chasing after him—Houston happened to be in the midst of a rabies outbreak at the time—but he darted down the street, disappearing behind a row of houses. Ducking into a phone booth alongside the cantina, I held the receiver away from my ear as a rabies task force specialist yelled at me that I had to find that dog. Night after night, for a full week, I closed down that cantina in hopes of finding either the dog's owner or the menacing beast himself, and then, at the exact same hour on the following Friday, there he was, sitting out front in the bright sunlight. I slipped back into the phone booth, called the rabies task force specialist. "He's here," I whispered. "I'm looking right at him." "What's he doing?" he asked. "Well," I said, "I think he's waiting to bite me again." "Then he's fine. If that dog's still up and around, he's fine."

I figured that night to be my first truly sound sleep in a week. The dogs, however, had a different agenda. They were up to all hours, barking and howling. I waited well toward morning for them to finally retire. One never did. He was tied to the post of a makeshift car park just up the block, his barks like a hammer against the tin sides. I put on some clothes and stumbled up the block. It was the banshee. Who, I asked myself, would reclaim this monster? Nobody answered at what I assumed to be the dog's home, so I decided to paste a note to a car park post just out of bite range, asking if the dog could please be kept inside at night. On my way to campus later that afternoon, I noticed another note taped over mine: "This dog no bother you," it began, "As you must talk. A dog must bark."

And must now—lest we have hordes of disaffected dogs jumping from windows and truly running roughshod over our lives—also have ample space in our society to walk, and run, and play, vent their pent-up energy and frustrations, tend to their daily toilette, and, when standard modern medicine fails them, have ready access to alternative methods.

Through a contact made at the FIDO Web site, I found the name of a holistic veterinarian named Dr. Alberto G. Gil. His office is out in Old Westbury, Long Island, but the doctor told me that he does make house calls and was, in fact, going to be in Brooklyn the following Monday. I felt compelled to ask him his rates. We already foot a fairly substantial yearly bill with our "traditional" vet, and take ourselves to a doctor only in dire emergencies. One hundred dollars, I was told, for the house call. Additional charges would vary depending on the length of the visit and type of treatment rendered.

We determined to limit the first visit to "a consult," in which the doctor would chat with us and get a general sense of my dogs and their dispositions and what types of treatments might be in order. Their names are Roz and Gus. They were both adopted from shelters and are—due in large part, no doubt, to the incivility of their previous owners—deeply unbalanced, emotionally and psychologically. My wife and I got Gus (a Labrador–Springer Spaniel mix as far as anyone can tell) just over a year ago from the North Shore Animal League in Long Island. He'd been left tied to a tree outside the shelter in the middle of the night. Gus is deeply wary of this world, to the point of near sleeplessness. His first few weeks with us, in fact, he'd keep waking himself up from his naps, so mistrustful was he of humans. To this day he often doesn't seem to recognize me, or to believe I really exist, suddenly sitting up and fixing me with a trembling, wide-eyed stare that's quite unsettling for someone with as tenuous a hold on reality as I have. Gus, it also bears mentioning, can only walk along the far right side of any hallway and only through the very bottom right corner of a doorway. Roz has no problem with hallways or doors. She simply can't tolerate being left. We got Roz six months ago from a shelter in Quebec during our yearly summer stay there, a seven-month-old, pint-sized Terrier-Beagle mix who'd survived a Canadian winter on the streets. Roz has the gentlest disposition, but the minute we leave the apartment, she becomes a dervish, an inspired master of the explosive, multimedia collage.

Dr. Gil, a short, handsome, dark-haired man in his late thirties, arrived toting a traditional black doctor's bag. My two wary and wired charges sniffed him up and down, then took their usual places at either end of the living room sofa and watched as he took a seat opposite theirs and stared back. "This one," he said, nodding at Gus, "seems very fearful. But otherwise his coat is pretty good." "And Roz?" my wife asked. Dr. Gil paused a moment, then got up and walked over to Roz. He picked her up, studied her coat, looked in her eyes, smelled her breath, then placed her back down. "This one," he began, "has a definite pathology. Her coat is a bit dull, her eyes a little red, her breath doggy." For the next hour or more the doctor discussed with us our dogs' diet and medical history. He asked if we'd had them vaccinated. "Of course," I said. "Hmmm," he said. "That's not good." Vaccinations, he explained, have a variety of chemical agents that can cause severe allergic reactions, compromise an animal's immune system, and even be a cause of emotional imbalance. While we went back and forth about the pros and cons of traditional Western medicine versus alternative methods of healing, the main subjects of the discussion drifted in and out of sleep on the sofa. All of this was on my dime, of course, so I made a point of steering our little "consult" back to the matter at hand, asking the doctor about some generic approaches for improving their overall health and physical appearance. He suggested things like making the gradual transition to raw meat and vegetables, herbs, and dietary supplements. The doctor stayed nearly two hours that night. The total bill came to $290.

In the two weeks since his visit, my dogs have made a more or less uneventful transition to a variety of raw and/or cooked meats—beef, tripe, turkey, the occasional stewed chicken with vegetables. Perhaps I'm imagining things, but both Roz's and Gus's coats do appear to be a bit more shiny now, their eyes brighter, and Roz's breath has improved. As for their psyches, I recently initiated my very own herbal-intake/touch-therapy/subliminal-suggestion program. First, I purchased a book on natural remedies for dogs, a vial of flower distillate labeled "Calming Essence," and a Separation Anxiety CD called *Fear Faders,* "a specially blended mix of music and rhythmic heartbeats . . . designed to ease the transition between homes." We had our first session just the other night. My wife was out with some friends. I sat down with Gus and Roz on the sofa, placed a drop of calming essence under each of their tongues, and put on *Fear Faders.* The CD jacket advises that for "conditioning to be most effective, praise your pet while listening." The sound effects, it explains, will gradually increase "from subliminal to audible." It sounds something like a suburban-wedding string quartet whose members all have bad indigestion. Roz's head spun toward the stereo speakers the minute it came on. Gus seemed only mildly interested. I gently stroked their heads, telling them, over and over again, what very good dogs they are. Within minutes, I was sound asleep. I've no idea what effect this had on the dogs, but when I woke, I found them both positioned at the living room windows, paws up on the sill, staring out, longingly, toward the lights of Manhattan.

lessons

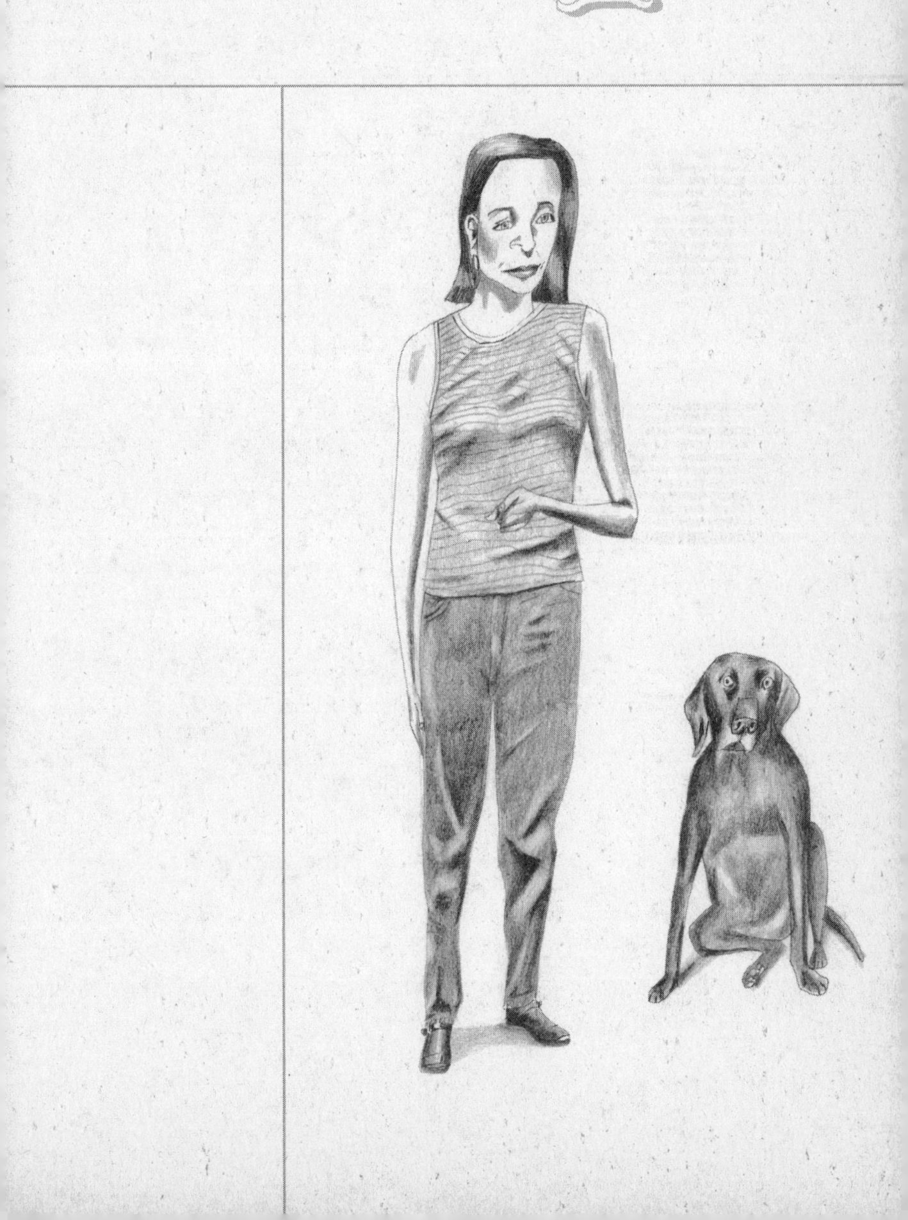

Ten Things My Dog Taught Me That Made It Possible for Me to Get Married

Pam Houston

MY HUSBAND AND I SLEEP WITH AN IRISH WOLFHOUND NAMED Dante in a wrought-iron queen-sized bed. Our combined weight is somewhere in the vicinity of five hundred pounds, and while I don't know enough math to tell you how much square footage of the bed's surface we cover, I *can* tell you that when we are all in there, it is impossible to determine the color of the bottom sheet.

We start out at bedtime in a fairly organized fashion. I get in bed first, in the very center, and lie on my side, facing the center of the room. Dante gets in next, and spoons his long body in front of mine, facing the same direction. Since he gave up all doglike postures years ago in favor of human ones, and since he and I are approximately the same length, we are toe-to-toe at the foot of the bed. My nose comes down right at the back of his head, so I can fall asleep to the cinnamon smell of his ears. Martin squeezes into bed between me and the wall, and I am in my favorite place, the meat of the sandwich between the two pieces of bread I love most in the world.

Where we end up, by morning, is anybody's guess. Dante has a habit of encroaching, and I, ever fearful of inadvertently pushing him off the bed, have been successfully trained to scoot—at the slightest provocation—nearer to the wall without really waking up. That leaves Martin wedged in the crack between the wall and the bed, which he sometimes responds to by reversing direction and wrapping his similarly long torso around Dante's and my feet.

Dante, meanwhile, will have decided that he and I are not quite close enough, and will have rolled over to face me, slinging his front leg over my shoulder and his back leg across my knees, burying his often drippy nose into my neck and blowing damp little snot bubbles for the rest of the night.

I often wake to Dante chasing rabbits in a dream, his back paws kick-kick-kicking at my shin bones, his nose twitching rapidly against my cheek. Martin's big toe will be stuck in my ear, and the comforter will have disappeared entirely. Dante will have somehow managed to get all four pillows under his body, and if I try to extricate one of them he will resort to what we call "gravity dog mode," in which he somehow triples his body weight without ever opening his eyes. Sometimes when I wake up I'm in the crack, Dante is diagonal across the entire bed, and Martin has given up and gone to the couch.

I can almost hear your head shaking, hear you pronouncing my marriage doomed. But neither Martin nor I would ever think of changing the sleeping arrangements, and we figure whatever we lose in sleep we make up for in other ways. Martin says, "What's a few nights on the couch in exchange for what so far is turning out to be a pretty great marriage?" We both know that if it wasn't for all the things that living with Dante has taught me, I would have never figured out how to be the marrying kind.

LESSON #1: That if your paws are too big to fit in your ears, you have to get someone else to do the scratching.

God played a dirty trick on the Wolfhounds. He gave them huge Marmaduke clubs for paws and these silky delicate ears with tiny openings. When they try to scratch it looks like somebody trying to tweeze their eyebrows with barbecue tongs. There are an infinite number of reasons why humans need Wolfhounds, but the one undeniable reason Wolfhounds need humans is so that the humans can scratch their ears. The two methods Dante prefers are as follows: the knuckle of the forefinger, bent hard and rubbed around the outermost section of the inner ear; or, the thumb and forefinger stretched over the back of the head and massaging the skin directly behind the ear cavity. When I hit the right spot, Dante leans hard into my hand, makes little grunts of happiness, and gets a faraway look in his eye.

My father is a man who takes selfishness to almost bizarre extremes. When I was a kid he used to say, "Pam, one day you'll realize you spend your whole life lying in the gutter with somebody else's foot on your neck." More recently he called to say, "I'm just sitting here looking over my life insurance policy and realizing that there is no way I'm going to reap the rewards of the money I'm putting in here, so if you want the thirty grand after I'm dead, you are going to have to start making these payments."

I knew his worldview was wrong, even as a kid; I just didn't know in how many ways. I used to believe his selfishness was getting him somewhere, allowing him to rip off the world in some way that he found satisfying. And even though I had no desire to emulate it, I saw it as a tactic that worked for him, and later—although I was ashamed of this—one that had dramatically influenced me.

I've spent a lifetime unlearning the things my father taught me: *Life 101* for those who speak generosity as a second language. When I'm scratching Dante's ears I begin to understand just how much my father's selfishness cost him. I understand—in the simple language of a born-again kleptomaniac—that it really is better to give than to receive. Not because of what you might get back, not because of some kind of karmic balance, but because it simply is. Dante always receives the scratching with such simple gratitude, with such total pleasure, and that pleasure comes straight back into me, multiplied one hundred times.

> LESSON #2: That if you want your hand to be licked, you might have to put it under somebody's nose.

Another place Dante and I spend a great deal of time together is the car. I put on about forty thousand miles a year, and for most of those, he is with me. He rides in the backseat of my Toyota Forerunner, with the luggage stuffed down on the floor in front of the backseat, so that he can lay across it and put his head and shoulders between the bucket seats in the front.

Sometimes he rests his heavy chin on my shoulder and looks out the windshield with me, and that is as close to heaven as anything I know. Other times I'll put my arm in the backseat and he'll lick it—he especially seems to like the taste of my watch—for several minutes before he finishes and I pull it back.

I've never been very good at asking anybody for anything. In fact, I'm one of those people who has taken self-sufficiency to some kind of outrageous extreme. This is a great tactic when you are trying to survive an abusive childhood, but not so great when you are contemplating marriage to a kind and loving man.

Dante attends to me in ways I've only recently gotten used to. When I'm sad, he'll lay in bed and press his big black nose flaps against my cheek, and stare calm and goodness into my eyes. If he thinks I need to be playful, he'll go outside and do his happy dance all over the lawn. If I need to get work done, he'll curl up on the couch and not disturb me. When we are in the same room together and both awake, his eyes never leave my face.

We are codependent, you are thinking, and you're right, but in all the best ways, and with none of the consequences. I almost just wrote *Dante was the first person I relied upon other than myself.* But that's only half of the story. What happened next asked me to be equally reliable in turn.

> LESSON #3: That the exact right dog will always come into your life just when you need him most.

I first laid eyes on Dante in the parking lot of a Gibson's discount store in Montrose, Colorado, when his breeder brought him to meet me at the agreed-upon time. A man I met briefly had just lost a Wolfhound named Zaephod, and though this man and I had nothing whatsoever in common, and I would not have even considered taking a restaurant recommendation from him, there was something about the way he talked about Zaephod that stayed with me for years. I knew nothing of breeders and their varying scruples at the time, as all my other dogs had been pound rescues. I saw an ad for Wolfhound puppies in the *Denver Post* one day and without doing the slightest bit of research, called the number and bought a dog.

In the seven years since that day, I have heard many things about various breeders, few of them complimentary. I have heard the words *puppy mill* used in connection with their names. I have heard about those who breed sick dogs to sick dogs to make a buck or two off the litter, with little or no regard for the future of the puppies that they sell. I have no way of knowing whether any of that is true of Dante's breeder, but it strikes me that if you're out to make a buck, breeding dogs who eat enough to double their body weight six times during the first twelve weeks of their lives might not be the very best strategy.

What I do know is that Dante has had chronic health problems since he was a little more than a year old. The first thing we discovered was that his heart is unnaturally large, irregular, and growing; his heart function dips as low as 18 percent of normal from time to time. The second thing was cancer: He was diagnosed with osteosarcoma during the week that he turned four.

For his heart he takes digoxin and enalapril, a combination of fairly sophisticated drugs that keeps his heart function stabilized around 40 percent without any dramatic side effects, and he gets an ultrasound scan twice a year. For his osteosarcoma he had four failed limb-sparing surgeries, an eventual amputation, six rounds of chemotherapy (which did have rather severe side effects), and he now needs a follow-up chest X ray every three months, which will continue for the rest of his life.

Because we spend half the year in Colorado and half the year in California, Dante has two sets of specialists: oncologists, radiologists, cardiologists, orthopedic surgeons, chiropractors, massage therapists, and reiki masters. To speak in the leftover language of my father, Dante is currently a thirty-thousand-dollar dog.

Having said all that, would I have traded him for a healthy dog from a breeder who only fed the puppies organic wheat germ, and kept perfect records, and refused to breed any dog that had a shadow of disease anywhere in his genealogy? Never in a thousand billion years.

I don't really expect you to believe me, but I've got to say it anyway: Dante is the wisest, kindest, most loving, most elegant dog to have ever graced this planet. If on top of cardiomyopathy and osteosarcoma he had diabetes, leukemia, hip dysplasia, a liver shunt, gingivitis, and a tape worm, I would still have considered myself the luckiest girl in the universe to have known him, to have learned from him, during his much-too-short time here on earth.

If the gods bring to you
a strange and frightening creature,
accept the gift
as if it were one you had chosen.

So begins one of my favorite poems, "Each Moment a White Bull Steps Shining into the World," by Jane Hirshfield. The world gives us everything we need just when we need it, and when we are really lucky, it takes the form of a big gray three-legged drippy-nosed dog.

> LESSON #4: That loving, in the face of inevitable loss, is the single most important challenge of our lives.

When Dante came home from our walk on the evening of his fourth birthday and I noticed that his front leg was quivering—just a little—cancer was the last thing I thought of. Which is odd, since of all the potential disasters spinning constantly in the disaster rolodex that is my brain, cancer is the one that comes up most often. But Dante was only four, after all, and what I imagined instead was an injury . . . a too-much-walking-on-the-pavement injury, or at the very worst arthritis, something congenital that lived in his joints.

On a Friday afternoon, over the phone, a vet I didn't know (it was only my second year teaching at UC Davis, and I still thought of Colorado as my only home) said, "You better get him in, that sounds like osteosarcoma." It was harder to stay in denial at that point, but I was somewhat successful at focusing all my energy that weekend on hating the unknown vet.

When I did take Dante in on Monday, the vet opened the door and from across the room said, "That's what I was afraid of." He gave me some Tahitian Noni juice and Chinese mushrooms, and sent me to the Veterinary Medical Teaching Hospital at Davis for the biopsy and the final diagnosis. The next five days I don't remember at all.

When something bad happens in my life, when something I love is threatened, I become, instantaneously, eight years old. Ten years ago when my best friend was diagnosed with cancer, any number of times when one man or another announces he is leaving me, this summer when the Colorado wildfires came within a few miles of my ranch, I became paralyzed, zombified. It is one of the things I like least about myself.

It is not entirely my fault, I have been told by therapists. This ability to freeze in place is probably the reason I survived (literally . . . physically) my childhood. As an adult this ability is a bit more problematic. I often manage to remain in this frozen state so long that I all but miss the terrible thing. I was frozen through my mother's funeral, for example, frozen for the last months of my dear friend Sally's life, and again for my friend Shelton's. I've been frozen while any number of men shout and throw any number of things into their suitcases, and I was frozen for the five days after Dante's biopsy came back.

At the end of the five days I made a decision. However long Dante had to live, I was going to bring myself back to life and stay there. I was going to be emotionally present every minute, right up to the lethal injection, if that's what it came to, through every surgery, every infection, every difficult decision, every howl of pain. For the first time in my life, this willful thawing was available to me (probably because of the four years of love that I had at that point received from Dante) and I recognized it for the lifeline that it was.

Did I wish I could have gone back and made the same decision with Sally and Shelton? Of course I did. But I kept my promise with Dante, I keep it still, and I believe it to be the first of many. This summer, when we had wildfire in wilderness areas eight miles to the west of us, and eleven miles to the east, it took me only three days to snap back to the living and start packing into boxes all the things I wanted to save.

> LESSON #5: That all your new habits, like weeping and praying and talking about your feelings, will actually endear you to more people than they will drive away.

This waking-up thing, this being present to my emotions even when they are inconvenient to the task at hand, has had some interesting side effects. It lost me my then-boyfriend, for example, which was all for the best, and it gained me some new friends of the variety that aren't nearly as perfect as I had been at keeping emotions at bay—which is better still.

When I sobbed all through my consultation with Dr. Peter Walsh of the UC Davis Veterinary Medical Teaching Hospital—in my opinion the world's best veterinary surgeon—I thought he would throw us out of his office and tell us to never come back. In fact it was the beginning of a very unique and wonderful friendship, full of trust and mutual respect, but conducted almost entirely in dog language, nearly empty of words.

I suddenly had something huge and awe-inspiring in common with a lot of other people—someone we loved desperately was gravely ill—and I understood that we could be a tremendous help to one another. Dante got himself a pen pal through YAPS (Youth and Pet Survivors Program), a little girl with osteosarcoma named Meaghan, and we all got invited to a place called the Silver Lining Ranch in Aspen, Colorado, where kids with cancer of all kinds go for a week of fun and emotional healing. It's run by Andrea Jaeger, who is less like a person and more like a force of nature, a human light source who is pure dedication, the generous ying to my father's selfish yang, and the best living example I've ever seen of the unlimited yield on kindness. When one of the kids she'd brought to the Silver Lining, a little girl named Christine who was suffering from three kinds of cancer simultaneously, was asked if God had a plan for her, she said, with a big smile on her face, "Sure, it's to make all the people who don't have cancer understand that they have to love each other every day."

> LESSON #6: That sitting in the grass together doing nothing isn't really doing nothing at all.

After Dante's first big reconstructive surgery, he developed the mother of all postsurgical infections, a wound so long and so deep, a bacteria so flesh-devouring, that you could see right down to the steel plate and screws with which doctor Peter Walsh tried to rebuild his leg. An infection so ghastly that the thousand-dollars-a-dose antibiotic didn't seem to be having any effect on it. A hole so large that it had to be flushed, disinfected, and rewrapped three times a day for a month.

During that time Dante lived in the veterinary hospital at Davis. Each day I would stop in to see him, let him out of his cage, and sit on the grass with him from about five o'clock until eight. Every day his cast was wrapped with a different color vet wrap, the odds and ends Dr. Walsh collected in a futile but kind attempt to keep my costs down. Every day one veterinary student or another came outside to tell me what a remarkable dog he was.

I've never been a person who sits still very well. I have never, for example, taken a nap in my adult life. You would be far more likely to find me doing three things at once—driving a car, painting my toenails, and reading a manuscript for instance—than you would be to find me doing nothing at all. If you break down my life, I am a person with approximately three and a half full-time jobs.

Before Dante's operation, if someone had told me I would spend twenty-one hours a week sitting on the grass, petting a dog, and watching the house wrens flutter from maple to maple outside the veterinary hospital, watching the clouds blow across the sky, I would have said you were crazy. But I loved those days on the grass with Dante. I loved hearing about the Mormon grandmother of this vet student, the cheating boyfriend of that one, while scratching an ear or rubbing a belly, or scratching the place where toenail meets toe. I loved the way Dante kept his dignity, even when he was sick or in pain, the way he made the transition so effortlessly, from a dog who wanted to run from one end of the state of Colorado to another, to a dog that was appreciative of a few hours on the hospital grass. I loved feeding him lamb from New Zealand, and Tahitian Noni juice for his immune system, and oatmeal cookies because they were his favorite, after the chemo had made him reluctant to eat. I loved the way Dante went back into the hospital willingly with Dr. Walsh at the end of three hours, so as not to make me cry, or hurt the doctor's feelings. Because of the infection, because of the cancer, because of the way one surgery led into the next, we lived with the idea that any day of lawn sitting and cloud watching might be the last. I loved the way Dante made me understand that in the name of love, I could sit still until the end of time.

LESSON #7: That if you love somebody deeply enough, cleaning up their diarrhea doesn't make you want to puke.

I've seen them. The mothers in the shopping mall bathrooms whipping those diapers off and on like they've lost all of their olfactory abilities. And now I get it. How if it is *their* baby, the diaper smells like fresh apple pie.

Chemo and its aftermath taught me about carpet cleaners in a whole new way, but I never saw it as a hassle. Dante was embarrassed every time it happened, and so cleaning it up quickly, and with a smile, was paramount, so as not to add to his discomfort, his shame. And when his final reconstructive surgery failed and Dr. Walsh and I faced the difficult decision to amputate, I never, for even a half a second, saw his three-leggedness as strange, or frightening, or ugly.

Dante is as beautiful on three legs as he was on four, only different. You should see him lift himself delicately over a 4-foot fence and come down on that one extra-strengthened front leg. You should see him outrun Rose, our four-legged Wolfhound, if there is a teasing squirrel involved.

Sometimes in a park someone will say, "Oh, that's so sad," when they see him, and I want to say, "No, idiot, this is the happy part."

Once, in the park, a Chinese man approached me and looked at Dante with nothing but approval in his eyes. "In Beijing, in the zoo," he said, "there is a Siberian tiger that only has three legs." He shook his head, "No pity," he said, and made a fist with his hand: "No pity." He touched the top of Dante's head lightly with the fist he had made and walked away.

LESSON #8: That in the end, the money doesn't matter a bit.

This was something I'd always suspected, having grown up in the household of a man who would drive to the next state to buy gas if it was three cents cheaper over there. My father may have resented my mother and I most of all because we cost him money (though we did our best not to cost him much of it). Thirty thousand dollars is a lot to spend on a dog, especially when you have to put it on your credit card. Especially when you are buying, according to the best veterinary journals, six months to a year at the most. Thirty thousand dollars is a lot, and it is nothing. If I had it all to do over again, I know that I would have spent that much if all it bought me was just one of those beautiful afternoons on the veterinary hospital lawn.

LESSON #9: That sometimes, even if you haven't acted perfectly, the good thing happens after all.

But it bought me way more than one of those afternoons. As of this minute, the care and love and expertise that the doctors at the UC Davis vet hospital and his follow-up–care doctors at the Veterinary Referral Center of Colorado have given him is two years and seven months of life that statistically he should not have had.

Given me.

Given us.

There are days when I think he stays alive just because he has more to teach me, that he doesn't trust me on my own yet, that he worries I'll go back to my closed-up, shut-down, selfish, and terrified pre-Dante ways. Sometimes I think he stays alive for his pen pal Meaghan, so that she knows she can stay alive, too. Sometimes I think he stays alive because he knows how magnificent he is. A big old Irish Wolfhound, minus one shoulder blade and all that attaches, cantering lightly across the pasture at sunset, a living miniseries about getting the most out of every day.

But sometimes I think he's alive because, in spite of everything I was told about the world, in spite of the house I grew up in and all of its large and tiny terrors, every now and then goodness is allowed to shine through. Even if I don't act perfectly. Even if I don't hold my breath for all eternity. Maybe Dante is still alive simply because he is good, and because I try to be good, and because we love each other so much, and somebody somewhere thinks we deserve a little more time to live in that love together.

I grew up believing that if I admitted I was hoping for something, the thing I hoped for would be swept away. And so I always prepared for the worst, and kept my hopes in the closet. Which is a terrible way to live, a terrible way to keep oneself from living.

Dante's life after cancer was the first really important thing I've allowed myself to hope for out loud, that I've dared even to pray for, and the fact that it came true is trying to turn that hope into something like belief, something like faith and gratitude. Faith enough to brave the vows of marriage. Gratitude enough to let a Wolfhound sleep all over the bed.

> LESSON #10: That everything is forgivable, that every moment contains eternity, and that loving unconditionally doesn't mean you are a self-annihilating fool.

Dante is lying here with me on the brand-new couch as I write this. We decided to try to keep dog paws off of this couch for at least a month, and here, on day two, Dante is obliging by dozing on his back with all three feet straight up in the air.

I ask him for a story that goes with lesson #10, and he says in his Zen-ish way that there isn't one story that goes with this rule because they all do. He says that lesson #10 is what every dog has been trying to teach every human since the very beginning of time.

Love Is Never Having to Say Anything at All

Patricia B. McConnell, Ph.D.

COOL HAND LUKE IS NOT GOING TO DIE. I WON'T STAND FOR IT. I know, of course, that he will, at least a part of me does. After all, he's eleven, he's a dog, and he's already cheated death from cancer, cars, and a 300-pound ram who was determined to kill him or me, whoever came first. I'm more grateful than I can say that Luke is still here. His front paws may be swollen with arthritis and he may tire more easily, but he still loves working sheep, fetching tennis balls, and sitting in silence with me in the rosy light of summertime sunsets. And I still love him so deeply and completely that I imagine his death to be as if all the oxygen in the air disappeared, and I was left to try to survive without it.

I'm not alone in this love affair. Everywhere I go I talk to people who have soul mates like Luke, dogs so special we get tears in our eyes just talking about them. This phenomenon is not particularly new—people have been in love with their dogs for centuries. Josephine was reportedly fonder of her Pug, Fortune, than she ever was of Napoleon. Nor is the love of pets, dogs included, unique to industrial societies—even hunter/gatherer societies have animal companions.

Of course, not everyone loves dogs. Even in countries like Britain and the United States, where many of us are happy to spend a sizable portion of our retirement savings on food and veterinary care for our dogs, there are people who simply don't like them. In some cultures, dogs are despised as vermin; in some others they're cherished—because they taste good. But the fact remains that there's a phenomenon that needs explaining here. Those of us who love dogs love them so deeply it hurts. It's easy to demean these feelings, as people who don't get it often do. Dog lovers have been described as neurotics or social incompetents, but though dog lovers can be just as emotionally illiterate as the rest of the world, loving dogs is not, in itself, the problem. There's something much bigger and better than neediness that drives our love of dogs. People all over the world have sought an answer to why we love dogs, perhaps an indication that the question is deeply rooted. I don't think it's a trivial question, either, and not just because I'm stupid in love with my dogs. I'm also a scientist and an applied animal behaviorist, and from the perspective of biology, the question is both interesting and important.

Indeed, biology itself provides some of the answers. One of the obvious connections between dogs and humans is our shared natural history. Dogs and people may be strikingly different in a lot of ways, but if you compare our behavior with that of other animals, we share more than we don't. We humans may not roll in cow pies or eat the placenta after giving birth, but like dogs, people sleep, eat, and hunt together, and that in itself is notable in the animal kingdom. Pandas are notoriously solitary. Feral cats can live in groups or live alone, but they don't hunt together. Butterflies are often seen together, but only because they're attracted to the same minerals in the puddle in your driveway. In contrast to animals who are seen together without social relationships, dogs and humans are so social that we even raise our young together, sometimes deferring our own reproduction in order to assist another member of the group. Individuals of both species will even nurse the young of another female, and that fact alone puts dogs and humans in a very special category.

Many other factors of our natural history have a profound effect on our relationship with dogs. Dogs, like people, live in social hierarchies, and are generally amenable to doing what high-status individuals ask of them. Both human beings and dogs are "Peter Pan animals," whose behavior is shaped by a process called *paedomorphism,* in which adult, sexually mature individuals retain the characteristics of adolescents, remaining curious and playful all their lives. It's easy to take playing with your dog for granted, but go ask a cow to play with you and see how far you get.

Equally important is our shared tendency to nurture needy individuals. In both species, offspring are born helpless, desperately in need of care and a safe environment in which to learn the many life lessons required for survival. Humans have such an extensive period of parental care that we are hard-wired to go weak-kneed at any animal who looks infantile. Advertisements for Kodak don't show us sun-drenched scenes of little boys playing with puppies for nothing. If you want people to feel all warm and gooey and nurturing, show them a baby mammal with a disproportionately large forehead and oversized eyes, and listen for the "Awww's" coming out of the crowd. It's such a primal part of who we are—this reaction to young, needy mammals—that psychologists even label it the "Aw phenomenon."

Dogs don't stay cute little puppies for long, but they remain dependent and nonverbal, much like very young children. Some of us may have tremendous respect for our dogs, as I do for Luke, but even though he can load the ram on the truck single-handedly, he still can't open doors or pull his dinner out from that magic place under the counter. Natural selection has emphasized nurturance in our species, and surely dogs have profited by it.

Yet somehow all of these characteristics don't seem enough to explain the passion that so many of us have for our dogs. A love of play and strategic hunting techniques may drive much of our relationship, but a shared natural history doesn't seem enough of an explanation when some big, strong fireman is sobbing in my office while discussing euthanizing his dog. The depth of the pain we dog lovers feel when facing losing one of our best friends can be overwhelming, and isn't unique to dog owners. I'm still grieving over the death of my beloved cat, Ayla, with a sorrow that lovers of cats, horses, and birds can well understand.

In some ways, the experience of losing a beloved pet is quite similar to the grief we feel when we lose a human loved one. When we lose a dog, we go through the same stages of grieving that we do when we lose a human, from denial to anger to acceptance, although usually in a much shorter period of time. But something not particularly obvious is different about our grief over losing a dog. People who've never cried in their lives cry over losing their dogs. I'll never forget an episode of the TV series *M*A*S*H* when, surrounded by the relentless agonies of injured and dying soldiers in Korea, the medical team coped with black humor, bravery, and stamina . . . until a little stray dog they'd adopted died. Then they fell apart. It may have only been television, but it reflected something universally true about the effect dogs have on us.

I remember watching the movie *My Dog Skip* with a friend and crying at the end with the same pure emotion I saw on that *M*A*S*H* episode. We weren't just crying about the loss of a dog, we were crying over loss itself, and somehow, when personified in a dog, that sense of loss was easier to let out. It was the kind of crying that is healing, painful though it may be. I think the tendency of humans to be able to grieve so deeply over a dog reflects that something very big and primal and important goes on between people and dogs that has as much to do with our emotions as our shared natural history.

So why is it, then, that dogs can elicit a purity of emotion that we often cover up in our human relationships? Perhaps, just perhaps, it is because dogs don't talk.

Okay, you already knew that dogs can't talk. But the more I think about the consequences of our nonverbal relationship with dogs, the more benefits I think there are. Psychologists have told us for years that dogs give us "nonjudgmental positive regard," and all dog lovers intuitively understand exactly what they mean. The pure and simple joy that radiates out from our dogs every time we come home is rarely duplicated in human greetings, and it can elicit the feeling of pure love that we all seek from infancy onward. I think that dogs do indeed love us with tremendous intensity, and the fact that they can't talk acts to underscore it, not diminish it.

Of course we can communicate with dogs, and of course they understand up to hundreds of the words we use, and get a tremendous amount of information from our intonation. But even the most avid dog lover can't sit down and have an in-depth conversation with her dog.

If dogs could talk, I suspect that things wouldn't feel so pure and simple. First of all, though most of our dogs love us deeply, they don't necessarily love us every second of the day. Cool Hand Luke can shoot me a look that can be summed up in two words: The second word is "you," but the first one is not "love." And why not? Why should intelligent, complicated individuals not make judgments about what happens to them? Surely our dogs can get frustrated if we delay that weekend walk in the woods for the phone call that came just as we were going out the door, just like our spouses or partners can. I don't say this cynically, and I don't want to burst any sacred bubbles, but perhaps what dogs give us is the *perception* of continual "non-judgmental positive regard." If I could teach Luke to talk, I'm not sure I'd always be happy about what he had to say.

A hurtful word can live a long time in the heart of the receiver, and influence the relationship forever after. In the case of dogs, perhaps it's easier to ignore an irritation here and a ruffled feather there, because our dogs can't put words to them. "Sticks and stones may break my bones but words will never hurt me" may be a common refrain, but it's not based in reality. Words can cause terrible damage, sometimes lasting a lifetime, and the fact that dogs can't use them may be a blessing.

Of course, our lack of a shared language is a profound disadvantage sometimes, causing us no end of grief when we're desperate to ask our dogs what's wrong with them, or yearning to explain why we're torturing them with yet another radiation treatment. Our ability to talk to one another may be one of the greatest accomplishments of the human species, and there are times when I'd give anything to be able to communicate with Luke in greater depth than I can now. But speech comes with a price. Being in conversation with even a good friend raises your blood pressure. It takes a lot of mental energy to make decisions about what words to say, how to string them together, what tone to use when you say them. That's the very same energy that spiritual leaders advise us to turn off as a way of revitalizing ourselves. The constant conversation that most of us have in our heads as we're driving, eating, and walking through the park can be exhausting ("Did I turn off the water in the herb garden? What should I do about Spot's arthritis? It's getting worse. Shoot, I forgot to get the oil checked when I got gas last night.") and is so inherent to the way our brains work that we actually have to *practice* turning it off. Anyone who's tried meditation knows how difficult it can be to shut off the internal chatter that comes with being verbal.

Experts at meditation can be "in the present," and free of mental noise for hours, but I'm thrilled to turn off my brain for a minute or two. That's because I'm a novice at a skill that we humans need to learn and practice. But I doubt that Luke has to practice meditating to be able to experience the kind of spiritual peace humans have to learn to find. Being nonverbal allows an otherwise intelligent, highly connected animal to live in the present without the hailstorm of internal conversations that complicate our human lives. If you think about it, most of what we "talk" about in our own heads isn't about the present, it's about the past or future. But dogs keep us firmly rooted in the here and now, and that, it turns out, is a notable accomplishment.

Where but with dogs (and selected other animals) can we have such a deep and meaningful relationship with so little baggage? Words may be wonderful things, but they carry weight with them, and there's a great lightness of being when they are discarded. The story of the Garden of Eden is a lovely allegory for the cost of cognition. Being able to use our brains the way that we do separates us from the rest of the animal world, and like most everything else in life, has its costs as well as its benefits.

And so, perhaps it's not just the things we share with dogs that wrap us together in mutual love. In the lovely balanced irony of yin and yang, it's the differences as much as the similarities that bring us together.

I do know that some of my happiest times are when Luke and I sit silently together, overlooking the green, rolling hills of southern Wisconsin. Our lack of language doesn't get in the way, but creates an opening for something else, something deep and pure and good. We dog lovers share a kind of Zen-like communion with our dogs, uncluttered by nouns and adverbs and dangling participles. This connection speaks to a part of us that needs to be nurtured and listened to, but that is so often drowned out in the cacophony of speech. Dogs remind us that we *are* being heard, without the additional weight of words. What a gift. No wonder we love them so much.

Watch the Animals: A Story

Alice Elliott Dark

WE HAD A TRYING RELATIONSHIP WITH DIANA FRICK. SHE WAS A moneyed blue blood, the descendant of a signer, who could have been one of our old guard except that she spurned the role. Instead, she was interested in animals to the point of obsession, which in our part of the country was saying a lot. There were few among us who hadn't mourned a loyal dog or put out scraps for a stray cat or developed a smooth working relationship with a horse. Animals had a place in our lives, to be sure, and we took seriously our responsibilities toward them. But Diana went further, and always had.

For decades she'd chosen the company of other species over companionship with her own kind, a preference we naturally took as a rejection. So after she was diagnosed with lung cancer and she began to seek homes for her menagerie in the event of her death, we didn't line up at her door. Why should we? We owed her nothing. Yet the woman was fading, and we'd known her all our lives. On the telephone, in the clubs, shops, and churchyards, we tried to decide what to do.

She first came around to plead her case in autumn when the lanes swelled with bright leaves. We couldn't help but examine her for signs of the illness, but nothing much showed; she'd always been spare. Her eyes shone blue as ever, that was the main thing. She appeared without calling first, the way we used to do when we were liable to be having tea or drinks in the afternoon and could easily accommodate company. Now we were busy but we didn't turn her away. Years of curiosity assured her a vigorous welcome.

"Let's sit outside," she said. "I've got the dogs, and I need a smoke." She noticed our raised eyebrows. "Well, I've got no reason *not* to smoke anymore, have I? I was planning to start again anyway when I turned eighty, but my schedule has been moved up a bit."

That was typical of her sense of humor—black, direct, laced with a stubbornly nonconformist aroma. We didn't smile, but she didn't care.

"Where are your bird feeders?" she asked as we walked around to the back. "It's going to get cold soon."

Her voice rasped now rather than boomed but it was still forceful.

"You put the porch furniture away already? But it's only October! Oh, all right then, we'll sit on the grass."

She always brought along at least two of her dog pack and spoke to them in a high whine to which they responded with a great deal of tongue-wagging enthusiasm. "Stop smiling!" she'd command. They'd shiver with pleasure. Often, she kissed them on their mouths.

When we were all settled and mugs of tea had been handed around, she made her play.

"I'm leaving money to cover their expenses," she told us. The days were over when it was considered impolite to talk about money, but she made her offer sound like a bribe. It was yet another example of how clumsy she was with people.

"I'll need a promise in return," she continued. "I don't want to have to look up from where I'll no doubt be burning to see them shunted around. If you take them, you keep them for the duration."

We said we'd think it over, then changed the subject. When would she begin treatments? we wondered.

"Statistically my chances aren't much better with chemo and cutting than they are just twiddling my thumbs, so I'm not going to let them touch me."

She shook her head in a manner that conveyed her thorough disapproval of standard medical remedies. Good old Diana. It was a conversation stopper. We fumbled to pat the dogs.

"They're incredible, aren't they?" She grinned at our attention to them. "I've got all the dogs working as therapy animals in nursing homes. They can relate to anybody. What heart they have, considering how they were treated. We should all be more like dogs when we grow up."

When we compared notes on these visits we couldn't help but bristle. It wasn't that it was unheard of to put conditions on a request, or to shore up a good deed with a financial benefit, but to do so successfully required finesse and subtlety. People want to believe they are high-minded and generous, not greedy and bought. A good monger could have offered us the same deal in terms that would have us not only clamoring to agree to it, but also feeling grateful she'd come to us.

Diana created no such feeling. The only positive we could find in her pitch was that at least she understood her animals required incentives to make them palatable. These were not purebreds, or even respectable mutts. She collected creatures that others had thrown away, the beasts left on the side of the highway or confiscated from horrific existences by her contacts at the ASPCA; the maimed sprung from labs; the exhausted retired from dog tracks; the unlucky blamed for the sins of the household and made to pay with their bodies, appetites, well-being. Immigrants from hell, she called them, and made a mission of acknowledging these crimes, beginning with naming them for their misfortunes. Thus a cat who'd been paralyzed by a motorcycle was called Harley; a dog whose leg had been chopped off by its owner earned the name Beaver Cleaver; a kitten whose eyes had been sewn shut as part of a research grant went by Kitty Wonder; and so on.

She took these animals that otherwise would have ended up euthanized at best, and she trained them and groomed them and nursed them and fed them home-cooked foods until—we had to admit—they bore a resemblance to the more fortunate of their species. They behaved, as far as we could tell. But from a practical standpoint, could they ever be considered truly trustworthy? Who knew what might set them off?

We had our children and grandchildren to consider, and guests, and pets of our own. It was not a commitment that could be made in a hurry. We told each other pretty much what we'd told her—that we'd think about it. That seemed a reasonable approach, everything considered. What else could she expect?

For a while we didn't see her much, but she became the central topic of conversation, a level of attention she'd earned several times before, usually when her books came out and we'd see or hear in interviews about her antihierarchical theories of nature, her view of animals that countered the harsh interpretations that science ascribed to their behavior, and her sorrow at the ways of the world—i.e., *our* world. She wasn't as contentious now, but we didn't believe she'd softened underneath; perhaps she was finally being a little smart, that was all. She wanted a favor, and she knew that she wasn't liable to get it if she didn't participate to some degree in normal human relations.

For the benefit of younger generations and those new to town, at dinner parties and on Sunday walks, we repeated her story—that is, how her early years had seemed to us. Her childhood didn't offer much. Her parents were jolly enough, if often absent, but so were a lot of ours. She went to Miss Dictor's, also like a lot of us, and she rode, skated, danced. In fact, she was popular—with the boys, naturally, because of her looks, but also with the girls, among whom she was known as a "good egg." Her coming-out party was of the spare-no-expense variety and she shone even in the requisite ivory, a hard color to wear; but she overcame it with tan arms, the radical touch of a bracelet clasped high on her bicep, and her thick brown hair worn long and loose.

We assumed she'd follow the path we all walked: marriage to someone like-minded, a house of her own but similar to her parents', children raised with the traditions that she remembered fondly, all the little habits that connect one generation to the next. Nothing we could see in her indicated she was headed anywhere but in that direction. Then her brother, the heir, died in a sailing accident, and her direction changed.

Her parents had no other children, so her father had to face the prospect of leaving all that money, albeit in trust, to a woman. He let it be known far and wide that he was not happy about this. He never said a word about losing his son, but the death of the line and his name—his hand strayed north to massage his aching heart when he spoke of it.

"Don't be ridiculous," we told him. "Diana will have children, and they'll be your descendants."

"But they won't be Fricks," he said dolefully.

We felt sorry for Caroline, his wife, and could only imagine the style of second-class citizenship in which she must live. Our efforts to bring his thinking into the modern world made no dent, however. He died only a few years later, full of self-pity to the end. We hoped Caroline would then become a merry widow, but as often happens, she followed him shortly to the grave.

Diana got everything.

She had suitors, of course; beauty and money is an attractive combination. Every so often a fellow would say he believed he was getting somewhere with her, but it never panned out. When an interviewer later asked why she'd never married, she replied that from childhood she knew she had a vocation and couldn't afford the distraction of human love—spoken as if she were a nun. But her calling was low rather than high, down at the level of the animals, and we couldn't help but think it a delusion and a waste.

She was in her early twenties when her first book appeared, an anthropomorphic children's tale, simply yet effectively illustrated, that caught on well enough to lead to another, and more after that, until the series was a standard in every nursery, a basic christening gift. The world loved them; we alone were ambivalent. How could we not be? The characters were a barnyard of familiar types, replete with our habits and belittled by suggestions of inbreeding and snobbery. We saw ourselves drawn with a harsh, loveless pen and felt stung by her portrayal—especially as we were *proud* of her.

We never spoke to her about our sense of injury, however. As we did with our own children, we showed what support we could while we waited for the day when she'd come to us offering thanks or forgiveness or perhaps a smaller token of reconciliation, a recognition in any case.

Meantime she bought a piece of land close to town and made it into a gentleman's farm, pruning the trees away until she had rolling vistas and putting in a pond and an off-limits strip of sod next to it to accommodate the nesting habits of Canada geese. In her forties, she took in a series of foster children and brought them to the club for swims; if she thought we'd complain, we disappointed her. Instead, we offered to make calls for them to the schools, but she turned us down flat.

"*I* believe in public education," she scolded, as if we didn't.

We sighed and went back to waiting, although with diminishing hope.

Perhaps if she'd been average we might not have been so bothered by her hostility. Diana was marvelous, however, in exactly the way we admired most. Hers was an artless, natural beauty that managed to get by the envy of other women while arousing in the men a filial pride—a desire for her success and happiness, as well as for her. We admired her work as well; the spirit of it if not the letter. We looked at her and saw ourselves at our best. She was the sum of our efforts over the last four hundred years in this country, and back into the past to Britain and the continent, Normandy, Saxony, the high, clear springs of our culture. We wanted to be able to trot her out at our ceremonies, to have her bend her long neck to the yoke of our charities and bow before our altars, cut ribbons at our dedication ceremonies, and stand side by side with us at our weddings and confirmations and graduations.

That she cared so little about those kinds of gatherings was irksome to say the least. People scrabbled all their lives for just a fraction of what was hers from the start, yet she didn't feel fortunate or grateful or privileged. She preferred to be in her barn prying stones out of her horses' hooves or sitting motionless by a closet door watching a new litter of kittens pump blindly at their mother. Those things were fine, in moderation. It was her excess that we didn't understand. Or maybe it was the opposite; we understood it all too well and were afraid of it.

We'd taken to heart the often repeated caveat from our childhoods that the elders applied to all manner of deviance—*think what would happen if everyone behaved like that!* The consequence was never exactly specified; for most of us, the implication of chaos and breakdown was enough. We knew our own bad thoughts, after all, knew what we had to suppress. We understood why we couldn't indulge our baser natures or the full range of our whims; we might lose what we had if we did. How had it happened that Diana didn't understand what was at stake?

The final straw came when she published her autobiography. At last we learned her gripes about us, and they cast a wide net. She recounted various instances of cruelty she'd observed as a child, among which were incidents that had bothered us, too. None of us had applauded Harold Johnson's shooting of his dog for eating the Thanksgiving turkey, nor were we amused when someone nailed a cat through its feet to a plank of wood. Yet did she extend us any credit for empathy and shock? No. We were a town without pity, a callous bunch who didn't realize, as she did, that animals have feelings and souls. Would we get rid of one of our children for taking a long time to be toilet trained or shedding too much? Would we call the police on a stranger for asking directions? Yet we perpetrated these evil deeds on animals without thinking twice.

Her arguments were silly, but the book became a hit. *Souls,* she claimed. That was the crux of what she had to tell the world. As always, she pushed it beyond the beyond.

The next foray in her campaign consisted of a mailing, eight double-sided pages of pictures and descriptions of her menagerie. The cover page sported the title "Full Disclosure," and as usual, Diana meant what she said. She was certainly no mistress of persuasion—we already knew that. Yet these pages set a new standard in their complete refusal to make even the smallest nod to the principles of salesmanship. Beneath a grainy picture of each animal she described their routines in detail—ear cleanings, pillings, and other noxious chores—as well as offered predictions as to what health problems they were likely to suffer in the future. Then there were their habits and eccentricities: This one had to drink from the tap in the kitchen, that one slept under the covers by Diana's knees, and on and on. For the armchair behaviorists among us, the document offered interesting anecdotal evidence of how creatures adapt to hardship and abuse/luxury and pampering—not to mention what it revealed about Diana. No wonder she never went out!

After receiving these pages we called to ask how she was. "Not bad, with the minor complication of stage-four lung cancer," she replied.

Wasn't she doing anything at all?

"I'm killing the pain. Of course, they're queer about that, never want to give you enough. What difference does it make if you become addicted to opiates when you're riddled with the big *C?* I have my sources, though. Veterinary drugs are easy to come by."

We told her we knew lots of doctors and had ins at the university hospital if she'd like us to make a few calls. She responded by lecturing us on birds and their need of water in the winter; we could buy solar birdbaths from such-and-such catalogs.

"So no decision yet?" she prompted.

Not yet, we replied.

"Don't wait too long, or I won't be around to hear it. But no pressure!" Ha ha ha.

Then she surprised us. We were at church for the children's choir service on Christmas Eve afternoon and were settling ourselves to the tune of the organist's prelude when Diana walked in and took a place on the aisle two thirds of the way back. For the next few moments the old cavernous nave rippled with elbowings and turnings around and head tiltings; immediately we began to compose comments for later about how she was the second-to-last person we expected to see there, as the old joke went—the last being Jesus. The organist struck the chord for the processional, but we took a beat longer to stand than was customary as we watched her kneel all the way to the ground to say her private prayer.

How beautiful she was—the picture of devotion, like Jennifer Jones in *The Song of Bernadette.* Then we stood and she disappeared beneath taller heads as the children came up the aisle clad in the garb of the ancient Israelites à la Italian medieval painting: drapes, drapes, drapes. They made faces and batted at the frankincense that one of the kings swung dramatically in a censer, and we gave them the usual pleased, encouraging smiles as they passed.

We loved them best, better than anything, but at that moment we were grateful when they were finally all up front posed in the familiar tableau so that we could gawk at Diana. It appeared that she'd bought a new suit for the occasion; we hadn't seen her legs in years. She participated fully in the service and afterward joined the crowd in the vestry who were waiting for children and grandchildren to drop backstage the raiments and constraints of their holy personae. We assumed she wanted to congratulate them on their performances, to play the village eccentric by speaking to them exclusively, but she turned quite amiably to us.

"Such wonderful music," she said.

"We have a new organist," we informed her—although in fact he may have been well down the line since she was last there.

"Lovely," she said. Then the children appeared and loudly gave their insiders' versions of the pageant. Diana was lost in the mayhem as we walked outside.

Dark had fallen by then, but the day was strangely balmy; there was a low moon in the purple sky. It wasn't the Currier & Ives Christmas we all held as the ideal but it was Christmas nonetheless. Our church was built of fieldstone. In the precincts of the churchyard, we may as well have been in the home counties. Even the graveyard did not betray us; the dates went back far enough to afford us a claim to a history and a past. We knew that teenagers sometimes went there at night to try to spook themselves—but that seemed an impulse, the flip side of Sunday morning, and the rector ignored them as long as they did no harm.

Many of us took a detour before going to our cars and walked for a few moments down the narrow pathways among the markers. Here were our parents, grandparents, ancestors. In spite of our tacit assumption that the here and now was the end of it, we found ourselves addressing them in our minds. "It's Christmas Eve again," we informed them, "and, as always, everything and nothing has changed." We didn't go in much for putting flowers on the graves but it was seemly to stop for a moment of acknowledgment. It was an interlude of calm before the revels, part of our yearly ritual.

Then Diana walked past us and made her way to the Frick family plot. We saw her bow her head, and her hands rise to her face. We winced. We'd all had the thought when standing by those graves that we'd be there soon enough ourselves, but for Diana the time was imminent. She wasn't toying with history as we were, but staring directly at her own extinction. It was natural, yes, but still awful. When she rejoined us we could see the disease in her. Without benefit of the flattering church light she appeared emaciated, her skin thin and gray.

"We're having cocktails at the Gardeners'. Why don't you come?" We didn't like the idea of her going home to an empty house. Not on Christmas. Even by choice.

She smelled like our adolescent girls who put vanilla on their pulse points in the summer.

"I thank you very much," she said, "but I have mouths to feed."

She said this plainly, imbuing it with no hint. Yet the spirit of the day was in us, and the favor she'd asked seemed logical rather than an imposing chore.

Laddie Phillips spoke first. "Look," he said. "I'll take that Greyhound. Rescued from a dog track, was he?"

Mina Jones, never one to be outdone, instantly said she'd take two cats—*at least,* she added, affording her room to maneuver in case anyone displayed a more impressive generosity.

Ben Knowlton, home from college, asked for the Pit Bull.

"The Staffordshire Terrier," Diana instructed. Then, as if coaching herself to be agreeable, she gave a shake of her head that ended in a softening of her expression. "But perhaps it's a good thing to say Pit Bull. You and she can be ambassadors for the breed."

And so it went until nearly every animal was spoken for, and promises made to find placements for the rest.

"So how about that drink?" we offered again.

There was a pause. How could she refuse? She couldn't, and finally, she understood that. She followed us out of the parking lot.

The next morning, after the presents had all been opened and the wrapping paper was blazing in the fireplace, we felt the usual letdown, not the smallest part of which was a bout of regret for having acted so impulsively with Diana. By lunchtime, however, we felt ourselves again and glad of our gesture. We'd opened a door that had been locked for decades. It seemed a good omen for the new year.

After that, we began calling to ask how she was. Soon, without calling first, we stopped by to drop off leftovers. We offered to take her dogs for a walk so she didn't have to go out in the rain. In other words, we did all in our power to show her that even if she had never taken our side, we were nevertheless on hers.

At first, predictably, she declined, and when we wouldn't hear of it, she flat-out refused our ministrations.

"Go away," she'd shout when we knocked on her windows. It was quite a picture seeing this frail shrinking creature waving her bird arms at us, as if she could keep us out. We no longer took it personally. She was dying and there was no time to dwell on slights or insults, no room for the luxuries of holding grudges and taking offense. She needed us at last, and her need was as good as an apology. We took her keys to the hardware store and made copies, then set up a schedule of rotating shifts so that except for at night after we'd tucked her into bed, she was never alone. It was a lot of work, but it was what we'd do for any sister or mother or aunt; it was simply right.

The one difficulty was her habit of sleeping with all the dogs arrayed around the room. We didn't think it was safe; if any one of them knocked her over, her bones would surely shatter. Before we left we put them in their cages, but when we arrived the next morning there they were, on her bed and all along the walls like wainscoting. No matter how patiently we explained the danger to her, she persisted in sneaking downstairs at night and letting them up.

"We're going to have to put you in a nursing home if you don't take care of yourself," we told her. We said it out of exasperation, the way we told the children that Santa wouldn't come if they were bad.

"Dogs go off on their own to die," she said.

"You're not a dog." It was like talking to a child, and we became childish ourselves, doing it. We wanted to wring her skinny neck.

"Leave me alone," she said.

We were tempted, but we couldn't. She had no one else.

One early-spring morning the house seemed unnaturally quiet. Usually Diana had let the dogs out by the time we arrived. It was the one part of her old routine she maintained even after she'd become too weak to manage their heavy bowls of food and water anymore. In our experience, she'd never kept them waiting past seven. And so we knew.

We weren't squeamish, yet we tiptoed up the stairs and approached her room with trepidation. We needn't have worried, though. The scene, when we finally faced it, was peaceful. Diana had that mythic look of death that apes sleep while the absence of her singular spirit made the room feel empty. The only disturbing note was that the dogs were still with her—the large ones in their customary spots along the walls, and the smaller creatures arrayed around her on the bed like a wreath. When we entered, they eyed us lugubriously.

"Out!" we commanded, but they didn't move.

Then we forgot them for some time as we began to piece together details we'd overlooked at first glance. We pulled the curtains and, in the early light, saw that a crust of powder ringed her lips, and scattered on the bedside table and the floor below lay dozens of gelatin capsules, all of them opened and empty. How typical of Diana to do things her way, regardless of any constraints of law or ethics. Yet we didn't disapprove of her for it. It was her choice, we decided, as we would want it to be for ourselves. There was no reason for anyone else to know, however. The world at large isn't always as understanding as one's own kind, and we feared they might judge her weak or criminal. We cleaned up the pill bottles, washed out the glass, and tucked the note she'd left in a pocket for disposal at home. She hadn't written much anyway, just three words: *Watch the dogs.* It was an odd exhortation as we'd already agreed to it. It reminded us, though, that they were still in the room.

"Shoo!" we ordered, with no luck. Then someone recalled the ironic command Diana used when she wanted them to hop in their crates. It might at least get them downstairs, where we could deal with them more easily.

"Prison time!" we said, imitating her singsong way of speaking to them. The phrase got some results; they stood and walked to the door. Then they stopped, though, and simply stared. Was there another command we should be giving? We racked our brains. Meanwhile, it was eerie how they looked at us. It was as if they understood they'd never see her again, and that within the day they'd be in strange houses, separated from each other, adjusting to new circumstances and people and demands.

"Prison time!" we said again.

This time they seemed ready to obey, but not before taking what appeared to be a last look back at Diana. Was it possible they had an inkling of what was happening? No doubt they recognized death; but the idea that they might feel *grief* was another matter. That was a notion from Diana's realm, not ours. We'd interpret the dogs' baleful behavior as consternation at a disruption in their routine. Diana would say they were bereft. Who was right? It occurred to us that the greatest tribute we could pay her would be to give her, for once, the benefit of the doubt. (Perhaps the only tribute—for she'd always said she wouldn't be caught dead having a funeral.) And why not? What could we lose by extending them our empathy; what would we gain by holding back? We afforded them a moment of silence. What went on during that time we would never know. The way they looked at us afterward, though: We didn't believe in an afterlife, not a corporeal one at least, but in spite of ourselves, we hoped she could see.

Finally we coaxed them outside and began to notify everyone. The man at the *New York Times* had a file on Diana already and rang back to verify the details.

"Name of hospital?" he asked.

Oh no, we said, no hospital, none of that. On the contrary, the end was quite soulful, what we'd all like when the time comes—to die at home, during sleep, surrounded by friends.

Darwin's Dogs

Mark Derr

EARLY IN *THE DESCENT OF MAN, AND SELECTION IN RELATION TO Sex,* Charles Darwin uncorks a passage to illustrate the capacity of dogs to love that is guaranteed to break the heart of all but the most unfeeling cad and should hang over the door of every laboratory engaged in experiments with animals. "In the agony of death a dog has been known to caress his master," he says, "and everyone has heard of the dog suffering under vivisection who licked the hand of the operator; this man, unless the operation was fully justified by an increase of our knowledge, or unless he had a heart of stone, must have felt remorse to the last hour of his life."

A casual reader of Darwin's collected works might assume that the man was obsessed with pigeons; indeed, he avidly bred and studied them, as models for his theories. But closer examination reveals the full depth of Darwin's affection for all animals and his special love for dogs, who bound through the pages of his work, illustrating his theories of evolution and domestication, as well as animal intelligence and emotion. After disembarking the *Beagle* in 1832 (although purely coincidental, what better name for a ship on which a naturalist is sniffing out the mysteries of evolution?) to explore Patagonia and environs, he made a special trip to investigate the shepherd dogs of South America, described a few years earlier by the great French naturalist Alcide Dessalines d'Orbigny.

I suspect that Darwin, a proper skeptic, was intrigued to see whether d'Orbigny's account of these mongrels, who were suckled on ewe's milk and raised with sheep from infancy, did indeed travel with their flock, taking it to pasture, bringing it home, protecting it from marauding wildlife and dogs. In their spare time they hunted partridges and jaguars for their masters, who abused them horribly, even to the point of slashing them with knives. In *The Voyage of the Beagle,* Darwin doesn't confirm the hunting and slashing, but he does observe that, after the shepherd dog brings the flock in, he goes to the house for a piece of meat and then skulks away with it, "as if ashamed of himself," pursued by "tyrannical" house dogs. But upon reaching his flock, the dog, which, like all its kind, was castrated at an early age, turns and routs the house dogs with a bark. Darwin saw the whole performance as an example of the dog's powers of affection and association, what today we call bonding and behavior modification by castration. It is a lesson that should by considered by everyone who considers the big white guarding dogs genetically preprogrammed to protect sheep.

Unfortunately, Darwin, like those other intellectual giants Marx and Freud, is seldom read but frequently invoked—wrongly—by his proponents and opponents alike. His classic phrase, *natural selection,* means simply, as he explained in *The Variation of Plants and Animals Under Domestication* (Vol. I), that those individuals "best fitted for the complex, and in the course of ages, changing conditions to which they are exposed, generally survive and procreate their kind." Those who survive to pass their genes on to the next generation are by definition the fittest. They need not be the biggest, strongest, boldest, brightest, or best at corralling millions in the stock market. Indeed, there are circumstances in which the meek and cautious survive while the marauding bullies perish, victims of their own aggression.

Operating slowly over a long time frame, natural selection is more potent than what we humans can accomplish through selective breeding of domestic animals. People can't create new traits for domesticated species,

Darwin said, they can only concentrate or de-emphasize those already expressed. Through "methodical," or conscious, selection, a breeder decides what characteristics he or she wants and then strives to reach them. "Unconscious" selection, on the other hand, involves "the preservation by man of the most valued, and the destruction of the least valued individuals, without any conscious intention on his part of altering the breed."

Usually the two worked in tandem in subtle ways. By Darwin's time, several Greyhound breeders had crossed their dogs with Bulldogs to add courage, Pointers were crossed with Foxhounds for speed and agility (to match faster horses), and Bulldogs were downsized after the demise of bull-baiting. The breeders doubtless were seeking to match the fastest dogs, for example, but they could hardly foresee what the animal would look like and it was, Darwin says, different from the old hound.

Absent any knowledge of genetics, Darwin demolishes the practice of inbreeding (called interbreeding or breeding in to in), saying it arises from a misbegotten belief in "purity of the blood," and extols the virtue of crossing and hybrids. Inbreeding may appear to work, he says, but in the long run it produces weak, infertile animals, prone to malformation and disease. On the other hand, too much outcrossing leads to reversion to the basic dog. The key to success was to choose the best, the fittest, and proceed. In *The Descent of Man,* he asserts that "hardly any one is so ignorant as to allow his worst animals to breed," meaning those that were unsound mentally or physically. (More than a few modern breeders should take heed.)

Although Darwin frequently used dogs as examples, they presented difficulties not found in pigeons. He recognized that variability was essential to the adaptability of wild species, and that domestication, for reasons we still don't understand, unloosed the variability inherent in the wild progenitor of an animal. But the astounding variety of dogs, from the noble Greyhound, "the perfect image of grace, symmetry, and vigor," to the mutant Bulldog with its exaggerated head and undershot jaw to the Turnspit with its dwarfed legs (literally it was used to turn spits), befuddled him. He could only conclude that they must have come from several different wild species, primarily the wolf and jackal, a notion we now know is incorrect.

Humans had succeeded with varying degrees of success in reordering the behavior of those wild progenitors. In *On the Origin of Species,* Darwin observes that pointing, encircling a herd or flock, and retrieving are among the general wolfish hunting and puppy-rearing traits that have been "rigorously" selected for by nature. "Less rigorously," or less precisely, humans had concentrated one or more of those traits in specialized breeds of dog. Other changes were more profound. He writes in *The Descent of Man* that dogs "may not have gained in cunning, and may have lost in wariness and suspicion, yet they have progressed in certain moral qualities, such as in affection, trust, worthiness, temper, and probably in general intelligence." They had also become more biddable, or trainable.

Underlying much of Darwin's thought was his profound belief, shared with other eighteenth- and nineteenth-century naturalists, that animals differed from humans largely in degree, not kind. He argued that as one moved from lower to higher orders of animals, the influence of instinct declined and intelligence increased, and dogs and horses were near the top of that hierarchy. In fact, Darwin believed domestic animals were generally more intelligent than their wild progenitors, a notion that in this century has been reversed—to the detriment of all animals.

In the opening chapters of *The Descent of Man,* he brilliantly argues, using dogs as a prime example, that animals feel "pleasure and pain, happiness and memory." They inherit the capacity for terror, suspicion, fear, deceit, timidity, bad and good temperament, rage, and vengefulness. More significantly, they possess the powers of reason, imagination, love, jealousy, and pride. They believe in the supernatural: "There must be something special, which causes dogs to howl in the night, and especially during moonlight, in that remarkable and melancholy manner called baying." They are also religious in a way, substituting the master for God. Not possessed of human language and learning, they nonetheless communicate—who among us can't recognize the meaning of our dogs' barks, chortles, growls, bays, yodels, and howls?—and learn in their world. When in response to a whispered "Where is it?" a dog charges from tree to tree, she proves that she has a notion that there is something to hunt or fetch; thus, she engages in a form of abstract thought.

Dogs, and other animals, possess a sense of beauty, or aesthetic appreciation, although mostly confined to sexual attraction. Their moral sensibility is manifest in their knowledge of right and wrong and their assistance to their family, pack, or herd. But they are also altruistic: "It must be called sympathy that leads a courageous dog to fly at any one who strikes his master, as he certainly will."

Darwin admits that animals may lack self-consciousness, the ability to reflect on the meaning of life and death, their place in the cosmos. "But," he then slyly asks, "how can we feel sure that an old dog with an excellent memory and some power of imagination, as shown by his dreams, never reflects on his past pleasures or pains in the chase?" How indeed?

Trust

Heather Houlahan

WE ARE CROSSING FROM THE OPEN WOODS INTO A MEADOW when Mel alerts into the top of a shallow drainage. It is choked with bramble and saplings—exactly the kind of place where a lost child might end up. Or where a crafty volunteer might hide during a training exercise.

Her nose rises and leads the rest of her body, taut and beautiful. She glides into the wind following the specter of scent that is her reality, my mystery. Back and forth across the scent, down into the thick underbrush, narrowing her casts, closing in. At such moments I have been known to forget about breathing.

As fast as that, the buck explodes out of the ravine.

I don't wait for Mel to give chase.

"LEAVE IT! Goddammit, Mel—NO! Come. Here. Now!"

She breaks off immediately, streaks back to me and spins in circles, licking, whining. One very upset dog.

I have her sit, to calm her down. "Dammit, Mel, stop apologizing. Just don't do it again."

We have had this conversation a thousand times in the past five years, over ravaged backpacks, plundered cupboards, barking jags. *Stop apologizing. Just don't do it again.* But not, for four years, over Bambi. I thought we were long ago done with that youthful indiscretion, the vice that nearly sidelined her career as a search dog. True, she had stopped as soon as I called her. But she had worked his scent as if he were her human quarry. Lied, in a way.

"Now go find." Mel springs to her feet and starts back to the head of the ravine. "NO—you leave that. Go find over here." She obeys reluctantly.

We continue; it's a blinded task. I don't know who might be out here to find, if anyone. We might search six hours and discover no one. I love these exercises, and they are the closest thing to real search tasks that we can devise. Three hours later, with our assignment nearly finished, Mel alerts into a stand of savage hawthorns and disappears. Minutes later she emerges, one happy dog—the spinning this time is her joyful answer to my question, "Did you find someone?"

"Show me!" By the time we reach our volunteer, I am crawling under the thorny branches. We devote the next five minutes to affirming Mel's status as The Best Dog in the Universe.

Then he breaks the news. Mel had been within 80 feet of another subject, who had heard me in the distance, calling her off. They've been talking on team radios.

I realize I have called her off only once.

We double-time back to the ravine. The wind has shifted, and Mel catches the scent from the bottom as we approach, dashes in, and returns only seconds later. She leads me to my teammate, who is enjoying a nap. Another session of The Best Dog in the Universe, made more sincere by my conviction that I am The Worst Handler Ever.

"Barb, why didn't you tell me you were right next to the deer when he flushed?" (Implicit: "Why didn't you stop me from making an ass of myself?")

"What deer?"

I circle her bivouac and find the buck's daybed about 30 feet away, surrounded by the shredded saplings he has been torturing during the rut. She never saw him, never heard him, had no idea why I was calling Mel. No more idea than my honest Mel had.

Mel is too gracious to tell me *Stop apologizing—just don't do it again.*

There's nothing about living as a "modern" industrialized human that prepared me for Mel. The message was clear from childhood: Serious people don't spend their time with animals, or thinking about them and their lives. That's childish stuff, Disney fiction. Dogs are a trivial diversion, and *dog* is synonymous with *pet.*

Oh—and animals don't have language. That's what makes us better than them.

There are some people who rely on a dog for their livelihood, like stock farmers and police officers. Others—like some blind and disabled people trust their dogs with their own lives—a dependence that is humbling in the best possible way.

Myself, I can't think of one instance in which one of my dogs has saved my life or averted a personal catastrophe. Instead, I rely on my dog to save other people's lives. She has to find human scent and follow it under every condition imaginable. She has to tell me about every person she has found. And she has to refrain from lying in order to cadge a reward, or "please" me. If I want to avoid ulcers before I'm forty, I'd better believe she can do it. I have to know her abilities, and I have to trust her honesty.

So I pick the best dog I can, and I train her as intelligently as I can, and, knowing too well the power of hope over reason, I subject us both to the scrutiny of peers before I field on a search. Of three partners, only Mel has seriously challenged my skills as a trainer, and that mostly because she is something of a delicate genius—brilliant, egotistical, and oblivious to adversity, but falls to shards at a harsh word from me. But also because it is in her nature to chase creatures.

The day that Bambi didn't exist for her turned it all back on me. I accused Mel of lying, and her response was forgiveness, automatic and thoughtless. Even God, they say, takes time to think about it.

The boy went missing two nights ago. There are many places to hide, but not many to shelter a runaway, deep in this West Virginia hollow, and we try not to think about how long an 85-pound boy can last after two freezing nights and heavy rain.

Mel pulled up lame in the shoulder yesterday but has just been cleared for light duty by another handler who is also a vet. The operations officer asks me to do a thorough search of neighbors' outbuildings. The largest barn has cattle on one side, pigs on the other. When I open the center door where hay is stored, chicken feathers rain on my head. Tight bales are stacked 12 feet high, past the rafters and almost to the roof.

My lame dog, nearly eight years old, levitates to the top of the pile and disappears; shortly she returns to the edge and beckons me up. I clamber after her, belly-crawling when I reach the top. Mel has already searched the entire barn, and is whining and burrowing down the joints between bales near the center. She has always whined like a lost puppy when she can't reach her subject, and is never satisfied until she licks his face.

"David, it's time to come out now. No one is angry with you; we are all very worried. My dog won't hurt you; she is very worried too. But you can't hide from her."

Nothing. I wonder if I am talking to myself. Perhaps the boy was here, but has left? I can see no break in the neat stack of bales. We go back down and circle the barn—through the steers, over the irate pigs—trying to find another entrance to the hay pile. There is none. Mel vaults to the top as we return to the door.

This time she nearly disappears down one gap, and for a moment I imagine her sliding face-first to the bottom and suffocating. I pull on her tail and she backs out. I stick my arm down to the shoulder, and feel nothing but hay. Pull out one bale and try again, down on my belly, while Mel whines and tries to follow my arm. My fingers touch soft cotton and the warm back of a silent, mortified child who believed he had found the best hiding place in the world.

Later, a searcher asks, "Weren't you nervous sticking your hand down there blind? What if there'd been a copperhead or a raccoon or something that your dog was trying to get?" A reasonable question.

Western travelers once told tales of fiendishly designed idols of the East—stick your hand into the mouth of the god, and if you are an unbeliever, or tell a lie, the spring-set blades within will remove it. Even the righteous and faithful could be forgiven for trembling as they offered forth their hands.

My hand was steady. Mel had given me her word.

Lala the Loot

Michelle Huneven

FOR A GOOD PART OF MY LIFE—SIXTEEN YEARS—I HAD A DOG named Lala. During our time together, she was stolen from me three times. Lala was not any kind of pedigree, but a small mixed breed, part Chihuahua, part Dachshund, and part something else, possibly German Shepherd. She looked like a miniature German Shepherd—blond with black tips—and weighed around eleven pounds. She was undeniably appealing—dark, expressive eyes, and chronic joyousness—but she was not the kind of dog you could fence for money.

With people, Lala was the friendliest, most loving dog imaginable; I've never met another dog with such a purely affectionate nature. She, in turn, inspired affection and even goodness in the most unlikely and even unlikable human beings. Although when it came to other dogs, Lala was fearless and ferocious. I used to say that her motto was twofold: Come from love *and* kill big dogs. If she'd had a different kind of owner (if, indeed, she'd stayed with her second captors) she might have become a bear dog, a fyce (as Faulkner calls them): one of those little yappy things that run right up to bears, barking and nipping, but are too small and too close to the ground for the bear to reach underneath and eviscerate with a swipe of its claws. As it was, I once had to pry an Airedale's teeth off her throat. Lala antagonized other dogs, especially those larger than herself.

But humans Lala adored and trusted indiscriminately. Once, in a supermarket parking lot, she shot out of my car and ran across two aisles to greet a family of strangers as if they were her own long-lost kin. She made human friends wherever we went.

I had found her at a small sawmill in the southern Sierra foothills. I routinely stopped by the mill to fill my trunk with wood scraps for my wood-burning stove. One day, a small puppy with an infected eye came up and licked my ankle. "Whose dog is this?" I asked the owner.

"Yours," he said. Then added, "Somebody left three puppies in the ditch. Please take her, or my wife will."

I took her and drove directly to the vet, who pulled a foxtail out of her eye, gave her puppy shots, and said that she was around four months old. Maybe two weeks later, she was stolen from me for the first time.

I was living in the country, among the oak-and-grass–covered foothills outside a small town I'll call Mayville on the banks of the Chula River. (I've changed the names to protect the guilty—and to protect myself from the guilty.) On Memorial Day, I drove into Mayville to see my friend Fanny. Her backyard was on the river. We spent the hot afternoon walking several hundred yards up the bank, then floating downstream in inner tubes. Fanny's two dogs and Lala ran up and down along the banks with us. People were in their yards barbecuing, and cooling off in the river. Lala made friends left and right, with families and retirees and an old hermit, and was an instant hit with a small pack of eight- to ten-year-old boys. But the dogs were always there to greet us as we pulled ourselves out of the water. Then, at one point, Lala wasn't with them.

Fanny and I spent the rest of the afternoon scouring Mayville, calling and whistling, to no avail. I came across the pack of boys who'd befriended Lala. They'd seen her, but couldn't say exactly where, or when, or agree which way she'd gone. I gave up searching after dark, and had a very bad night.

The next morning, Fanny called from work; she was a teacher's aide at the local school. One of the little boys, she said, had had an attack of conscience. He'd admitted that he and his friends had stolen Lala, and put her in an outbuilding behind his house in Mayville. Fanny gave me the address, directions, and the eight-year-old's description of the place. I drove into town.

I found the address easily—a house on an acre of shady land with at least five outbuildings on the property. Nobody answered the door of the main house, so I walked around to the back. Three sheds were locked, and another was an old outhouse filled with gardening tools. The last building was a small substandard dwelling—Mayville was filled with uninsulated shacks and shanties that people once vacationed in—and I was heading toward it when a woman came out of the main house. She was slim and good-looking, with black hair in the big, sprayed hairdo of a cocktail waitress. "What are you doing?" she said. Not friendly.

"I'm looking for my little blond dog," I said. "Your son said she's here, in one of the back buildings."

"No," said the woman. "I told him to take the dog back to you yesterday, and he did. There's no dog here."

"I'd just like to look in there," I said, pointing to the one unsearched building.

"I can't let you in there," said the woman. "It's not mine. And there's nothing in there, anyway. It's empty. You won't find anything."

I wavered. It felt rude to insist. The woman seemed so certain, and so hard. She was not someone to mess with.

Then I heard something. Or thought I did. A yip. Or a hunch of a yip.

"Still," I said, walking past the woman. "I'm going to look."

I reached the door and turned the knob. The door opened. I did not see an empty house. Rather, I took one step inside a room crammed with electronic equipment—televisions, stereos, soundboards, stacks and stacks of them. There was only a narrow aisle through all the stuff. And suddenly, swerving around a pillar of speakers and running full tilt, there was Lala.

The boys, when tired of her, had simply put her in with all the other stolen goods. Lala, wriggling with pleasure, let me kiss and pet her briefly, then ran outside, and took a good long pee on the lawn. (Now that's a good dog!)

"You have to go now," said the woman. I ignored her and, turning on a faucet, gave Lala water out of my hands (she was very thirsty). We left only after Lala drank her fill.

Mayville was a quirky little town; there were near-luxury homes and small ranchos in the nearby hills. Modest, well-tended riverfront properties alternated with falling-down, paint-thirsty, more rustic constructions. The town itself was a few blocks long, with few merchants and no prospects—no economic base, no industry. Locals either logged, or commuted twelve miles to the next, larger town to work. There were a couple bars, some small grocery stores, a gas station, a post office, a struggling café, two struggling dinner houses, a decent hardware store.

Juvenile dognappers and stolen-goods keepers were not, unfortunately, the town's only or worst criminal element. Mayville had its own, home-grown sociopath, who was in jail when I first moved there, but I heard all about him.

Wren Hickles was known for stealing, wrecking other people's property, running cars off the road, and sudden, unprovoked, violent assaults. He was prodigious in his antics and there was hardly a family in Mayville who had not suffered at his hands. For a long time, nobody would press charges against him; they were too afraid of him. Finally, a man whom Wren had beaten savagely for no reason, in broad daylight on Main Street, had him arrested, and convinced several reluctant witnesses to testify. Wren Hickles was sent to Soledad for three years.

As those years were coming to a close, a murmur rose in the town. His name came up more and more. The old stories recirculated. This wedding party ruined by drunken rampaging. That truckful of firewood forced off the mountain road. This house broken into and trashed. That bloody fist-fight.

And then Wren Hickles was back. The news rippled through the small community. He applied for a job in the hardware store—the owner, a friend of mine, said Wren seemed friendlier and smarter than before, and also funny. "One thing, though," said the owner. "He was leaning against that glass display of pocketknives while he was talking to me, and when he left, half the knives were gone as well." My boyfriend at the time was a local. It was his brother who had succeeded in having Wren Hickles sent to jail. "If you see him," my boyfriend said, "don't do anything to attract his notice."

Not long after his return, I saw Wren Hickles for the first time. I'd stopped at the convenience store to pump gas and there was a lean, snaggle-toothed guy, shirtless, his back tattooed with a clumsy lightning bolt and the word Mayville. A prison tattoo. He was smoking pot with another guy right by the pumps while, a few feet away, a woman wept in a car. A bad scene. I decided to get gas elsewhere.

I told my boyfriend that I'd finally laid eyes on the notorious parolee. "Stay below his radar," my boyfriend said. "Or, believe me, you'll regret it."

Lala disappeared on a weekday. I was driving in to work and was a little late, and she chased me farther than usual, past the gate on the edge of my property, and partway down the side road to the highway. I stopped the car and yelled at her and ordered her home. I wasn't worried she'd get lost. We often walked this far together, and every morning she and my Lab went for long exploratory runs in the barely populated hills. But when I came home nine hours later, my Lab, Olive, was there, and Lala was not. I drove around the neighborhood calling her, and the next morning I contacted all the neighbors. Nobody had seen her.

I made handbills and hung them up on telephone posts and fence posts, in the Mayville post office, on the supermarket bulletin board. Days passed. A week. Nobody phoned. Then, one day, I came home late at night to a message on my answering machine. "I know where yer dog's at," a man said in a thick backwoods drawl. "An' this is Lawrence . . ." No further message. No callback number. Just a click.

Lawrence. I didn't know any Lawrence. I asked around. There was a retired dentist named Lawrence. "This didn't sound like a dentist," I said. I played the message for my boyfriend and watched his face darken. "I'll handle it," he said.

I begged him not to. I promised to talk to the deputy sheriff the next morning. I promised I wouldn't approach Wren Hickles myself.

And promptly broke that promise. The next morning, I went into town to pick up my mail. I'd heard by then that Wren Hickles had a job at the Mobil station, so I drove on over. He was washing the window of the office. "Hi," I said. "Are you Lawrence?"

"Yes ma'am," he said, turning. He put the squeegee in his bucket and offered me his hand.

We shook. "I'm Michelle," I said. "I think you called me about my dog that's lost."

"I seen your sign in the post office," he said. "The Greens got her—you know the Greens?"

Of course I did. The Greens were a big notorious mountain family, all men, except for the mother whose name was—I kid you not—Ophelia. The father, Robert Green, was a hunting guide; one son was a logger, another was a tree surgeon, a third was the runt of the family who was actually called Pipsqueak—he was trustworthy and a hard worker, the one people hired for chores around the house and yard. The youngest son was a beautiful hunk who soon moved south to star in pornographic movies.

"I was gonna call you again," said Wren Hickles. "Nice little dog. You better get her quick, 'fore they get anymore attached to her."

I drove straight up the mountain road to the Greens. I parked behind a row of pickups and flatbeds. When I got out of the car, the first living thing I saw was Lala.

She took one look at me and tucked her tail between her legs, as if she'd done something very wrong.

"Oh, Lala," I said. "You're okay, I'm not mad." And shortly, she was there, licking my face.

With Lala in my arms, I knocked on the door. Only Ophelia was home. Her husband, Robert, she said, had found "Sunny" on the street where I lived. "She would've come home," I said.

"I thought she was someone's pet," Ophelia said vaguely. "We were going to put an ad in the paper."

When? I wondered.

Ophelia reached out and stroked Lala's head. "She's the first dog Robert's let in the house in years."

I took Lala home and she didn't get stolen again for another thirteen years. I did have one more exchange with Wren Hickles. He pulled up next to me in his car at a highway stop and asked if I got my dog back. Not long afterward, less than a year after his parole, he fled the state. He'd carjacked a vehicle, locked the owner in the trunk, and sent it off the side of a mountain. While the owner survived, Wren's parole was definitely violated. The last thing I heard, he was being extradited from Missouri.

Lala and I moved back to the city—first to Pasadena, where we lived for six years in a courtyard of Craftsman cottages. We didn't have a yard, so I walked Lala several times a day, and in mild weather, tied her to a faucet out front, so she could lie in the sun and greet her many friends going up and down the courtyard walkway. If I didn't put her out for a few days, it wasn't unusual for strangers to knock on the door and ask after her. Oh, Lala and her legion of friends.

From Pasadena we moved to Atwater, an odd little suburb of Los Angeles near Griffith Park. We had a huge fenced-in yard, and Lala took her responsibility—guarding the property—seriously, at least when it came to other dogs. Every perambulating canine was announced, and many barked back. Except for this constant vigilance, Lala befriended the entire neighborhood—which is more than I can say for myself.

We were happy in Atwater except for one thing. One major thing. We had a crazy next-door neighbor, a woman who had repeatedly been charged with being a "neighborhood nuisance." Therese was in her late seventies and surely mentally ill; she was filled with hatreds, resentments, and frustrations—and that's putting her pathology nicely. All my neighbors warned me about her. She called the authorities about everything, real and imagined, any infringement, no matter how small. When people, having forgotten something, pulled back in their driveways and ran into their houses, she called parking enforcement if they blocked the sidewalk. If a car was parked in one spot over the seventy-two-hour limit, or with a bumper in the red zone, or more than eighteen inches from the curb, she called to have them ticketed.

Therese must have had a list of every petty authority and enforcer in Los Angeles County. She called the county agriculture inspector many times about my garden—when I mulched my roses with straw (she believed mice live in straw and therefore, the day I mulched, called and told the inspector I had an infestation of vermin); she called him when I made a compost heap (she thought it was garbage), and when I fertilized with steer manure (she said I'd strewn excrement on the premises). When I first moved in, she phoned my landlord every time I had a houseguest or a visiting dog, and told him I had a new roommate and/or a new pet. He didn't care, and began hanging up on her. Everyone in the neighborhood avoided and ignored her as much as possible.

Except Lala, who was as happy to see old Therese as she was to see almost anybody. Also, despite my endless requests to the contrary, Therese constantly fed Lala table scraps. Lala was perhaps the only living creature who ever exhibited even the slightest pleasure at the sight of this bitter, vindictive old woman. (Therese's own husband, a timid man, would sometimes raise his voice in unmistakable agony, "Therese, you are an evil, evil person," an assessment with which we neighbors, wincing in sympathy, unanimously agreed.) Lala had more compassion and humanity—and a greater love of table scraps—than all of us combined.

One chilly Sunday afternoon, I was watching videos in bed with my boyfriend. We were watching the *Prime Suspect* miniseries, one episode after another. The only problem was that the phone kept ringing. And it was never anyone I wanted to talk to more than I wanted to watch Helen Mirren solve crimes. Finally, after someone called to ask how to make pot roast, my boyfriend said, "Don't answer it anymore, okay?"

Lala was in and out of the house at her whim, sometimes joining us on the bed, sometimes patrolling the yard. The phone rang several times over the period of an hour. "God, you get a lot of calls on a Sunday," said my boyfriend.

Then, someone was pounding on the door. I jumped up, pulled on a robe, and answered the door. It was Therese, with her weary, sagging face and hideously swollen legs. She was eighty by then and nearer the end of her life than we even hoped. My house sat deep in the lot; it must have been an enormous effort for her to walk all the way down my driveway. She'd been banging the door with her aluminum canes.

"A man stole Lala," she said. "I've been trying to call you. He just opened the gate and stepped in and picked her up. He had white hair and a white mustache and a whole bouquet of white flowers. He probably stole those too," she said.

My boyfriend and I moved into action. Dressed. Grabbed cell phones. We were so steeped in *Prime Suspect,* it seemed as if we were setting off into our own crime drama episode.

We drove my truck up and down the streets, stopping and interrogating every person we saw. "Have you seen a small blond dog with a white-haired man?" We asked maybe eight or ten people before we got the answer we wanted.

"I saw them," said the man. "I asked him, 'Where'd you get that dog?' and he said he'd found her in the street."

The thief, he went on to say, hung out at the liquor store over on Fletcher, by the Foster's Freeze. We drove off in hot pursuit.

We found our prime suspect sitting on a cinder-block wall at the Foster's. "Where's my dog?" I asked him.

"Your dog? I haven't seen your dog," he said.

And then, in the long grass behind him, I saw a familiar black-tipped tail. When he saw me spot her, he said, "I tried to call you and tell you I found her lost in the street."

I yelled Lala's name. She jumped off the wall and into my arms. I was shaking with fear and loss and relief.

The dognapper asked my boyfriend for a reward.

My boyfriend said something suitably macho and dramatic—"If I ever catch you anywhere near our house, or that dog again, you'll be sorry you ever walked down that street."

And thus was Lala restored to me, again through the agency of a public enemy. We laughed about it—the high drama, the solving of a crime—but I was also keenly aware that it could have turned out very badly indeed.

I had almost sixteen happy years with Lala. As with many dogs, she was a study in unconditional love, but in her case, it was unconditional love of the most extroverted and expressive variety. She could beguile and charm even the worst of human beings, and somehow make them behave admirably on her behalf. She forced me to see the faintest spark of goodness in people. She made it impossible for me to thoroughly despise some of the most feared and disliked citizens in my community, for she brought out the best in them, brought out whatever trace of affection and responsibility slumbered within them. An entire town feared and despised Wren Hickles, and for excellent reasons; but my interaction with him was only positive: He did me a great favor. And while I suffered living next door to horrible old Therese and was frankly relieved when she died, I cannot hate her unconditionally, for she did, when quite ill, make her long, slow way over to my house to tell me Lala had been taken.

Ah, Lala. You were a better human than I—except when it came to other dogs.

Bloodlines: A Story

Catherine Ryan Hyde

ME AND MY NEIGHBOR FRANK MAIN USED TO GET ALONG REAL good till the dog thing. We got two kids each, only a year apart in school, and his wife and my wife take turns sometimes driving carpool. I took his mail in every day for two weeks while they had their vacation, and once when I dropped an intake manifold on my foot, Frank mowed my lawn for five weeks running. I think he's one of those America-America guys, like, you're here now, so speak English, but in nine years he never made fun of my English—even at the beginning when it wasn't so good—or mentioned nothing about it. Like so long as I was trying, you know? I got mixed feelings about that but it never much got in our way.

Anyhow, a while back his boy, Eddie, got after him to get a dog. And I even put in my two cents. I said you'll never regret it, Frank, it's the best move ever. I said look what Blackie is to our family. The kids love her, she takes care of the house, she even gets me off my lazy behind to walk her every morning and every night and that's good for the both of us.

She's the best dog, Blackie, big as a house, nearly eighty pounds, I think, though I never picked her up and put her on a scale, but so gentle. Shepherd and some Labrador and maybe something else, too. She can see her favorite food in my son's hand, a big juicy piece of steak, maybe, and she'll take it so gentle he'll giggle because he says it tickles his hand. And to think a dog like that was on her last day at the pound. Just think, Frank, I said, you could save a life like that, too, and that dog'll pay you back in more ways than you even knew there were.

So I felt real good the day he leaned over the fence and said he found the perfect dog.

Great, I said, when are you bringing him home? I can't wait to see. Is it a male dog or female?

Not sure, he said. Haven't decided yet. The bitch is expected to whelp in three weeks, then the breeder likes to let 'em nurse seven or eight weeks before he weans 'em—that makes 'em nice and confident since they're born guard dogs—and then me and Eddie get our pick of the litter and we'll be bringing it on home.

Now wait, I said, now hold on a minute here, let me get something straight. You found the perfect dog but it isn't even born yet? He just smiled in a way that made me see the first of the trouble coming on. Then how do you know it's perfect? You got a crystal ball to look in?

Researched it, he said. Bloodlines. Pedigree papers. Red Doberman Pinscher, championship lines. Be a hell of a watchdog.

By now I could already feel things get hot behind my ears. This is never a good sign.

Blackie is a hell of a watchdog, I said. And she was nearly free, out of the county pound. One time Blackie just out of nowhere howled like a banshee and lit out across the yard and leaped up at a spot on the corner of the fence. Slammed right into the fence and brought us running. We had no idea why, but a few minutes later some creep was caught looking over the back fence at Widow Jesperson's place down the street.

Like I said, Blackie is big as a house, and if she were to say to you, *Stay out of my family's yard,* I just bet you would. I just damn well bet you would.

I didn't think I should ask how much this pure red Doberman was costing him, but I wanted to know real bad.

Anyhow, I could see things going in a wrong direction, so I just took a few big deep breaths and I said to myself, It's a free country, man can get any dog he wants. Man can do what he wants, even if it's stupid. So all I said was, Can't wait to see, Frank, and then I went inside to take it out on my poor wife.

If I made the America laws, I said to my poor wife, who was trying to finish the lunch dishes, a guy could still do what Frank is doing, only first he'd have to go to the pound and walk up and down all those rows and look in the eyes of all those smart, pretty dogs, and tell them why they're just not good enough. Why they gotta die while he's waiting for something better to get born. And another thing, I said. What kind of example is that to set for your kids? Here's how much we respect life, kids. Let's make sure lots of new dogs get born even though we're killing half the ones that are already here. 'Cause, you know, our dog has to be special. And another thing. I wonder what he's paying for that dog. What do you think, Sofi? Guess.

I couldn't guess, Cacho, she said. I got no idea. Probably a lot.

Just my point. Just what I'm saying. Probably a lot.

Then she dried her hands and touched my shoulder like she does when she wants me to breathe deep and think on happier things. And I swear I thought no more about it till that dog come home.

Now there are crimes against nature and there are crimes against nature, but please tell me why, if the good Lord put a certain set of parts on a dog, would a guy go and cut some of them off again? Would you tell me that, please? Does Frank Main know more about dogs than God does? Is that it? I'm not trying to be a smart-ass. I really want to know.

I seen lots of dogs with tails cut off but it's still a crime against nature if you ask me. But then Frank tells me he's going to have the vet cut off half of those pretty silky ears and tape what's left to splints so they'll stick up straight.

While he's telling me this the pup is sitting on one hip, all off at an angle, and she turns her head to follow some movement, a bird or a fly, I don't know, and almost falls right over. For all that money I don't think she's very smart. But that doesn't make it right what he's saying. She's flesh and blood, after all.

Why? I ask him. That's all I want to know. Why take a knife to a healthy pup?

She's purebred Dobie, he says. Got to at least look like one.

Then he goes inside before we can really talk anymore about it, and the pup—Gretta, he calls her—starts chewing on one of his wife's marigolds in the nice planted beds. I stand and watch over the fence, and she gets tired of the flower after a time and digs up the whole plant. Frank's wife, Sharon, loves those flowers. Doesn't he know you can't just leave a new pup alone like that? They need tending. Figures. Frank doesn't know nothing about dogs or he wouldn't be cutting parts off them. Anyhow, puppies are always trouble. Gotta watch them every minute. Blackie was fourteen months when we got her. It's better that way, because all those bad stages are over and besides, people don't like to take the grown ones. They die a lot more regular in the pound. It's stupid, too, because they're better dogs and they get to love you just fine and if you can't train them, it just means you don't know nothing about dogs. They're better dogs but they die a lot more regular.

Frank's pup looks up at me with eyes that don't look so smart for all that money. Blackie never digs up the yard. Blackie is a great dog.

Over the next month or two I get real good at how not to look over the fence. She may be raising hell over there, chewing up landscape and digging for China, but I'll say one thing for that dog, she never makes a sound. Never hear a bark out of her. Sometimes I used to hear Eddie come out and play with her, yell at her to fetch and stuff, but it seems like he never does no more. Like he's back playing with his friends and forgot all about her. The girl is a year younger. She used to go out on the weekend, but I guess that dog is too rough for her, because she always ran inside crying. This is all I can hear and I've taught myself not to look over the fence.

I think it's funny how this championship watchdog never barks.

One day I'm walking Blackie, Monday, a couple hours before work, and here comes Frank and Gretta. She looks nearly half-grown now, big enough to pull him down the street. Her ears are taped and she's just crazy. I mean this is one hyper dog. Since this is the first I bumped into them outside the yard, I guess I see why. I'm not saying they never went out before, just I never bumped into them and I'm out two times a day like clockwork. So we walk together for about three blocks, and the pup is scrambling, churning her legs three times for every one of Blackie's steps, like running in place, like overdrive. She's jumping up at Blackie, slamming at her side, and Blackie doesn't hardly notice. Frank is telling me how he hired some pro painter guys to come over and paint his house. I'm looking at the tape all around this poor dog's butchered ears and listening to the paint thing and thinking this just keeps getting stranger.

You should've told me, I say. I'd've pitched in. Two weekends we'd get it done.

No, that's okay, Frank says. Get the pros, they do a good job.

So for a minute I'm thinking, What, I wouldn't do a good job? And I almost say it. But then Frank turns for home. They been out all of six minutes.

What, that's it? I say. Poor dog needs more exercise than that.

I gotta go, he says. Gotta get to the office.

He never said the office before. He always called it work. Just work. He works in a big office on the sixteenth floor downtown and I work in a city garage, maintaining service vehicles. I call it work and he calls it work, but all of a sudden it's the office. Then I think maybe I'm reading too much in.

Let me have her, then, I say. Blackie and me are going all the way down to Figueroa. I'll put her in your yard after.

Sure, I guess, he says. Thanks. Yeah, good. Thanks.

He turns back and I take hold of this little hellion by her stitched leather leash, and man, can that little girl pull. After a while I get tired of hearing her choke herself, so I break from a walk to a jog. It's been a while since I jogged. Months, and even then it wasn't regular. So it hurts my chest but feels kind of good, too, and I go through that wall like I always used to. You know, where you think you can't go more but you do, and then you settle in and get past it and kind of chug along. Blackie loves it. She's loping like a rocking horse, throwing herself up in the air instead of stretching out, so she won't get ahead of me.

I should get back to jogging, I decide. Every day.

A young woman comes out on her stoop to get her morning paper, and while she bends over she sees Gretta and her ear tape and gives me a bad look. One of those "How could you?" looks.

Not my dog, I say.

Either she doesn't believe me or she's mad at me anyhow.

When we get back, Frank is just heading out to his car for work. Oh, excuse me, the office.

You know, it's not just me, I say, and he looks at me funny. I say, Wherever I went with this dog, people think it's not right to put her through that.

Through what? Frank says.

The cropping.

That's what Frank calls it. Cropping. I call it taking a scalpel and slicing up one of God's perfect creatures, but I'm trying to have a civil conversation with the guy.

Oh, that, he says. It's part of what makes 'em good dogs. Makes 'em more stoic, you know?

Actually, I'm not sure I do. I heard the word *stoic* before, and maybe I knew what it meant at the time, but I can't make it come back to me now.

Frank keeps talking. They get used to pain, and they're better dogs for it.

Stoic. Right. I got it now. All of a sudden I'm mad. Real mad. Last time I got this mad I was still living with my father in Argentina. Now that my father is far away I don't get so mad anymore. Till now. I say something really loud. I say, What? Really loud I yell it and Gretta pees, right there, without even squatting down. It just leaks right out of her. I'm right up in Frank's face and I don't even remember how I got there. My brain knows I'm not going to hit him but my fist can remember how it will feel.

Want me to make you stoic, Frank? I ask him that. I say, You'll be a better man for it.

I just want him to think what he's saying, that's all. How it sounds, what he's saying.

You do it, he says, and I'll have the cops on you so fast.

Then he goes to his car. Leaves me to put his prize dog away in the yard.

We don't talk again for three months. Every morning and every night I take Gretta out of his yard and she jogs with us, but we never talk, me and Frank.

You never know who somebody is. You think you know, but you don't.

Then after three months I come home from our run and I have to talk to Frank, to tell him Gretta's spotting. Tell him I can't take her for runs till she's done being in heat because I can't defend her. Had to practically kick two big males to keep them away. We barely made it home. Poor Gretta. She's gotta feel bad when she loses those runs. It's pretty much all she's got.

So I knock on his door.

I tell him all the stuff the vet told us about Blackie. Tell him it can happen to anybody, that our Blackie got in one surprise heat, too, before we got her spayed. That she has to be locked in the house or she'll get pregnant, and now the vet won't spay her till the heat is over.

From the look on Frank's face you'd think I just explained the whole thing to him in Spanish.

Spay? he says.

Yeah. Spay. Fix. Neuter.

Spay? he says again. He just can't seem to wrap his head around that word. You think I'm going to get a two-thousand-dollar dog spayed?

Two thousand dollars. Two thousand dollars is more than I ever thought, even when I was guessing high. And I decide I'm not going to say all the stuff I want to say to him because he will never see a thing my way. We'll just keep banging heads. I'll say there's too many puppies in the world and he'll say people want champion Dobies, so these'll get homes. And I'll say that don't matter, it's still homes snatched right out from under those that're already here, and he'll say the people who buy his puppies were never headed for the pound no matter what. And then he'll slam the door in my face. Or worse yet, I'll really hit him this time, and the cops will come, and I'll be the wrong one, and all the shame will be mine.

Better keep her locked up in the house, then, I say.

Sharon doesn't like her in the house. Dog won't housebreak.

All dogs housebreak. I don't say this out loud, but it's true. Any dog'll housebreak. Just lots of people don't know how to go about it.

Might have to build her a five-sided run, then, I say.

I see in Frank's face that he doesn't want my advice, any of it, never did. Two thousand dollars. I bought my last car for less than that and it's a good car. Sofi drives it now and it still runs good.

The yard is nice and secure, he says.

I start up to tell him that he doesn't know what a female in heat will do to get out, what the males will do to get at her. But Frank closes the door. Doesn't slam it, but closes it, and me and Blackie and Gretta are on the street on our own. Doesn't even take his damn two-thousand-dollar dog back. I have to put her away in the yard.

While I do I look at Frank's house, all nice with its new paint, and I realize his house is a little nicer than mine. I never noticed that before it was painted. I knew it was bigger but I didn't think about it as nicer. And even in the month or so since the pro paint job, it's sort of been there to see without me seeing it.

Like a lot of other things I guess.

The next thing that happens is so not avoidable I almost don't have to tell it. It practically tells itself. I'm in the back room that Saturday with the windows open for air, and I hear some commotion, some scuffling and whimpering, so I go out, and I look over the fence. A dog is digging through from the other side. I can see his nose now and then, and his paws flying, and Gretta right at the fence cheering him on. Digging from her side, too. Then he tries to squeeze through, doesn't make it on the first try, has to back out and dig more. But I get a good look. And I run get my Polaroid.

When you work on cars, a Polaroid is a good thing to have. Take pictures of all the smog fittings and stuff or you won't never get them back where they go. Take pictures of parts and then post them for sale. Take pictures of ugly mongrel dogs in your neighbor's yard with his prize bitch.

I get back out and the dog is through the fence and Gretta and him are going at it and let me tell you, he's even uglier than I thought. He's got some wire-haired something in him, but a big head like a Bassett mixed with an Airedale and a million other things. I'm a big lover of dogs and no stickler for beautiful, but this is an eyesore of a dog if there ever was one. You almost got to love him for looking so bad.

They're holding still now and they're in that part I think where they're tied and they couldn't come apart if they tried. People don't know that. They'll turn a hose on two dogs and think they're just too into it to stop, but that male is tied in there till it goes down and he's not going nowhere till it's over. I snap off a couple of shots.

I take them inside and watch them turn into pictures, and they come out pretty good. First I think I just won't tell him. After all, I warned him once already. If I told him, he could go to the vet and get it aborted early. If I don't we all get to see what those damn puppies look like. That brings a smile on my face, I got to admit. But then I think it wouldn't be Frank to get hurt, it would be the puppies. One thing I know for damn sure, two people get into it over a dog, the loser will be the dog.

But I don't want any fistfights, so I tell Sharon. I wait till the next morning, when she's out tending the garden. Trying to put it back to where it was before Gretta, I should say. Sharon is crouching down, sweaty, and Gretta is on a chain.

Good morning, I say.

She jumps. Oh. Hi. Yeah.

Why is Gretta chained? I didn't mean to ask. This will get us off on a bad foot.

Oh. Frank said she tried to dig out under the fence.

She didn't, though. I tell Sharon that. I say, A male dug in and got her pregnant. I just wanted you guys to know that. So you can figure what you want to do.

See? After all that's happened I'm still trying to be a good neighbor to this man. That's who I am. Whatever Frank is, that's what I am. The dirt has been half-assed filled in where it was dug.

Sharon wipes her face off on the back of a gardening glove. Frank says Gretta tried to dig out, she says.

I stand there and say nothing. She doesn't believe me. I can't believe this. She thinks I'm lying? All I have to do is go inside and get those pictures. Polaroids never lie. But I don't. Because, you know why? Because I'm doing too much already, to be a good neighbor. And Frank, he's doing not enough. So, Frank, you got some really ugly mutt puppies in your future and it's nobody's fault but your own.

When Gretta starts to show, Frank calls me at my house. Talks to Sofi. Sofi covers the phone and says Frank wants to know if I actually saw a dog in his yard. If I know anything about who his dog might've bred with.

Tell him to go to hell, I say.

She doesn't. She tells him I don't remember.

Now I make it sound like we are the only two people in the neighborhood, me and Frank, but of course not. There's lots of others, they just don't figure in about the dog. Till after she gets pregnant. Then Frank is all over asking people if they saw whose dog it was. Acting as if I saw but won't talk. Acting as if he could've got to the situation in time if I'd talked. How'd it take him so long to figure out the dog was pregnant anyways? I mean, doesn't he ever go out there and look at her?

Anyhow, my neighbors on the other side are the Li family. I don't talk much with them, mainly because they won't talk to me or much of anybody else. Sometimes I try to talk to them about neighborhood things, good things that will help, but they don't want trouble. They don't say it like that but I can see. They say things like Thank you and Yes, yes, over and over and hurry back in the house. But they got a son, Richie, I known him since he was in high school, since they first come here from China, and now he's in graduate school but home for the summer. He wants trouble, if it's the right kind. If it's his kind of trouble.

Richie knocks on our door one night after dinner.

I send the kids upstairs to do homework and I sit with Richie in the family room and Sofi worries around getting us brandy while he tells me Frank came to see him.

Richie says, Like it's my problem his stupid dog got knocked up. Know how much he paid for that dog? Four thousand dollars.

I heard two.

You heard wrong.

Frank told me. Two.

Then that's all he wants you to know.

But also, I think, sometimes things go too many places around a neighborhood, and while they're traveling they get too big.

Richie looks so grown up now. His hair is parted on one side and slicked over. He grew up handsome. He's going to be a businessman. A good one.

I didn't know you don't like Frank, I say, because it's coming out while he talks.

Of course I don't like him, he's a bigot. You don't like him, do you?

Well, I guess I used to, I say. I don't think he's a bigot exactly. Just stupid. Especially about dogs. And maybe a little . . . like he's better than I am.

Richie sits back with his brandy and we both know I just said it. Frank is a bigot. I always knew it, but till I said it out loud to Richie Li, I didn't know. Explain a thing like that.

The purebred dog thing is a riot, Richie says. That dog is so stupid. And a total failure as a watchdog. I hope the ugliest mutt in the world knocked her up.

Probably I shouldn't have done what I did next but it was hard not to.

Wait, I said. Wait till you see.

And I went and got the pictures of the dogs going at it. I guess that's why I took them. 'Cause that dog was ugly in a way I could never describe. Richie just howled with laughing. I never heard nobody laugh so hard for such a time. And I looked again and it was even funnier with Richie here, because we neither one of us like Frank.

Oh, please can I have one of these? he said.

Don't show Frank, though.

Why not?

And miss the look on his face when he sees those puppies?

But I did give Richie one, and he took it to his father's copy place and made color photocopies, and gave them to all the neighbors that didn't like Frank. You know, people like us and not like Frank. I guess I always knew the block was divided into some like me and some like him but I never felt it deep till this dog thing.

Then every time Frank took this big pregnant dog for a walk, which wasn't very much, the neighbors who were like us got a good laugh behind their hand. I guess it was mean but I didn't do it, anyhow. Richie Li did it. And also Frank deserves it because he's stupid, especially about dogs, and besides he's a bigot.

Now it seems to me that anytime you do something you probably shouldn't do, you can bet it will come around to bite you.

So a couple evenings before Gretta is due to whelp I get a big knock at my door. The whole family jumps, because it's one of those police knocks. Either that or fire people to say get out right away. One of those shocking trouble knocks.

I answer the door and there stands Frank. He has a paper in his hand, and he holds it up about an inch in front of my face and it's one of the copies Richie Li made from the dog picture. I step out onto the dark front yard and close the door behind me to spare the family from trouble. While I do I'm feeling that cold flutter when you know things are coming to battle. I notice a couple of the neighbors out already. That police knock sure gets attention.

Frank is yelling at me. Yelling that he's trying to sue the people whose dog got into his yard, and here I have evidence and I don't give it to him, I give it to other people in the neighborhood so they can laugh at him. Loud enough so more neighbors come. And it seems funny how they come. Maybe it's just chance but the people behind Frank are people more like Frank. The people behind me I can only guess, because it's getting to be that dog-fighting thing where you don't look away.

None of this seems very much real.

He holds the picture in my face again. You think this is funny? he screams.

God help me, I crack a smile, I can't stop.

It's a little funny, I say. Yes.

Then just as I expect the fight to start for real I hear the voice of Richie Li behind me. Richie says, I think it's fucking hilarious.

That slows things down because Frank can't swing on two men at once.

Richie says, Frank, you know what? No wonder you got no sense of humor about that picture. Because you're a mongrel yourself and you know it.

Frank's face twists around and I notice that I can see the veins under his forehead. Even just with the streetlight I can see. His face is red and there are veins in his temples and it's because his skin is so white.

Excuse me? he says to Richie.

Just what I said, Frank. My family has been nothing but Chinese for eons. My friend here is from pure Argentine stock. But the only purebred American is the Indian and you're just a big mix of all those people who came later on a boat.

There are more people behind me than I thought and I know they are people like me because I can hear them saying yeah.

Richie says, Isn't that right, Cacho? and slaps a hand down on my shoulder.

Yes, I say. That's right.

It is right, but it's wrong, too, because if somebody looked at Blackie and said mutt like a bad thing I'd kick his ass. But I'm with Richie. But I feel a little bit like I know what it means to be a gun. Like there's a bigger fight and it's not so much about me but I'm the trigger gets pulled.

Frank throws the picture at my face. It's on a heavy stock like thin cardboard and the corner hits my eye. It's a shock to all of a sudden hurt so this must be the fight.

We weave and circle a little on the lawn with our fists ready, not up exactly but balled up and ready. I don't dare look away but I see Sofi standing on our stoop. See her at the corner of my eye, as she was when I raised fists to my father. Back then I looked over to see her face, asking me to please not. Then I looked back at the face of my father and saw all cold. When I did it, he wouldn't hit me back or call the police, only close his heart to me. Which in most ways he already had. Maybe that's why I was mad enough to hit. Maybe that's why I'm here again now. I didn't give Sofi her wish that day. Instead we gather up and run to this country. But I'm running low on countries where I think I can live.

My fists go straight, turn back to hands. I turn my head to look at my wife. To let her know the moment passed this time on its own.

As I do, Frank's fist slams my cheekbone. A good solid punch, enough to knock me back, slap on my brain. But it doesn't knock me down. I was in fighting stand, one leg well back, feet out. I just snap back and then straight again. I hear a little Oooh from the crowd because he really did it, then a sprinkle of cheer from the people more like me because I'm still on my feet. It does make me seem sort of unbeatable.

I turn my back on Frank and go inside with my wife. I will not hit him back. Just go inside with my wife and put ice on my face. He will be the one that hit. He will always have to live with being the one that hit.

It's hard being the one that hit. I almost feel sorry for Frank.

Three days later a FOR SALE sign goes up on Frank's lawn. But that's not the strangest thing. I come home from work that day and there's no car in his driveway, no dog in the yard. No curtains, and through the windows you can see no nothing. The house is empty. How did he get out so fast? Maybe packed in private for three days, then a moving company took it all while I worked? I never saw nobody move that fast.

Nobody in the neighborhood knows either, but we talk plenty about it.

Then about a couple months later I see Eddie Main down in front of the home improvement store. He's with a box of puppies to give away.

Hey, Eddie, I say, and he goes quiet like maybe he shouldn't talk to me but I can see that for his own money he'll talk to me fine.

I look at the puppies, and there's just two. They're really not so ugly. No puppy is ugly. Puppies are always cute. They're hairy, with brown goofy eyes.

I ask Eddie how many did there used to be.

Only three, he says. Small first litter. Dad palmed one off on a guy at work. This one maybe I found him somebody. They keep coming by and looking. I bet they like him but maybe they wanted something prettier. But maybe they'll come back.

I ask him where his family has been living.

He says they're in a rented place in the valley, but now they bought a house in Chicago.

Chicago, I say. Wow. Such a long way.

Dad says it'll be better there.

It won't, but I don't tell this to Eddie. It will be the same because Frank will bring himself along.

Good luck with the puppies, I say. What if nobody takes them?

Dad says at the end of the day they have to go to the pound.

Of course. That's what always happens to the puppies, I don't say.

Next day before work I go to the pound. Sure enough there's one of Gretta's puppies, sitting in a cage with a whole ocean of pretty Australian puppies with blue-and-white coats and blue eyes. With that same goofy look on his face.

I say to the pound lady, I'll take that one.

That one, she says. Really.

Of course she's surprised, but he's my fault. My pighead temper got him born so now he's my job.

But you know, he turns out to be a pretty good dog. Not super-smart but smart enough. Not the prettiest dog, but the kids love him and he's a great companion to Blackie and a pretty decent watchdog.

I think he gets that from the father's side.

Breathe

Donna Kelleher, D.V.M.

BRIDGET HAD BUT ONE MISSION THE NIGHT I SAW HER: TO breathe. A strange mix of Shepherd and Terrier, her hair jutted from her half-pricked ears in every direction as if electrified. Her head and neck straining forward, her chest heaved with each inhalation. I still can hear her labored breath echoing through the examination room and see the bloodshot panic in her sweet brown eyes.

Bridget's allergic bronchitis left her breathless every few months. "Her breathing is worse this time," Sam said. "I don't know how long we can go on this way." In the past, Sam had been more tolerant of Bridget's disease, but the antihistamines, corticosteroids, and allergy shots that had seemed to help before were becoming less and less effective so that by now the agony of her symptoms governed both of their lives.

While examining the patient, I noticed that her gum and tongue color was cyanotic, tinged blue. This was a bad sign because it meant Bridget was not getting enough oxygen into her body. Worried that this attack was his fault, Sam admitted that he'd fed her two Saltine crackers, a variation from her strict diet of duck and potato. "It was only two!" Sam said, but he was not the only one feeling guilty. Why couldn't I prevent Bridget's attacks? This time, it might have been wheat, but the time before it had been pollen. Surely the real problem was Bridget's ever-weakening immune system.

Bridget knew the drill. We rushed her to the back treatment area, fitted an oxygen mask over her nose, and shaved her front leg for an intravenous catheter. We would give her more injections and keep her overnight in the oxygen chamber for observation. I watched her labored breathing, noting her respiration rate on her record. Bridget's gaze was distracted and fixed.

I placed my stethoscope against the tired dog's heaving chest, just as my childhood doctor had on my own asthmatic chest some twenty years earlier. I knew just what Bridget was going through, struggling desperately for each molecule of air. I, too, have had many close calls throughout my life. My asthma was diagnosed in the middle of the night when I was two years old and coughed so hard my parents had to rush me to the emergency room.

Every week or so my mom and I made the lengthy commute to see Dr. Kraus—a portly, stubborn matron with a guttural German accent and a curt yet overbearing bedside manner. My childhood was spent wheezing and gagging with a seemingly endless series of allergy shots, reactions, and attacks.

Often when Dr. Kraus put her cold stethoscope to my chest, her face would go blank, and she would diagnose me with another bout of pneumonia. In no time at all, she'd toss me onto the steel table and pound on my back to loosen the phlegm. "She has pneumonia." Dr. Kraus always talked about me like I wasn't there. "She'll need antibiotics again." My mother and I did the best we could to treat my recurrent pneumonia and ongoing asthma. I took my medications, but was never completely healthy.

I knew firsthand corticosteroid-induced irritability and the grip of my stomach after antibiotics. Two of the medications prescribed to me during childhood were taken off the market years ago because they cause hallucinations. Decades after my childhood diagnosis, Western medicine has made little progress in the treatment of many chronic respiratory diseases.

Back in the ER, the weight of Bridget's stare through the steel bars of her oxygen chamber seemed to cry out with no words and no sounds. I saw past her written record and treatment protocol. She was afraid to lie down because even the slightest pressure on her lungs would render breathing impossible. An hour after Bridget's arrival, she continued heaving and struggling almost as if she'd received no medical attention at all. I knew exactly how she felt, how constricted breathing sends suffocating chills down the spine. I worried that she was not improving.

Sometimes compassion drives us to ask critical questions: Was there some other way to treat Bridget that might be more effective in preventing these bouts of allergic bronchitis? Why was her immune system so unbalanced?

In veterinary school, we were taught to view chronic disease processes as "progressive" and "degenerative." This paradigm was so entrenched that I came to believe that many diseases, including allergic bronchitis, simply could not improve. At best, symptoms could be suppressed. We learned to practice fear-based medicine, meaning that if we didn't treat certain conditions, they would irreversibly worsen and lawsuits might ensue. Medical decisions became less about what was right for the animal than about what could happen without conventional treatment. My medical decisions became governed by "what ifs." *What if Bridget had cancer or heart disease along with allergies? What if I don't recommend enough diagnostic procedures? What if I miss something?* This thinking meant that if my own pet had an infection, I would use five days of antibiotics, but if a client's animal had the same infection, I thought it best to prescribe many more days of medication, increasing the risk of potential side effects.

We did not learn about acupuncture or any other holistic approach in veterinary school. Consequently—in the early years at least—I never dreamed I would practice holistic medicine myself. In my own experience, however, I'd discovered that acupuncture and herbs worked better in preventing my asthma attacks than any conventional approach. Even in my veterinary classes, something did not sit right with me. My mother had taught me to objectively question everything in life, so when I heard of diseases with "poor outcomes," like allergies and arthritis, I scratched my head, thinking, There must be some other way to treat animals. Our veterinary library subscribed to a rarely read journal from the International Veterinary Acupuncture Society (I.V.A.S.) and there I read about alternative ways to treat chronic problems. I spent a summer observing well-known holistic veterinarian and author Dr. Allen Schoen. I spoke with his clients about their pets. I listened to their stories and saw for myself the vibrant condition of their animals. One thing lead to another and I soon applied for and received a scholarship to an acupuncture course offered by I.V.A.S. It was frightening to think of trying acupuncture at such a critical moment for Bridget since I had never used acupuncture in the ER.

But I knew a dramatic change was needed in Bridget's medical program if we were going to save her. I telephoned Sam. "Bridget is feeling a little better," I told him. I could sense his fearful thoughts in the sigh at the other end of the phone, for as much as he loved Bridget, I knew that part of him would find relief if she would simply die, taking the difficult decisions about her fate out of his hands.

Desperation gave me newfound courage. "Sam, I want to try acupuncture on her," I said. I was afraid of his response. I knew my veterinary boss thought acupuncture was nothing short of witchcraft hocus-pocus. My job could be jeopardized. It took 150 years to scientifically explain how aspirin works, but was it any less effective during the many years when its beneficial effects could not be explained? There was a long pause at the other end of the phone. . . .

"Well, we sure have tried everything else," said Sam, "so go right ahead. We've gotta do something." I rummaged through an old bag I had buried in my car and found two boxes of sterile acupuncture needles. After struggling with the decision over size and type, I brought some into the clinic. It was 4:30 A.M. which was good because no one would walk in on me. We could keep this acupuncture treatment quiet.

I propped up two Chinese body meridian atlases by the oxygen chamber. I felt a little uneasy, but could hear the painful rattle of Bridget's labored breathing, which reminded me there was little time to change my mind. I knelt into the cage with my patient. I slipped the first needle into Bladder 13, the association point for the lung, right above Bridget's shoulder blades, and I had to flatten her coat to find it. She looked at me as if she knew that I was trying to help her. I put needles into Lung 7, on the inside of both front legs, Kidney 6, to aid the kidney in accepting fluid from the lung and excreting it from the body. I used a point in the middle of the front of her chest, Conception Vessel 17, which expands and relaxes the chest, and diffuses Qi, life's energy force, in the lung. Patting Bridget on the head to reassure her, I quietly shut the oxygen chamber door, still watching her closely.

At first she looked suspiciously at all her pins. They must have felt funny, perhaps tingly, and she investigated each one, but did not tamper with their placement. She looked at me in bewilderment. I was worried that I had chosen the wrong points. Maybe Bridget's breathing was too far gone and her immune system too suppressed with medication to allow the treatment to work. Perhaps I had to consider the possibility that acupuncture just didn't work. I heard again my vet school teachers and my boss criticizing any form of medicine they could not explain.

But after about fifteen minutes, I saw my patient lie down for the first time. Bridget's breathing became deeper and her respiration rate slowed. As I saw her begin to relax, I remembered how afraid I used to be when Dr. Kraus would pound my chest. Now, watching Bridget, I felt myself relax as well, and leaned back beside Bridget's chamber.

After another twenty minutes with the needles in place, Bridget looked up at me, wagging her tail for the first time since her emergency arrival earlier on. I opened the cage to check her gum color and, to my astonishment, her gums were pinker. The voices of all the skeptics that ran through my head were suddenly hushed and those of my acupuncture teachers rose to surface. *Acupuncture must really work!* Bridget and I took a long sigh together.

I looked up at the clock: 5:20 A.M. I was wide awake and hastened to the phone on the other side of the room. "Sam, Bridget is okay. It's a miracle. She responded to the acupuncture and oxygen. I think she can go home."

Sam's groggy voice replied, "Wow! Thank you. . . . I'll be right in. I couldn't really sleep without Bridget in her usual spot on the bed anyway. . . . Thank you so much." I looked over at Bridget pawing at the door of her chamber. She barked, restoring all the usual wiggle and chaos to her stray facial hairs.

Bridget went on to have weekly acupuncture treatments and herbs and never needed another late-night trip to the ER. Whenever she comes in for her treatments, she sits squarely in front of me, her fuzzy tail rotating in big circles like a windmill—the only thanks I ever need.

The Bite

Alexandra Styron

LOS ANGELES WAS A DRY, BROWN SUMMER SCORCH. IN SEARCH of some relief, my roommate Beth and I had decided that morning to drive to the beach with the dog, but by 11 A.M., all three of us were wrung out and frayed. Traffic was down to a crawl from Shutters all the way up to the emerald skirts of Pepperdine and my old Volvo blowing a Freon-resistant sirocco around us. On the backseat was Wally, keyed up, panting hard, her muzzle moving up and down with every tap of the brake.

By then, Wally and I had been together for a little over a year. I'd clipped an ad in the paper—*Top AKC Lab puppies ready to go!*—and driven to Anaheim for an exploratory visit. I was only "thinking" about getting a dog. Out near Disneyland I found a dismal kennel on a treeless plot across the street from a fast-food restaurant. A dozen adult dogs threw themselves against their cages as I pulled into the driveway, barking like maniacs. It took all my resolve not to turn and run. The proprietor, a slatternly woman missing a bunch of her teeth, emerged from a camper. She took me to a shed and gestured to where a litter of five yellow beauties huddled behind a steel fence. Choosing a timid, big-eyed female, I brought her out onto a little patch of grass. Terrified, she wobbled and blinked, obviously unused to the sunlight and soft turf.

Well.

My heart tugged in my chest so hard that when I gave her back and went for lunch, I couldn't eat a thing. I was single then, in my mid-twenties, and living in Los Angeles only temporarily. I couldn't really manage responsibility for a shell-shocked ball of fluff, so what was I *thinking* driving to this puppy mill? I returned to the kennel for one more look. At her pen I called out gently: "Hey, puppy."

Hearing my voice, the little girl untangled herself from her siblings and pushed up against the fence. Her enormous eyes looked at me with what I can only describe as a frank plea. So she ended up in the back of my Volvo, where she retched and cried piteously. I pulled her onto my lap with one arm while doing sixty on the Anaheim Freeway. She slept the rest of the way home.

For the next couple of weeks, as we got to know each other, lap-driving became our preferred mode of travel. Then, one morning, as we were going downhill on La Cienega approaching a red light at Melrose, my increasingly confident puppy decided to hop down and inspect the clutch. From below. In another hair-raising move, I managed to pull her free just before slamming into the bumper in front of us. After that, Wally was relegated to the backseat, on the right side, where we could both keep an eye on each other. This became her spot, from which she would not be moved, and from where she monitored our progress on that blazing Sunday in July.

It was early afternoon by the time Beth, Wally, and I finally pulled into our friend Sam's driveway in Malibu. Piling out, Wally took a sniff of the briney air, then shot through the bougainvillea for the beach. I stopped for a quick hello before following after her.

This was what I'd begun to live for. Wally's unerring joy, her excitement for what lay ahead; her crazy ardor had become a singular force in my life, a foil for my own misaligned mental state. I'd been walking a perilous course since my move to L.A. two years prior, a road I traversed with one hand over my eyes so I wouldn't have to see what lay in my path. Shortly after arriving from New York, a rotten love affair got its grip on me and continued to hold me in its thrall. I pretended to myself and others that it was over, but I was unable to extricate myself, and everyone knew it. Surely my friends were as tired of me as I was of myself. Wally was just about the only sensate being in my life to whom I didn't feel the need to apologize or lie.

Another fact I was pretending not to notice: the quickly dimming prospects of my career as an actor. I was twenty-seven at the time. Not exactly old, nor beyond the point of possible future success, but I didn't really want it anymore, didn't have the appetite. The consequences of my changing heart frightened me too much to admit. I had decided I would be an actor when I was twelve years old, pursued a drama degree in college, and afterward cofounded a small theatre company in New York. I loved the excitement of live theatre, but off-off Broadway is a punishing venue and no one expects to *stay* there. Beyond my self-created opportunities, I hadn't made much headway. Other things interested me—politics, literature—but I didn't have the confidence to diverge from my stumbling path. Time was wasting, so I moved to Los Angeles. Honestly, I didn't know what else to do and thought *something* might happen to me out there. Of course, a great many things happened. It's just that none of them were what I'd expected.

Wally and I took a long walk on the beach beyond Sam's. This was what we did together. Walked. All the time. For long hours in the mornings and again before sundown, my dog and I tromped all over L.A., each with our own agenda. Exercising and exorcising. Runyon Canyon. Griffith Park. The Reservoir. I'd found the perfect companion and the only way to stave off my despair. In the hills, my mind traveled in great loops, plotting, playing, fixing. I fiddled with stories in my head, replaying real ones and mapping out the imaginary. The life I was living seemed totally out of control. By pulling me ahead, Wally became the engine for new ideas. One day, charging alongside her through the underbrush, I had decided I would try to write.

I didn't have any grand ambitions. On the contrary, I had no plan at all. But I needed to make my ideas vivid. I bought a stack of legal pads and began. After a while, a small green shoot of hope bloomed as I discovered a passion I'd never had as an actor. All through that fall and winter, I put my shoulder to it, performing without an audience. Unless you count Wally, who was usually asleep. There beside me through the quiet mornings, she made this solitary pursuit—the exact opposite of what I thought I'd wanted—bearable. But still, I was an actor. My profession was a costume, and it protected me.

North of Sam's, I threw sticks into the ocean and admired Wally as she expertly assessed the break of the surf. Timing her moves so as not to get sucked under an incoming wave, she leapt above the white crests and brought back her quarry over and over again. After each retrieval, she would throw herself onto the ground, rubbing her back in the sand in a delirious frenzy. When she rose, her hindquarters shimmied with delight, a move that caused my sister-in-law to name her "The Wiggler." Wally's devotion and plain satisfaction were exquisite, her pleasure my own. When we returned, happy and tired, Sam and Beth were waiting for us on the porch and the sun still burned high in the hills.

Now, a full eight years later, I still remember with perfect clarity the decision we made to take a hike that afternoon. Even at the seaside, the day was monstrously hot. Wally, wet and contented, had fallen asleep in the shade. I knew she didn't need more exercise, but Beth and I had set our minds on the trails of Charmlee State Park, just beyond Sam's house. We ate a late lunch and waited for the temperature to drop. At four o'clock, Beth and I set off with Wally, promising Sam that we'd return in an hour.

The parking lot at Charmlee was empty. The park service booth was deserted and the bathrooms were locked. It was just too hot. I parked the car and glanced back at Wally with a surge of apprehension, but she was pressing up against the door, wagging her butt and ready to go. Letting her take the lead, we took off along the rocky path to the far end of the park.

Like many dogs on open terrain, Wally liked to charge ahead, then double back to make certain we were coming along. She led us at last to a promontory and a sun setting magnificently over the Pacific. We were all parched and spent, but the hike had been worth it. "Go on, Wally," I said after we'd taken a few minutes to admire the vista. Sam would be expecting us back. Following the same path back, the dog took off.

Beth and I followed, engaged in a deep conversation about something or other, and twenty minutes or so passed. The bald mountainside gave way to a rocky bowl of sagebrush with a thin strip cut through it, barely wide enough for one person to pass through. Single file was the only way to go and I had taken the lead. Periodically, Wally would gallop back toward us until she had us in her view and then run up the trail again. She was nowhere in sight as we headed down into the bottom of the valley. I was jabbering away, looking down at my footing when an unexpected shape caught my eye. I stopped hard and Beth bumped up behind me. A few feet in front of us a snake lay horizontally across the path, head and tail hidden by the brush. It could have been a stick, it lay so still.

Beth and I are both from New England. Not exactly venomous viper territory. We had no idea how snakes behaved, though it was Beth's inexpert belief that they travel in pairs, making it too risky for us to walk through the tall grass on either side of the path. We stood there, frozen, trying to guess the species while weighing our options. I thought of Wally and felt a gust of dread. It would only be a matter of minutes before she ran back to find us.

"We have to get around it," I kept saying to Beth.

She suggested we throw a rock.

I cast a stone, which glanced against the snake and landed in the dust with a quiet thud. The snake didn't flinch.

"Maybe it's dead," I said.

"Doubt it," Beth replied.

Then, as I knew she would, Wally came bounding down the other side of the hill heading right for us. I screamed at her to stop. To my amazement, she did. Stopping just two feet on the other side of the snake, Wally sat, panting furiously, oblivious to the danger that lay between us. I hadn't trained her with any great precision and knew she wouldn't stay there for long. Beth picked up another rock and tossed it.

Finally, of course, Wally saw the snake.

The afternoon heat seemed to bunch around us, rippling everything as if we were under water. Time decelerated. Wally got up and, oblivious to my shouting, began to sniff the strange stick before her. In an instant, the flat, featureless object sprang up and embedded its fangs into Wally's muzzle. She yelped. I screamed. The snake pulled back, coiling and hissing, its knobby rattle terrifyingly revealed. Backed on to her haunches, Wally sat stunned, two bright drops of blood leaking from her nose. She lifted a paw to rub at herself while the snake continued to menace her. Beth and I were still stuck on the other side. *I can't believe this is happening,* was all I could think as I stood there, dumbstruck.

Unable to bear another encounter, Beth and I broke away from the path and ran through the high brush, giving the snake a wide berth. Back on the narrow trail just behind Wally, we shouted at her to come. She followed and, moments later, we stopped on a plateau well above the angry snake. We were, however, still a mile from the trailhead and our car.

I inspected the holes in Wally's muzzle. They were tiny, barely bleeding. Somewhere I'd read that after a rattlesnake bite, you were supposed to apply a tourniquet and keep the patient immobile so the venom wouldn't travel through the bloodstream. Wrapping a tourniquet around Wally's nose didn't really seem like an option. I began to panic.

"We have to carry her," I told Beth. "We have to, or she'll die."

But hauling an unwilling seventy-pound Labrador a rocky mile uphill in 90-degree heat quickly proved too much for us. Putting her down, we began to walk. With each step I imagined the drops of poison pulsing along, moving ever closer to Wally's heart. By the time we finally reached the car I was speechless and in tears. Wally's pace had slowed some by the end, and her nose had begun to swell. But still she wagged her tail gamely, and obediently jumped in the back of the car. I threw Beth the keys. I couldn't drive.

Why is that medical mishaps always seem to happen on Sundays? As Beth drove down the winding mountainside, I picked up the car phone and got listings of every veterinarian in Malibu. No one was open. After three or four calls, I at last got hold of an answering service. The nearest veterinary hospital was nearly an hour away, in Woodland Hills. I scribbled down directions and Beth began the drive north through the canyons.

Crises present great lessons in human character. Situations that bring out the best in some expose the worst failings in others. What that day revealed to me about myself still makes me ashamed. During all those phone calls and all of that direction taking, I remained in the passenger seat, unable to sit in the back with Wally. I had no idea how long this awful poisoning process would take, but I couldn't bring myself to witness it. Every few minutes during that endless drive to Woodland Hills, I would say, looking straight ahead through the windshield, "Beth, look back there. Is she still alive? Is she dead yet?" I couldn't even look at her.

I was completely in love with that dog. She filled so many holes in my life, met so many needs. I got from Wally what no one else was willing to give. Now I was going to lose her, and I couldn't look. At the moment I needed to be my best, I turned out to be a complete coward.

Wally was still alive when we got to the hospital, though by then her muzzle had ballooned to grotesque proportions and she was having trouble keeping her eyes open. She looked like a prize fighter. Two veterinary assistants came out and carried her from the car. The doctors were kind and swift, giving me an honest if inconclusive prognosis. They put a tube down her throat to keep it open and applied an antivenin IV—or so they told me; I didn't actually go back to watch. Go home, they advised me. I could give them a call later, but they wouldn't know anything for certain until the next day. If she lived that long.

It was evening by then, and since I would surely have to return the next morning, good news or bad, Beth and I decided to go back to Sam's. At midnight, I called the hospital. Wally was stable but not out of the woods. I went to bed, but didn't sleep. Instead, I made desperate bargains with a god I rarely spoke to, and dwelt on the profundity of what this animal meant to me.

Daybreak, making its final appointment on the continent, came at last. During the night, I had begun to understand the ineluctable magnitude of the situation: I had to be prepared to let go of what I loved most. I couldn't turn away from it and I couldn't pretend. At six-thirty that morning, I called the hospital. The receptionist put me on hold for several minutes before returning to the phone. I held my breath and hung on.

"It looks like Wally's going to be fine," she said. "You can come pick her up whenever you like."

Rain is pitching down outside the window as I write this. It's June in New England, and I am home in my study. Behind me Wally lies, snorfelling in her sleep, dreaming perhaps of the beach walk we'll take later today when the weather clears. She's nine now and not as spry as she used to be. But she's just as game, living for her daily swim and ecstatic rolls in the sand. As for me, I gave up acting in favor of a career as a writer. I also gave up bad love and married a man who spoils the dog worse than I do. We left Los Angeles years ago, Wally and I in the Volvo, not at all sure of what we might encounter next but certain of what we'd left behind.

God Is *Dog* Spelled Properly

Lama Surya Das

A FEW YEARS AGO, I WAS DRIVING TO WESTERN MASSACHUSETTS with my dog, and when I looked in the rearview mirror, I was delighted to behold her big, serene face staring back. I felt so happy at that moment, so blissful and content, it was as if suddenly all was right with the world. *I'm driving my dog, Chandi,* I thought. *My life has meaning.* And then it dawned on me that I used to feel exactly the same way when I drove around my late teacher, the Dzogchen master Nyoshul Khenpo Rinpoche. He would come from Bhutan to visit, and I would escort him around the northeastern United States, all the while filled with a joyful sense of Serving, of being in the Presence. And now, driving in my red Plymouth with Chandi—my snow white, six-year-old Shuvacz—I realized I was experiencing the same kind of inner delight. "Am I crazy or what?" I asked myself. "Is there no difference between my relationship with a holy Tibetan lama and my dog?"

I quickly recognized that what I was responding to was the sense of peace, joy, and unconditional love that Chandi (whose name means "Moon Goddess" in Sanskrit) always emanates and simultaneously evokes in me. But that moment has stayed with me, and has left me to ponder one of life's great conundrums: Can one's spiritual master be a dog?

Dogs, first of all, teach us how to connect with the most basic and universal of spiritual practices: connecting with nature. Just take regular walks with your teacher, and let the natural spirituality ensue. I walk long twice a day with my god. Chandi runs always alongside like a loyal sidekick, accomplice, protector, bodyguard, and heart opener, with only an occasional sidetrack to sniff out a pungent morsel of garbage or some carcass in the woods near home. These walks teach me every day to find joy in the simplest things—even just going outside, regardless of the weather, is an epiphany when I go with her. Here is a being that bounds through the rain, sleet, snow, and hail with indomitable enthusiasm, happy to be outside regardless of the weather; happy to just be. And her enthusiasm helps remind me that sacred altars and shrines are everywhere, great and small. What might have been a boring, preoccupied walk to the post office or bank becomes, with Chandi, an epic journey of discovery and delight.

Chandi is my Muse. When she walks the Path at my side, she also inspires me to remember that we never walk alone. Better than any escort service, my eternal escort takes me out each morning and evening to explore the altar of this earth, when I might otherwise have remained indoors, dogging it, chained to desk or couch.

"A master," Buddha says in the sacred text the Dhammapada, "gives himself to whatever the moment brings him. He doesn't think about his actions; rather, they flow from the core of his being." Watch a dog leap for a Frisbee and you will grasp what this teaching means. As a Buddhist, I aspire to a Right way of living: Right Effort, Right Mindfulness, Right Intention (there are eight "official" steps on the path to enlightenment, but I'll stop here). It can take many lifetimes to get all these Rights right. But then I look at Chandi bounding through the woods—or later, curled up contentedly at the foot of my bed—and I think, She is Right without even trying. She just is. My dog Chandi lives in the holy now. She daily instructs me, without words or lesson plans, in the meaning of the golden eternity, here and now, every single day. Divinity gleams in a dog's eye.

Buddhists practice being mindful—which means, at its simplest, to live in the moment and to be aware. Dogs are naturally mindful. Dogs also teach us that the body is an enormous storehouse of wisdom and intelligence of various subtle kinds. Watch a dog explore his or her world, and you will soon learn to follow suit. Dogs use all their senses in a way I can only aspire to. Buddha talked about higher powers, including divine eye (clairvoyance) and divine ear (clairaudience) and divine nose; I think I know what he might have meant when I see Chandi pricking up her nose, like a mystic, at the scent of the invisible indivisible. The nose knows, dogs seem to say, as if heaven scent.

My own late Tibetan Dzogchen master Khyentse Rinpoche said that dogs can perceive the clear light, the inner luminosity—which is a reflection of the in-dwelling spirit or higher mind in each and every one of us. I believe that dogs have a visionary life, be it of the ears and nose. Have you ever noticed how they know when the master is coming home before any outward signs are evident to us ordinary creatures, how they can discern the presence of ghosts and spirits, how they will never accompany you into danger but will only go along if dragged kicking and screaming? This is the wisdom of Dogs. Some psychics are too preoccupied with the other world to sense what is right beneath their noses, but not Dog.

Talking to dogs reminds me of spiritual prayer. It matters little whether an answer comes; what matters is the act itself. Dogs teach us about faith, trust, and devotion; how never to give up; and how to keep coming back and just showing up, which is more than half the battle. They teach us how to devotedly serve a higher master, how to attend and wait, and how to let go of a grudge. But most of all, they teach us about the meaning and experience of unconditional love. You will find all of these tenets at the basis of any religion, any spiritual practice. And the remarkable thing is dogs do this all effortlessly, automatically, with utmost purity and grace.

On the subject of unconditional love, we all have plenty to learn, lama or not. And perhaps we could all start by loving ourselves. The Dalai Lama was astounded—and saddened—to learn that many Americans suffer from low self-esteem. In his country there is no such thing as low self-esteem, because everyone is taught at an early age to honor themselves. To love themselves. They are taught that life is infinitely precious and meaningful.

Before gurus such as Chandi and Nyoshul Khenpo entered my life, I did not know that I was like a shining golden god, worthy of slavish devotion. I thought it was going to take lifetimes of spiritual effort to achieve anything approaching that exalted status! Chandi has kindly taught me otherwise. She doesn't care how much money I make, or how I dress, or who I vote for, or how enlightened I am, or even how I feel. She is a saintly, white-robed swami, whose only goal to is to love and to serve.

Dog lovers tell me with one voice that the unconditional love and closeness they share with their dogs leads them right to their higher selves, because it helps them feel more worthy and more directly connected to the inexhaustible source of all good things. Chandi helped my preteen goddaughter feel good about herself simply by licking her, Patricia's, face every day. Scratch a dog and you'll find God.

A Zen master once remarked, when asked the secret of enlightenment: "When tired, I sleep; when hungry, I eat." I notice that my dog understands and embodies that profoundly meaningful utterance. Without priestly instruction, Chandi cuts right to the bone.

Any spiritual practice will ask you to look within yourself, and recognize your own inner wisdom; your own inner strength. Buddha said: "Your work is to discover your work and then with all your heart give yourself to it." I like how dogs seem to specialize in some hobby or sport or canine art form, and then loyally stick to it. Some dogs protect sheep or herd cattle; some dogs pull sleds or flush game. And most dogs these days—especially American dogs—simply chase sticks and fetch balls and take naps for a living; but the point is, watching these dogs has helped me learn how to better focus my own talents, such as they are. Dogs never feel the need to move house or change jobs. They don't suffer from doubt, or pretense, or hesitation or vacillation. You're not going to find a Border Collie on an analyst's couch, saying, "Maybe I should have pursued acting." She simply does what she is bred to do. Dogs, therefore, are holy because they are wholly themselves.

Perhaps we can all find peace if we simply do what we were bred to do. In Buddhism, and in many other religions, that means serving others, striving toward enlightenment, and being a decent human being. And the further you pull away from that, the more lost you are apt to feel.

It is important, I think, to recognize that we are all interconnected. All beings are God's creatures; all beings are endowed with the luminous Buddha-nature (or "innate goodness" in the American vernacular). One widespread belief in some Christian circles is that humans alone possess immortal souls. Buddhists, however, believe that All Are One. Mahatma

Gandhi once said, "There is little that separates humans from other sentient beings—we all feel pain, we all feel joy, we all deeply crave to be alive and to live freely, and we all share this planet together."

What we seek, we are; it is all within. Dogs know this. The Buddhist practice of bowing and reverencing the spirit in each being encountered comes naturally to dogs, who bow and say bowwow to any and all comers.

Gandhi also said, "The greatness of a nation and its moral progress can be measured by the way in which its animals are treated." Because we—you and I and our dogs—recognize the divinity and soulfulness of all creatures, we are helping to make the world a better and more sacred place. In the presence of a dog, you love and are loved. And all that love helps purify our karma.

Recently I visited Saint Johnsbury, Vermont, and happened upon a place called the Dog Chapel—an old, white-frame New England church taken over by artist Stephen Huneck and transformed into a place where people can commune spiritually with their dogs (whether alive or dead). Among the chapel's many doggie delights—too numerous to mention here—is an announcement board out front that you would expect to list prayer services and sermon times. Instead, the board says: WELCOME. ALL CREEDS. ALL BREEDS. NO DOGMAS ALLOWED. This tickled me because I aspire to Doghood myself. For I see daily that my dog attends, lives for, and serves at the pleasure of a Higher Power. She awaits grace from above, while waiting for nothing; she simply attends. Chandi follows her own special creed: "I run, therefore I am. I have no appointments, no disappointments. I am always ready for anything. Embracing the firmament called Now, I rest in that numinous, weightless, stressless zone beyond the gravitas of this world. Fleas, heat, and the sound of your car leaving are my only enemies. My friends are all things. I am one with All. Yes is my name. I am at peace at the foot of your bed."

Now, I am not an advocate of joining or forming any dog cults, but I do think dogs have an extra dollop of divinity. When Chandi and I are together, regardless of where, we have our full medicine, and nothing more is needed. So if I tend to wax grandiloquent about this particular species of sentient being, it is because I lose my head around her! In short, Chandi gets me out of my head, and into a heart space where we can play as if no one is watching. She brings out the Dog in me, and brings me bones and sticks too. What more could I want? I want to be the man she thinks I am.

In the interest of full disclosure, my given name is Jeff Miller. Lama Surya Das is just what it says on my Buddhist dogtags. While I did not grow up with dogs, I did grow up chasing balls—base, foot, basket, golf, tennis, billiard, bowling, etc. This closely aligns me with the long lineage of canine inanity. I also spent a lot of time chasing God and the Truth, and as a teenager I was a veritable mutt, chasing my own tail half the time, often in life's doghouse, writing doggerel until the early hours dawned. But I am much less dogged now and I must, in many ways, thank Chandi for that. It is not simply that I become like a little boy again with my dog. It is that she awakens the Buddha within me, here and now. She both lightens up and enlightens the spiritual path on which I walk. Chandi makes me a jolly lama.

When we play fetch, she seems to think the object of the game is to get *me* to chase *her* along with the stick or ball we have under discussion. I am reminded, during these games, of my pursuit of God, which I have realized of late needs to include the oft-overlooked fact that she is chasing me. When one slows down and tunes in, meetings can more easily occur.

In a famous teaching tale, from the Hindu text the Mahabharata, the warrior Yudhishtira is returning home after a long, bloody war. It is an arduous journey and all the while Yudhishtira is accompanied by an old, faithful dog. Finally, Yudhishtira makes it to the Gates of Heaven, only to be told his dog cannot come along. "But he is a faithful and true companion," Yudhishtira says. "Sorry," the gatekeeper answers. "No dogs allowed." So Yudhishtira decides that if his dog cannot accompany him, they will stay together behind. The dog, at that moment, reveals himself to be an incarnation of the god Dharma—Yudhishtira's physical father and spiritual guide—and they enter the gates together. I want to go like that, with my loyal dog alongside.

My first guru in India, Neem Karoli Baba, was renowned for stating "Don't become attached to wealth, people, or pets." But—how could he say such a thing? My dog is attached to my heart and soul by an infinite, luminous umbilical cord, although I have long tried to let go of all my attachments like a good Buddhist should. I suppose this is a cross I'll just have to carry, all the way to the Buddhist Pure Land. But I also suppose if there is any attachment worth holding on to, it is love of my dog. It may be the last bond to go.

One Hundred Demons: Dogs!

Lynda Barry

WE HAVE THREE. WHEN THE DOORBELL RINGS, THEY ALL GO BERZERK. THEY DO THIS EVEN IF SOMEONE RINGS A DOORBELL ON TV.
DING DONG!
RAWF! ROWF! RAWF!
KNOCK IT OFF!
RARK! RARK! WROW!
RARK! RARK!
ROWA! WAOR!
MY RESPONSE, OF COURSE, IS THE WRONG ONE. I YELL AT THEM. LOUDLY. REPEATEDLY. THE DOG BOOKS ALL SAY NEVER SHOUT AND DO NOT REPEAT COMMANDS.
LULU! OOOLA! ED! HEY! KNOCK IT OFF! HEY! STOP THAT! IT'S THE TV, YOU GOOFS!
DOG BOOKS GIVE SOUND ADVICE BUT THEY DO NOT MENTION THE TWO MOST IMPORTANT THINGS: YOUR DOG'S HISTORY AND ITS NATURE, AND OF COURSE, YOUR OWN.
LASSIE! LASSIE! COME HOME!
N'AKO LYNDA! IT'S JUST TELEVISION! YOU CRY FOR THAT DOG?! ESTUPIDO!! THAT DOG MAKES MORE MONEY THAN I DO!
HISTORY, AS WE KNOW, REPEATS ITSELF. THIS GOES FOR GOOD AS WELL AS BAD. I WAS SHOUTED AT A LOT. BUT OTHER THINGS HAPPENED TOO. I HAD SOME GOOD LUCK AT SCHOOL.
Cc Hh Ii Jj Kk Ll M
IT'S FOR YOU, MRS. LESENE.
WHY, IT'S LASSIE.
I SAW IT ON TV.
SUCH A SAD STORY. BUT THE ENDING WAS HAPPY. I LIKE THIS PICTURE. LET'S PUT IT UP.
MY HUSBAND AND I HAVE TWO CAREFREE DOGS THAT HAD VERY GOOD BEGINNINGS. OUR OTHER DOG, OOOLA, HAS A HISTORY AND A NATURE WHICH IS MORE LIKE OUR OWN.
HAPPY, PLAYFUL, SPONTANEOUS
OBSERVANT, MOODY, SOCIALLY UNPREDICTABLE (AKA "ARTISTIC")
ED MARTIN
Lulu
OOOLA
OOOLA IS FROM A SHELTER. SHE BELONGED TO A MAN AND A WOMAN WHO GOT IN A FIGHT AND THE MAN THREW OOOLA OUT OF A SECOND FLOOR WINDOW TO PROVE SOME SORT OF POINT. SHE WAS FOUR MONTHS OLD.
(HER LEG WAS BROKEN)

THE DOG BOOKS ALL WARN AGAINST CHOOSING A DOG OUT OF SYMPATHY. ABUSED DOGS ARE LIKELY TO HAVE BEHAVIOR PROBLEMS. THEY MAY BE VERY TIMID OR QUITE AGGRESSIVE OR BOTH AT ONCE
RRRRRRRRRR RRRRRRRRRR
YOW! YOU BIT ME!
BUT I ALSO GREW UP IN A VIOLENT HOUSE. SHE WAS A FEAR-BITER. SHE DIDN'T WAG HER TAIL. SHE WAS NERVOUS ABOUT BEING TOUCHED. I UNDERSTOOD THAT.
WE ALREADY ADOPTED HER OUT ONCE. THEY RETURNED HER. SHE'S GOING TO HAVE TROUBLE BUT IF SHE CAN FIND THE RIGHT HOME SHE'LL BE A GREAT DOG.
VOLUNTEER
LORI
WHEN I WAS IN THE 2ND GRADE I HAD A TEACHER WHO FELT A CERTAIN SYMPATHY FOR ME. BACK THEN THEY CALLED MY KIND OF TROUBLE "EMOTIONAL PROBLEMS." SHE TURNED MY LIFE AROUND.
WHY DON'T YOU STAY AND MAKE A PICTURE FOR ME? YOU DON'T HAVE TO GO OUT TO RECESS IF YOU DON'T WANT TO.
THE SMALLEST THINGS THREW ME OFF. MAYBE IT WAS MY NATURE. MAYBE IT WAS MY HOMELIFE. BUT IT WAS MRS. LESENE'S AFFECTION AND INTEREST THAT MADE ALL THE DIFFERENCE. I WASN'T A VERY LIKEABLE KID. SHE LIKED ME ANYWAY.
NO! PLEASE! DON'T! I'M SORRY! PLEASE!
IT'S JUST A LITTLE SPILLED PAINT. I'M NOT MAD AT YOU. MRS. LESENE ISN'T MAD. I KNOW IT WAS AN ACCIDENT, HONEY.
SHE LET ME COME IN EARLY AND STAY LATE. THERE WAS A SPECIAL ART TABLE AT THE BACK OF THE ROOM. I SPENT A LOT OF TIME THERE. SHE GAVE ME SOMETHING NO ONE COULD TAKE AWAY.
NAKO! MY STATIONARY! IDIOT! WHAT ARE YOU DOING?
MAKING A PICTURE FOR MY TEACHER.
ESTUPIDO! YOU'RE WASTING IT!
THE DOG I HAD WHEN I WAS A KID WAS A SHELTER DOG TOO. I DON'T THINK I WOULD HAVE MADE IT THROUGH THOSE YEARS WITHOUT HIM. I WISH I COULD SAY I WAS ALWAYS AS LOVING TO HIM AS HE WAS TO ME. I REGRET SO MANY THINGS.
?
IDIOT! WHATS WRONG WITH YOU?! ESTUPIDO!
SELFISH! NO RESPECT! YOU WANT SOMETHING TO CRY ABOUT, HUH? ANSWER ME!

OOOLA CAME HOME WITH US AND BROUGHT HER TROUBLE WITH HER. SHE GROWLED AND SNAPPED. ALL OF OUR DOG BOOKS SAID WE HAD TO ESTABLISH DOMINANCE. THERE WERE RULES ABOUT HOW TO DO THIS.
THE ALPHA STARE DOWN
RRR RRR RRR RRR
NO!
THE FIRM COMMAND SPOKEN ONCE
THERE WERE PINCH COLLARS TO BUY AND DOGGIE KUNG FU MOVES INVOLVING GETTING HER IN A SUBMISSIVE POSE AND HOLDING HER THERE UNTIL SHE CALMED DOWN. IT MADE US ALL MISERABLE AND IT DIDN'T WORK.
RRRRRR RRRRRRR RRRRRR
NO!
IF WE HAD BEEN THINKING, IF WE HAD BEEN REMEMBERING, WE'D HAVE REALIZED WE WERE DOING EXACTLY THE WRONG THING FOR A DOG LIKE OOOLA. MY 3RD GRADE TEACHER HAD A SIMILAR APPROACH. IT WAS OK FOR SOME KIDS. IT WAS TERRIBLE FOR ME.
STAY IN AND DRAW?
NO. WHY DO YOU NEED SPECIAL TREATMENT? I'M NOT MRS. LESENE. I DON'T SPOIL MY STUDENTS. GET OUT THERE.
WE CRINGE WHEN WE THINK OF OUR BY-THE-BOOK TREATMENT OF OOOLA. WHAT SHE NEEDED WAS A CHANCE TO START OVER AGAIN, BE A BABY AGAIN. SOME MAY CALL IT "SPOILING." I'M GLAD WE STOPPED SEEING IT THAT WAY.
LOOK. SHE CAN'T BELIEVE SHE'S ON THE BED.
IT'S OK SWEETIE. YOU CAN SLEEP HERE. C'MON OOOLA.
SHE GOT BETTER. WE KEPT HER HISTORY IN MIND AND SHE REVEALED HER NATURE TO US. UNDER THE FEAR AND DEFENSIVENESS WAS A SWEET AND NOBLE CHARACTER. A GOOD DOG. A GREAT DOG.
THUMP THUMP THUMP
(REALLY "SPOILED")
ALL SHE NEEDED WAS TO FIND THE RIGHT HOME. BUT THAT'S TRUE FOR ALL OF US, ISN'T IT?

passages

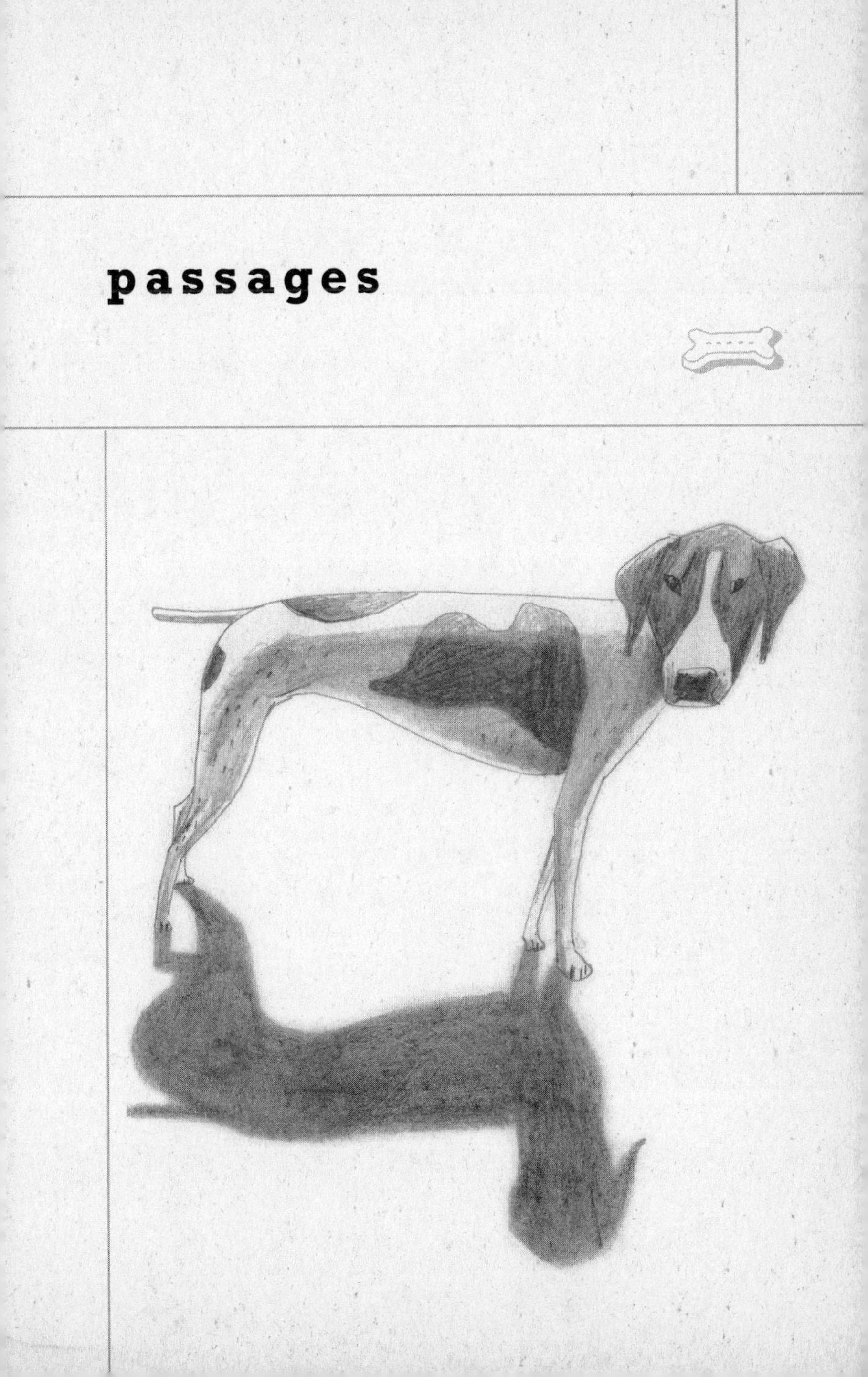

The Second Sheilah

Elizabeth Marshall Thomas

A DOG NAMED SHEILAH WAS THE LOVE OF MY LIFE. AN Australian Cattle Dog, she was very beautiful, with little white spots in her red-gold fur. She was joyous, gentle, kind, sunny, cooperative, and extremely intelligent. Although she came to us as a stray without household skills, in less than a day she knew her name and also our names, she realized that she shouldn't relieve herself indoors, and she figured out the dog door and the stairs. During this time she had noticed things about our house that even after twenty years of residence, we scarcely knew ourselves. In the afternoon of that first day, she became interested in a newcomer who was approaching the front door. Wanting to watch the newcomer, Sheilah at first stood on her hind legs to look out a downstairs window. But when the newcomer moved out of sight, the dog surprised us by turning around and running directly away from the window, out of the room, down a hall, and up the stairs to a second-floor dormer window, recessed but with a wide sill, onto which she jumped. From this vantage point, she had a perfect view of the newcomer. The remarkable thing was that she had never before looked out of that window. She had merely walked near it once, when following us on the previous night. Dogs don't often look up, but if she had looked up as she passed under the window, she would have seen only the sky. But perhaps she saw the window from the outside, when she herself was standing where the newcomer stood, and perhaps had noted the window for future reference.

Sheilah was everything I ever dreamed of in a dog. I loved her madly, deeply. She also loved me. If we had belonged to the same species but were of different genders instead of the other way around, if we could have overlooked the sixty-five-year difference in our ages, and if both of us were single, not just Sheilah, we would have gotten married. I had waited all my life for such a special dog, so when at last I found her, I was happy. She was happy, too. We rejoiced together whenever our eyes met. But within a year, she was killed in an accident and I entered a period of mourning from which I believed I would never quite emerge.

Nor did I. At the time of this writing, the pain of her loss is as fresh in my mind as it was when I last saw her, stiff in death, lying in her grave at the edge of our field with dirt in her bright fur. I hope that some day my ashes will be scattered near her. The pain of her loss was so terrible that I needed desperately to mitigate it, and I began casting about for something that would give even a small measure of relief.

But in my confusion I did all the wrong things. I desperately set out to replace her, even though I already had three other wonderful dogs, and even though I knew perfectly well that no living thing is replaceable, and certainly not a dog like my Sheilah. But the loss was so great that I was experiencing a kind of madness. Perhaps I could replace *something,* I thought. Perhaps I could find a dog almost as smart as Sheilah, or almost as beautiful, or almost as joyous, or almost as much fun. I made all kinds of plans, none of them practical. When I learned of another stray, another Australian Cattle Dog who had been found wandering in the streets of Philadelphia and might be available for adoption, I spoke with representatives of the rescue organization that had found her. I learned that they were going to attend a field trial and dog show in Maryland, and would bring her with them. If I met the standards of the rescue organization, I could meet them there and take the dog. Her name was Fawn, they said.

In recent years, certain members of the dog establishment have looked on me with opprobrium. Who can blame them? In the two books I have written on the subject of the dog, I seem to be at considerable variance with some people's most cherished beliefs. On raising dogs, I hold, for instance, that mixed-breed dogs are just as good and sometimes better than purebred dogs, that judging dogs by AKC standards is the same as judging people by their looks, by which any high school cheerleader would rank far above Eleanor Roosevelt or Albert Einstein. As a result, I hold that raising a mixed-breed dog for brains and ability is just as virtuous as raising a purebred dog for its much touted "breed conformity," and sometimes more so. This last belief has led me into what some consider to be an almost criminal activity—I intentionally allowed a dog to choose her own mate, and permitted the birth of unpedigreed puppies! To be sure, I kept most of the pups myself and found loving homes for the others, but according to certain dog fanciers, my deed was the moral equivalent of armed robbery.

And then as if I had not made enemies enough, I also antagonized some of the dog trainers by claiming that people need not try to dominate their dogs, that the training problems are with the people, not with the dogs, because most dogs—certainly the young, mentally undamaged dogs—are only too touchingly willing to please us. And last of all, as a final affront, I said that dogs can learn good household behavior from other dogs just as well or better than they can learn from people. For these and other opinions, the mere mention of my name raises the hackles of some of the people who attend events such as the dog show in Maryland. "Aren't you the woman who wrote those books?" they ask, eying me suspiciously.

As a result, I may have been a bit vague about my identity when I applied to the Australian Cattle Dog rescue society. I gave my first and last names only, as they are common enough and could designate any number of people, and evidently I got away with it, as nobody angrily asked if any books were attributable to me. Unsure that I was doing the right thing, but nevertheless compelled to try, I booked a hotel room in Maryland and got in the car.

Fawn. Wasn't she the girlfriend of the infamous Oliver North? In the hallway outside my hotel room, someone was yapping hysterically at full volume, a most unpromising sound. I opened the door. A little red dog was standing uneasily behind the legs of some people, and she threw herself down on her back the moment she saw me. Her body went completely rigid—even her eyelids were stiff—and her face wore an anxious grimace. Evidently, her way of coping with our species was to scream bloody murder, then grovel abjectly and hope for the best. My Sheilah would never have done such a thing—she would never have subordinated herself to a stranger. But my Sheilah had self-assurance. Fawn, in contrast, continued to lie on the floor as if cast in bronze, perhaps because she didn't know what to do next. I had initially assumed she was named Fawn because of her faint spots and her reddish coloring—I suppose one could say that remotely she resembled a fawn—but she could just as well have been named for her behavior. She was fawning. I didn't think I'd like her very much, but before I knew it, I heard myself agreeing to take her. Her foster people waited a few minutes, perhaps not quite believing that anyone would want this bizarre little foundling, but because they had come to Maryland for the dog show, which was at that moment in process elsewhere in the hotel, they soon went off to the show ring, leaving Fawn with me.

She tried to follow her foster people but the door shut in her face. Aghast at first, almost frozen with anxiety, she stared, unbelieving, at the closed door. There she was, suddenly without a friend, without a home, without food or water or a way to get any, abandoned to a total stranger who didn't seem to like her yet was towering above her in a room with no escape. Fawn cocked her head, perhaps hoping to hear that her foster people were returning, that they had left her behind by mistake. As her hope faded, she turned to face me, cringing with worry. Someone had cut off her tail. Tentatively, she wagged the stump.

In the next room, other dogs suddenly began barking. Startled, Fawn screamed at the top of her lungs, then rushed toward the sound. Or so she thought. Actually, she ran in the opposite direction. For this mistake, there was just one explanation—she was deaf in one ear, a disability quite common in her breed but which her rescuers hadn't mentioned. Perhaps they hadn't noticed, or perhaps they hoped I wouldn't notice. Not many people want a partly deaf dog.

Nor had they mentioned her nearly psychotic nervous tension, or that the very thought of other dogs made her wild. However, perhaps I should have foreseen these problems. The rescue group had already told me that Fawn was almost certainly the product of one of the many puppy farms that infest Pennsylvania. If so, she would have been taken from her mother much too soon and sold to a pet shop, where, like most other pet-store puppies, she would have been imprisoned alone in a cage—a baby in solitary confinement. Since anyone who buys a puppy from a pet store knows very little about dogs, it is quite probable that the people who bought her then added to her troubles by mishandling her. Their mishandling made her unlikable, and then, of course, they didn't like her and they tossed her out. I didn't really like her either, so I changed her name to Sheilah, hoping to soften my own heart.

The prospect of spending the day in a small room with her nonstop, high-pitched bark was daunting. Believing that a distraction would help us both, I took her to the field trial even though Hurricane Hugo was in process, even though rain was flooding the roads and the gusting, 80 mph wind was ripping the seats from the deserted observation stand. Yet despite the weather, the authorities had directed the competition to continue unless the governor ordered an evacuation, so the trials went on, although the competing dogs could scarcely hear the commands of their handlers against the roar of the wind.

They could, however, hear little Sheilah barking. We were asked to leave. Ashamed, we slunk far away to a neighboring field. The distance from the other dogs quieted Sheilah, but didn't help the competitors, who still couldn't hear their handlers and still couldn't drive the anxious, rain-soaked cows into the receiving pen before the time was up and the bell sounded. As each competitor failed and was removed by the disappointed handler, a big black-and-white Border Collie would run out, round up the scattered cows, and hustle them into the pen, quickly preparing the arena for the next competitor.

It saddened me to compare that black-and-white marvel with the ignorant, yapping fice I seemed to have acquired. Wet and windblown, Sheilah was saddened too. She pressed close to my heel as we left the field to look for my car in the parking area and once inside it, she insisted on licking my face as I drove, obstructing my view of the road. I tried to push her away but she wouldn't take no for an answer. Again and again, as I tried my best to fend her off, her little tongue annoyingly touched my lips and her little nostrils blew two streams of carbon dioxide into mine. She was beseeching me for something—for love, for reassurance—and despite my efforts to discourage her, she kept it up all the way home.

Who was this little Sheilah, formerly Fawn? And why did she rudely challenge my three other dogs the moment she saw them? These other dogs, all females, were a pack, a team, and every one of them was bigger than Sheilah, yet she leaped from the car and rudely rushed up to them, yapping and staring, showing them that she considered herself Dog One. Dignified ladies though they were, the three mature dogs could not, of course, passively accept this horrible behavior, and they attacked Sheilah. I let them maul her for a while before I pulled them away, hoping that she would learn to respect them. This was futile. Not five minutes later she was again staring and yapping. Here was a dog of a kind very seldom encountered—a dog with no social skills whatever, and no judgment.

Unpleasant as her behavior was, it said a great deal about her, and confirmed the theory that she had been raised alone. A study of infant dingos has shown that if they are raised in isolation from other dogs, they grow up to believe they are alpha adults, and nothing convinces them otherwise. While this characteristic may be softened by the long domestication of most kinds of dogs, Australian Cattle Dogs are very close to dingos (the breed results from a dingo-dog cross) and retain some wild characteristics, including, it would seem, the conviction that they are Dog One despite overwhelming evidence to the contrary. This certainly was the case with Sheilah. Younger than the other dogs by many years, she lacked their experience and their knowledge. She also lacked their poise and confidence. That she should consider herself their social superior was astonishing. If she had been a more secure dog, willing to slip politely into the group and wait to seek her true rank later, the other dogs would have accepted her. As it was, she was like a noisy child in elementary school who is bossy and scornful to adults—she was obnoxious. The other dogs avoided her to prevent themselves from attacking her, just as human adults would avoid the bossy child.

The three elderly females soon came to hate Sheilah. Now and then, when pushed beyond endurance, they would attack her. Sheilah of course became very upset when all of them turned against her, but she didn't seem to know what had provoked them. She was being the only way she knew to be, snarling and bristling at the other dogs, groveling insincerely for the people. Soon she had alienated almost everyone in our household, which made her sad and very lonely. Hoping to improve her situation she intensified her frantic efforts to elevate her status. But no one really liked her except my husband, and he was often away.

We didn't like her, and she didn't like us. She wanted different owners and a new home, so she began asking our visitors to adopt her. When a newcomer would arrive, she would grovel in front of that person, slavishly follow wherever the person went, and follow the car when the person drove away. Our visitors thought she was bizarre, and laughed at her. I thought of returning her to the rescue group.

That was back in 1999. At the time of this writing, almost three years later, little Sheilah is relaxing peacefully on the dog bed under my desk, her head resting on my foot. In the eyes of the people and most of the dogs, she is an accepted member of our household, growing calmer and more agreeable with each passing day. She's very pretty—not with the lanky elegance of her gorgeous predecessor, but with a compact little body and a wonderful pair of hind legs. The centers of her little round feet are directly below her hip joints so that her legs are straight from hip to sole, rather like a person's. She lies on the floor with her right legs neatly tucked under her body and her left legs fully extended, one straight out front, and one straight out behind. No matter what she does, she is charming. How did we get from there to here?

Not by means of one trainer's suggestion, that she wear a shock collar and we zap her whenever she challenged another dog or started her high-pitched yapping. Painful shocks might stop certain behaviors, but would leave her with nothing. She knew no alternative behavior. As a motherless pup in a pet shop, misunderstood by the people who bought her, then alone and homeless on the city streets, she spent her childhood without guidance. With no one to help her, she had formed herself. Therefore, even if we had managed to squelch her, we would not have replaced one form of behavior with another since she had no "good" behavior waiting in the wings to take the place of her bad behavior. We would have stripped her of her only coping mechanism. We saw that we would have to start fresh, giving her a chance to develop better coping mechanisms. And this would take time.

We began with a tranquilizer. When the little dog got very nervous, which usually happened around dog dinnertime, we fed her an hors d'oeuvre of cheese that contained a tranquilizer. She'd soon seem a little less nervous, a little less likely to scream challenges at the other dogs, a little less likely to push and paw at me and the other people. She'd calm down. Then maybe she'd eat a little of her dinner. Soon she was eating more, and eventually she was eating enthusiastically. She rounded out like a little barrel. The extra weight wasn't unattractive—she became a bit chunky without being obese—and the well-fed feeling from the extra food also helped to calm her.

Our next move was to take long walks. At the time, nine dogs were associated with our household, and seven of them would join the walk, which usually took place in the evening on a path that led through a field and a forest, crossing several brooks and ending at a cabin by a stream. Little Sheilah would yap blue murder each time we started out, screaming at the top of her lungs, dashing back and forth as we crossed the field, trying her best to control the other dogs. But the dark woods had their effect on Sheilah—the tall trees, the softly flowing water in the brooks, the moist air, the scent of leaves and mushrooms, the spongy forest floor still holding the sign of every animal who had passed there, all combined to fill her with wonder, so that once we were among the trees she would trot silently beside me, her head forward, her ears up and her eyes wide, looking at everything, pausing now and then to inhale and consider the signals left by the forest animals. She'd puzzle over these scents, but also would take note of the behavior of the other dogs, learning from them what to make of the odors. Dogs who live together may feel great rivalry among themselves when they're at home in familiar settings, but once they're afoot, out in the woods, off on a journey, they usually come together and act as a group. By the time we had gone a quarter mile or so, Sheilah would be one of the pack. If a dog up ahead alerted us to something unusual, such as a coyote sign, she would be the first to run to that dog's side, ready to help with a possible confrontation. None came, of course—what wild animal would confront seven dogs? But Sheilah's action was positive, and her reception by the dog she'd gone to help was also positive—the other dog would usually turn toward her, making eye contact to learn how Sheilah viewed the situation, and would see not a hostile adversary, but a group member ready to help if the need arose. All this made Sheilah very happy. When we returned from the walks, she'd stretch out on the kitchen floor and fall into a peaceful sleep.

And finally, at night we let her lie on our bed. We were advised by many people not to do this—a dog with inflated ideas of her own importance should be humbled by being made to lie on the floor, not elevated by being allowed to lie beside the people—and yet this also helped. Often at night I'd feel her little body pressed against me, and I'd put my hand on her to feel her gentle breathing. I'd always find her facing away from the direction I was facing, as if between us, we were keeping watch for danger, even in our sleep. My touch would wake her. She'd turn her head and give my hand a little, warm kiss.

And so, over time, she grew calmer. The other dogs came to tolerate her, and she them. She became proficient in the woods, and even helped me to track a bear that had been hit by a car—she helped me confirm that the bear had not been hurt too badly, and had left the area safely on his own. She also is the first to bark when visitors come, seeing them less as potential owners and more as a threat to her group. She has become useful, and she knows it. She is a contributing member of our household, a dog with a lot to give. And this was what she needed, really—not more training, and certainly not electric shocks. She needed time to find herself.

Was she the same as the first Sheilah? Could she take her namesake's place?

Of course not, and I was foolish to expect it. She was herself, and she made her own place. Yes, we gave her a certain amount of security, but the most important achievement was hers—she conquered her anxieties, and untwisted herself. Today, she can best be described as joyous, gentle, kind, sunny, cooperative, and extremely intelligent. And she's beautiful, too, with little brown spots in her red-gold fur. I love her madly, deeply. And she also loves me. If we were the same species but different genders, if not for the sixty-six-year difference in our ages, and if both of us were single, not just Sheilah, we'd get married.

As for her deaf ear, it's not important. On her first day with us she heard a sound that interested her, and, thinking she was running toward it, she ran in the opposite direction, just as she had done in the hotel room when she heard dogs barking. Yet in each place, she made her only mistake within moments after she had arrived on the scene, and in each setting, her first mistake was her last. Within a very few minutes after her arrival in any new location, she can assess her environment, recalculate what her hearing seems to be telling her, and make the necessary adjustments. Very few dogs seem to notice that she's partly deaf, and people never notice. After all, it's not the hand you're dealt, it's how you play it.

The Children Are Very Quiet When They Are Away

Maeve Brennan

IT IS A WINTER-AFTERNOON SKY, VERY DARK, AND LOWERING itself now to thicken the heavy mist that is gathering over the dunes. The Atlantic Ocean, hidden by the fading dunes, is thundering today. The line of the dunes is growing dimmer, and the huge house that stands up there over the sea is becoming ghostly. It is an enormously clumsy house, with hundreds of diamond-paned windows and a massive front door that has flights of stone steps going up to it. Inside, there must be at least eighty or ninety rooms, all of different shapes and some with balconies. In clear weather, some of the balconies can be seen from here.

"Here" is a small lawn that stretches its little length with modest satisfaction in front of a fat, romantic cottage that is very closely related to the amiable monstrosity on the dunes. The cottage might have been baked from a bit of dough left over after the giant's place on the dunes was made. They are alike, and the cottage has its own massive doorway and its diamond-paned windows and its big beams and its gingerbread roof.

The giant house is inhabited in the summertime by seven children, and the cottage is the home of a black Labrador Retriever and five handsome mongrel cats. The Retriever's name is Bluebell and she is almost six years old. On a bleak day like today, the cats stay indoors. They are asleep around the house, or they are at the windows, attentive to nothing. But at the edge of the driveway that separates the small lawn from the great one leading to the dunes, Bluebell lies on guard, with a large hollow bone between her front paws and her head turned toward the big house away up there in the distance. Bluebell must wonder why the children do not appear. They were always appearing, from all directions, and descending on her, when she did not reach them first. They used to swoop down from their house and across the lawn in a flight of white shorts and white shirts, and Bluebell never crossed the driveway to trespass on their grass until she was certain they were coming to her. They used to call her name as they ran for her, and as their breath shortened and their voices came closer, her name sounded louder, and the sound of it filled her with a joy that could only increase, because there was no limit to the children's energy or to their affection for her. "Bluebell. *Good* Bluebell. Good *Bluebell.*" There had never been so many voices calling her all at once, or so many legs to charge at and then avoid, or so many admiring faces to watch and please. Please them all, always please, that was her duty, her only duty, and she had never before seen it so plain, or felt it to be so simple, or so interesting, or felt herself so valuable. She was a dog and she performed like a dog. She forgot her middle age and her extra weight and her gray muzzle, and she frolicked like a puppy, and like a mustang, and like a kitten.

She found a treasure in the short grass and then, after smelling it importantly, she tormented it for a few seconds with her paws before she pranced away and left it as it was, invisible. She entertained like a dog. She lay stretched on her back with her huge chest heaving dramatically. Upside down she is grotesque, a vulnerable monster. She might be a sacrifice, on the lawn, in the sunlight. Her front paws hang in the air empty and aimless, and the big, soft ears that make her look demure and mournful fall away, inside out, and leave her face exposed and wild. And her eyes are wild; they look at nothing. The children are astonished to see their familiar turn mysterious, and they make a circle around her. They are embarrassed, because she is shameless, and they try to clear the air with their laughter. "Look at Bluebell. She is *funny.*" Who is Bluebell now, and what is she? She is not herself. The smallest girl decides that Bluebell is a bench, and she sits heavily down on the softest place, the stomach. Bluebell springs rudely up and resumes her proper shape. Now she is a dog again, and she stands on four legs again. The children welcome her return by telling her her name: Bluebell, Bluebell, Bluebell. Bluebell brandishes her heavy tail and challenges with her eyes the eyes that watch her, and then she races away and they all race after her. She has never been so pursued. She has never been so famous or so celebrated. Her name is on every lip. She has come into her own. She is the only dog in the world.

But here it is winter, with the cold winter weather that is so good for playing in, and she has been waiting for hours, ever since last summer, and the children have not appeared. If she watches faithfully, they will appear. They generally come out around this time. Whenever they come out is this time. Bluebell moves the old bone over to the middle of the driveway, and then she resumes her dignified attitude, with her paws precisely arranged, as though she were lying in wait on her own tomb. Her head is turned to the house on the dunes. It is lost in the mist. The house is gone. There is no sound except the pounding of the sea in the distance, and that sound means nothing to Bluebell. What use to plunge into the sea and brave the waves when she has no witnesses? The lawn is empty, shrinking away into the mist, and the air has turned to silence. No voice is calling from up there on the dunes. There is no Bluebell. Her name is lost. She was the only dog in the world, but now she is only a dog. It is all the children's fault, all this absence. It is all their fault. They are too quiet. All this silence can be blamed on them, and all this waste. Bluebell takes her eyes from the dunes and puts her chin on the empty bone between her paws. She drowses. It is all the children's fault. Everything is too quiet. It is all their fault. The children are quiet because they are away. But what is away, and then, what is here? Bluebell is here. Bluebell sleeps. Now Bluebell is away where the children are who are so quiet here.

Uncle Harry

Donald McCaig

AFTER TWENTY YEARS' TRAINING AND TRIALING SHEEPDOGS, I cannot understand why so many people assume a dog's emotional life is poorer than our own.

Harry is a powerful, short-coated, ugly, black-and-tan Border Collie. His head's so broad I've been asked if he "has any Pit Bull in him." Every day Harry and I work sheep on our farm, and on weekends to relax, we go to sheepdog trials. Harry's a natural dog: At a year old, before I started training, he'd sweep out in a great arc behind his sheep and bring them directly to my feet. Like most naturals, Harry resented interference and when I made suggestions, sometimes he'd sulk and go home. In time, he came to agree that my suggestions made things go a bit smoother, but he never lost his preference for working on his own.

Harry loves the trials. When I start packing, I can't keep him out of the car. As soon as we arrive at the trial grounds he jumps out to greet all those beautiful, supple, talented, charming, albeit less-than-compliant bitches. When it's his turn next, he whines his pleasure.

By three years old, he'd won trials and qualified to run in the National Finals Sheepdog Trials. The National Finals, held that year at Lexington, Kentucky, is the World Series of sheepdog trials—Harry would run against 180 of the best sheepdogs in North America.

Harry made his natural outrun and fetch, turned his sheep around me, and set out on a horrendous drive the British judge said was the longest he'd ever seen. Near the end, Harry was losing faith, but I said cheerful things to him and he finished the drive, brought them into the shedding ring, made his split, his pen, and his shed. As I walked off the course a friend came over to congratulate us and told me, "You were hyperventilating so bad in the shedding ring. I was afraid you'd pass out." I do recall that at the time, my vision was getting fuzzy at the edges, but so long as I could still see Harry and the sheep, I didn't care.

Harry is our oldest male and acts as shop steward for our six Border Collies. When I scold some dog malefactor, Harry puts his heavy head on my knee and urges forbearance. Our last litter of pups was born in the deep dark winter and sometimes you have to put those pups outdoors RIGHT NOW, but our farm borders twelve thousand acres of State Game Commission land and to a hungry bobcat, fat puppies look like breakfast. Midnight or daylight, whenever we put the puppies out into the snow, Uncle Harry went along to protect them and make sure they didn't stray. Harry took to the work. Whenever a puppy started fussing in the house—be it two or three in the morning—Harry would bump open the bedroom door and jump on my chest to tell me about the puppy in distress.

Harry is my literary dog and accompanies me on book tours and readings. Harry doesn't particularly like hundreds of strangers making a fuss over him but he'll put up with it, and since many people mistake Harry's natural courtesy for fondness, he gets along fine. Harry's limits are met sooner than mine, however: At a Baltimore NPR studio, three weeks into my last book tour, Harry went into the corner, faced away, and wouldn't come out again. I did the last two weeks of the tour alone.

With Harry snoozing on the front seat beside me, we've traveled thousands of miles to dog and book events.

Harry knows how to act, off lead, in motels, livestock markets, bookstores, tents, libraries, loading chutes, TV stations, B&B's, college classrooms, Greenwich Village, dozens of different trial fields, and once, on the sixth floor of the National Geographic Society in Washington, D.C.

While traveling, I take one motel bed, Harry hops up on the other. One night, in upstate New York, people in the next room had their new puppy with them and at four in the morning, Harry was pawing my chest, wondering why I wasn't letting that poor puppy outside, was I deaf or something?

Two years after his brilliant run at Lexington Harry's runs started falling apart. He'd be his old self at home, but on the trial field he'd wallow around like he couldn't hear my whistles or, worse; he'd take matters into his own hands. I figured it was a training problem—that his old sulkiness was returning in spades. At home, on our small training field, he'd not set a paw wrong and when we walked to the post at a trial, Harry'd look at me and say, *Of course I can do it. For goodness' sake, you've seen me do it often enough.* And then Harry would wreck.

I was looking forward to the Edgeworth Trial. Good sheep, beautiful course, and, not incidentally, a trial that rewards natural dogs. It's a 650-yard outrun up a breathtakingly steep hill and the dog is out of sight of the handler until it reaches its sheep. Four years ago, when Harry ran that course, he was beautiful and if I'd needed two commands to bring the sheep to my feet, I'd not needed three.

On Saturday when Harry ran, it was cool and though a light wind made the sheep spooky, they weren't too bad. It takes nearly two minutes for the dog to get up that hill behind his sheep and those minutes seemed long to me, a lifetime. Harry made a perfect outrun and with my eyes shaded, I could see Harry and two sheep drifting off downhill, but three remained and I whistled Harry to stop and go back for them but he paid me no heed and his two sheep dawdled on down the slope. Harry was with them, sure, but he had no control of them.

We retired. One of the three ewes he'd shunned had been a tough old beast and I figured Harry had opted for the two drifting off as the easier task. A sheepdog who doesn't bring all his sheep is a moral failure, sure, but every dog has his off days.

On Sunday there was no wind, cool air, terrific sheep—a chance for a fine run. Harry went out wider than before and it was easily three minutes before the sheep started to move. I whistled Harry to where he needed to be, but he lagged. I yelled, "Hey!" and "Harry!" I shouted his commands. He took my commands too late or not at all, put no pressure on the sheep, and for the second day in a row they simply drifted.

I haven't been so angry at a dog in years. After we came off the field another handler said, "That dog needs an attitude adjustment."

No, I didn't lay a hand on Harry, physical or verbal, because there's no point making a correction unless you know what you're correcting. I had run out of dog and had no idea in the world why.

I did manage to pat Harry's head before I went to bed, but it was an effort.

The next day our vet told me Harry has a heart murmur, a leaky mitral valve. That long, hard outrun was too much; I ran out of dog because Harry ran out of heart. I suppose one might imagine Harry's emotions alone on that hill as his genes, his skills, and his distant handler cried to him while his oxygen-starved heart confounded his body and mind—I don't want to think about it.

I am grateful that in my anger, I didn't raise my hand to Harry. When things go badly and an attitude adjustment is required, it isn't always the dog who requires it.

Harry won't go to trials anymore. He'll live out his life on the farm and do simple chore work. Until I pack my bags to take some other dog to a sheepdog trial or literary event, I believe he'll be happy.

Last January, Harry and I stayed with friends in Charlottesville. At midnight, when we went outside, snow was falling, two or three inches, muffling the suburbs. I walked down the middle of the unmarked street while Harry ranged on both sides, over whitened lawns, underneath snow-bulked pine trees.

Some of the houses had security lights with motion sensors and wherever Harry ranged, lights blinked on. Everything ahead of us was darkness. Behind, wherever Harry had passed, it was light.

Accident

Mark Doty

BUT AS THE SEASON TURNS, DARKENING INTO A LATE BUT RAW winter, so do we. Our golden autumn's gone gray and severe. Our neighborhood, out at the end of town, is empty save for us, the windows of summer houses shuttered tight. The dry canes of the climbing roses rattle, and wind whistles in the wires in the masts of the moored catamarans, a chilly singing. Wally's mood shifts. He'd planned, these months when he wasn't working (no shops which could use his skills would be open till April), to paint and sketch, maybe to continue doing some writing, but what he does is walk, whole days of dog walking, and when I come home from my two days of teaching each week there's a heaviness and darkness in him, even though I know he's glad to see me. It feels as if his life is a weight he has to lift, to carry, and he doesn't quite seem to have the strength. The days I'm away the weight seems to become heavier; free of the distraction of company, he sinks further into himself, into uncertainty, into depression.

And then one morning early in January Wally's walking Arden, on the way home from the lush wrack and tumble of the salt marsh. They're crossing a lawn that is separated from the road by a tall hedge when Arden spies a rabbit, object of wonder and delight, and bolts unstoppably after it, right through the hedge and into the road. Wally, left on the other side, hears the sickening screech of brakes, and then, worse, the sound of a body being struck, and then a cry—pain, confusion, terror? He runs to the road. The car has stopped, but Arden isn't there; Wally looks up to see him racing away down Commercial Street, toward town, and though Wally runs after him shouting Arden's name till he thinks his heart will burst, the dog can't hear him. There's nothing for him but panic's imperative, nothing but flight.

The driver of the car and his passenger, two kind and concerned men, drive Wally around the neighborhood, stopping to ask people if they've seen a dog. Someone says they thought they saw a black dog racing up Franklin Street—in the direction of the dunes and woods, a refuge, but only if Arden also crossed the town's busiest streets.

No sign of him.

Soon Wally's calling me at my office; only one other time, two years later, will a telephone call be so terrifying. There are great huge silences between words, when he cannot still his sobs enough to continue.

"Babe . . ." Long silence, the intake of Wally's breath. I'm thinking, My God, what's happened?

"Arden . . . got hit . . . by a . . . car."

Slowly, my questions get the rest of the story out. I think it's probably a good sign that Arden could run, and has; at least he was able to, though we're both terrified that he's injured internally, that he's hiding somewhere, in pain, where we can't get to him. And I'm frightened by this wild panic in Wally's voice, which is somehow like nothing I've heard before, more desperate, more empty, as if the bottom has fallen out of the world.

It takes me six hours to get home. During this time, Wally's combed the streets, calling till he's hoarse. No luck. He's also called his friend Bobby, who's driven down from Boston; always wanting to please, to make himself indispensable, Bobby shows up all excited saying he's found Arden, who's waiting out in the car. Wally rushes out, but the dog in the front seat is someone else's black pooch, who was perfectly happy to jump into Bobby's station wagon. Later, Wally will tell me how his knees buckled when he saw that it wasn't our dog. Bobby wasn't a stranger to Arden; what was he thinking? Was he so desperate to help that he'd pick up *any* black dog? Certainly he could behave thoughtlessly, but I think now he must have picked up on that panic in Wally's voice, that nearly unbearable note of pain. I would have done anything to salve that, too, but confronting the wrong dog only made Wally's spirits sink more deeply. Bobby has to go home, just after I return, and I'm glad.

We comb the town again, hoping that a new voice might reach Arden; if he's hiding, panicked or wounded, can I draw him out? We call the police and the radio station and make signs to post all over town: at the A&P, the post office, the café bulletin board. Arden's not a dog who's been out in the world on his own. With Wally or me since he was a puppy, carried home in our laps from the animal shelter, he's bound to us by deep ties, and though he likes exploring, he's never evidenced the least desire to wander around without us. He *is* in relation to us; that's his life.

And though I am frantic with worry for him myself, what I hear in Wally's voice, what shows in his face, is some panic and terror more primal than mine, a pain that seems to go all the way to the root of him. We drive through the parking lot at Herring Cove Beach, a place we often walk, thinking perhaps he might have run there. A town eccentric—a former therapist, I've heard, who's become a vision of Father Christmas in his long white hair and beard, who dresses all in white and walks with a tall walking stick—is crossing the parking lot, and when we pull up beside him Wally rolls down the window and says, "Have you seen my dog?" It's the voice of a terrified little boy, helpless, utterly alone.

Back home, having accomplished nothing, we're looking down into the rough January water of the bay churning against the breakwater stones. "Where is he?" Wally demands, as if I or anyone could answer. "Where is he?"

Our descent seemed a long, imperceptible downward glide, but I can see now there were indeed precipitous drops, moments when we stepped down to a new level, a greater depth.

Arden's accident was such a moment. In Reinaldo Arenas's memoir *Before Night Falls* there's a weird and chilling scene when thunder shatters a glass of water on a bedside table; it is, somehow, the beginning of the speaker's misfortune, the physical manifestation of his illness beginning. A glass shatters and a room goes dark; nothing is ever the same again.

What opened in Wally then was a depth of vulnerability and despair like nothing I'd ever seen in him before. It was about the real loss—was it?—of Arden, of course, but it was more than that, too; Arden and Wally both struck, everything out of his control, everything veering into his life, unstoppable, an event from which he couldn't be rescued. We didn't know where Arden was or how badly he might be hurt—did we know where Wally was, or how much he'd been harmed?

We tried to sleep that night, and did, fitfully. I remember walking the beach at five, a bleary dawn, whistling and calling. Late in the morning, the phone rang. Some neighbors, down for the weekend, had gone to town for breakfast, because it was a warm and sunny morning. Reading the bulletin board in front of the café, they'd recognized Arden's name and description. Then, walking homeward, in front of the bank, Arden appeared, walking—with a rather confused and tentative look, they thought—in the same direction they were going.

"Arden?" they asked. And it seemed his name brought him back from wherever he'd been to the world of connection. He shook his head, as if clearing it, and looked at them uncertainly, and when they said it again, he began to wag his tail and step toward them.

He wasn't hurt; the vet's poking and prodding later that day wouldn't reveal a thing. He must have run in sheer terror, and hidden, not knowing where the familiar might be, not knowing how to return to his name.

The men stroked and talked to him until I got there. Wally said he couldn't handle going, he was so afraid it would be another mistake, the wrong black dog, and he couldn't bear it again. So I went alone. When I stepped out of the car onto the sidewalk Arden came hurrying to me, and leaned all his weight against me, and buried his face in my coat.

Later, when both Wally and I were dealing perhaps most directly with the prospect of his dying (not the literal, actual illness, but the preparatory work, the—what to call it? consideration?—which went on about a year and a half ahead of his death), we both struggled in dreams to come to terms. And the dream that shook me most, night after night, centered on Arden. We were walking in a field, the three of us, near a highway, happy, at ease, and then Arden would catch a scent and bound ahead, wild with it, no calling him back, onto the road. He'd be hit, but in each dream there would be a variation—struck and killed, or run away, his situation unknown. I'd wake up in horror, afraid to sleep because I was afraid the dream would start again. I thought of lines from a poem of James Merrill's:

> *the mere word "animal" a skin*
> *through which its old sense glimmers, of the soul.*

Always exploring ahead of us on our walks—the walks Wally couldn't take anymore—Arden was our future's dark vessel, the part of us that would scout ahead, sniffing out what's to come. He was, in my dream, where we were about to be struck.

Dog Town

Alysia Gray Painter

I LOOKED DOWN AT THE LITTER BOX, THEN AT MY DOG, AND put my face in my hands, trying to decide if I was going to bawl small or bawl big. If our lives turn on a million moments we hardly notice, this was moment number 345,921 and I noticed it, if only because it had just kicked me in the shin. Granted, there were plenty of other things wrong besides the fact that I'd just bought a litter box for a dog. I was a Westerner not in the West, a writer not employed, and a renter short of cash. But my moment of reckoning arrived the moment my dog, Gladys, filled with shame, first stepped into that litter box, and cry I did.

Moving is tough. My husband and I had just left New Mexico for New York, because that's what writers in their twenties do more often than not—leave *X* for *Y*, with *Y* being New York about 100 percent of the time. But what of the animals who must move with them? Do they notice? Do they care? Do they miss their old yard? Do they hate their new litter box so much, hate it in the worst way? Who thinks of these questions as they optimistically load up that U-Haul?

One bright, baffling day in our new town, Brooklyn, these questions were answered in a terrible rush. We awoke to find that all the trees on our block were encircled by newly built colossal fences. Whether it was because a local congressperson believed that urban residents were having too much contact with nature I can't be sure, but it certainly put a crimp in potty time. Gladys, a princessy Pug, won't go on concrete or asphalt. The spot must be pliant and organic, hopefully grass, possibly dirt, ideally hyacinths. I've cajoled, she sulks . . . what can I do?

The boarded-up trees posed an instant dilemma. We didn't have our own yard, and places where a Pug might politely squat were gravely limited. There was a picturesque park three blocks away, but we both demurred. Two young ladies—one on two feet, the other flat of snout—could hardly risk traipsing along dark winding paths for a late-night tinkle.

So I bought a litter box and placed the dreaded object on our balcony, no more than a coffin-shaped fenced ledge, really, in full view of a hundred different neighbors, some with telescopes, others with cameras, all with malevolent intentions. I filled the litter box with dirt and grass and lessons were begun without aid of textbooks, instructional films, or pride.

I won't elaborate, except to say that Gladys eventually learned to employ the litter box for her nightly needs in full view of a dozen brownstones. But I knew we'd have to move to a roomier residence, a home with a yard, a place with space. Perhaps it was because Gladys wouldn't look me in the face. Admittedly, I too had trouble meeting her enormous wet eyes. Treat time grew awkward. *Wuv you wuv bug* cuddle hugs immediately ceased. Often, when I went to clean the litter box, the Pug and I would pass each other in the kitchen and she'd thoroughly examine a floor tile, or the oven, or the ceiling, but never me. I vowed no dog of mine would ever have to play cat ever again.

For the first time, it became clear that dogs respond to place, in much the same way that people mirror—or deflect—their surroundings. I have friends who are very Chicago or so Seattle, but it wasn't until this Brooklyn experience that I began to appreciate that pets too can be associated with locales. Our big move showed me that it isn't necessarily breed that connects a dog to its surroundings but temperament, lifestyle, and character. An enlightening discovery, but it still didn't answer the question at hand—where did our Gladys belong?

Months after the Litter Box Fiasco, we moved again, this time to Los Angeles. Job prospects took us there, homesickness for the West took us there, but mostly Glady's craving for a humble patch of grass took us there. We picked up another Pug, Jerome, a companion for Gladys. Exhausted from this second move, and from the hardscrabble, nearly checkless writer's life, and from constantly inveigling Gladys to use a cat's toilet, I thought little of what a second move might mean for her. She'd have a small yard in L.A. What could go wrong?

I found out on one of our first walks around our new neighborhood. Several films had recently come out starring Pugs, and a Beverly Hills matron stopped us to visit with Gladys. "Aren't these dogs trendy now!" she smiled-hissed, and my face screwed up the way it used to when I cleaned the dog's litter box. Trendy! Is that some sort of compliment? Gladys pranced around—*I'm trendy, I'm trendy!*—and the woman slithered along her Prada-pretty path, a harbinger of things to come.

Unlike New Mexico, where making it day to day, being with nature, going out to eat, and seeing friends are the things that most folks think about, the obsession in Los Angeles is, How do I break in and make a million today? And that goes for dogs, too. Strangers kept telling me to get my pups into films while Pug Fever was still on, next year it would be Malamute Mania, we were missing our boat—or yacht, rather. I looked at Gladys, who wouldn't pick up a dollar with her mouth if it was soaked in beef broth, and sighed. If I wasn't very L.A., she really wasn't.

I tried to finish this sentence: Gladys is so—where? She'd never really tuned into New York, but, then, she was never really New Mexico, either. She hadn't made many friends at our local park, preferring the company of her "parents." Her size, demeanor, and breed were, in fact, particularly incongruous in the Land of Enchantment. Anyone who has spent time in the Southwest knows there are laws against driving a pickup without a huge, furry, kerchief-wearing tongue-panter riding shotgun. Cops'll pull you over for not owning a happy, slobbery Chow named Durango or Luna or Kiva.

In fact, nearly every dog in New Mexico, Colorado, and Utah is part Chow, likely all descended from the same legendary explorer Chow who helped settle the West centuries ago. Today, this venerable Chow can be seen in its countless descendants sunning in driveways throughout Albuquerque, Denver, and Flagstaff in much the same way their forefathers sunned. Even if a Southwestern dog *isn't* a Chow, it is. Just peek at that Park City Poodle's tongue and you'll see the evidence in black and purple.

Gladys was never in touch with her inner Chow, so I felt okay about moving her from the only place she'd ever known. But was she happier? She certainly equated Brooklyn with that blasted litter box and a lack of nature. In Los Angeles, she's a trendy, usable commodity. Obviously our dogs belong with us, but do we belong in the same places as our dogs?

Strangely, our second Pug, Jerome, a native New Mexican, is quite Los Angeles in every way. He seems thrilled to be here, interested in shiny objects (the number-one trait of all successful studio executives) and superfriendly to the point of schmooziness. If Jerome were to whip out his card or cell phone, I wouldn't be surprised. Just a wisp of a dog, he's brave enough to network with even the most intimidating, drooling beasts that rule at that hip dog park off famous Mulholland Drive. I've actually seen him air-kiss—or, rather, air-lick—people. Jerome's a player.

Several months ago, for the fun of it and because it was free, my husband and I started compiling a list of Jerome's favorite directors, films, and actors. It was determined, unanimously, that Jerome loves splashy, special effects–packed movies like *Speed,* and hopes Stallone will make a deserved comeback.

We didn't draw up a similar list for Gladys, who doesn't have a favorite movie and doesn't like L. A., although in looks and personality she resembles Baby Jane, the infamous burned-out, bitchy Hollywood starlet played by Bette Davis in *Whatever Happened to Baby Jane?,* the gothic camp classic. Like Baby Jane, Gladys likes to stay holed up in her 1920s house near Sunset Boulevard, lounging languidly, musing darkly about her past.

Perhaps we'll move again one day. If we do, Jerome will miss the celebrity lifestyle, but then lots of Tinseltown types downsize to deluxe, redwood-accented cabins in Idaho, or Santa Fe adobes. He'll be fine with leaving the bright lights as long as he knows he'll live on in the hearts of those he's met in Hollywood. I won't tell him that the duration of "living on" in the hearts of Hollywood is exactly sixteen seconds.

And Gladys? Well, there's got to be a place for her somewhere. I imagine it's atmospheric and rainy, a place where the natives eat lots of buttery bread and sausages, which, due to the damp environment, fall easily from their slippery hands and into Glady's waiting maw. There'll be more laps for her sleeping pleasure in this mythical land, and no more unguents or eye drops ever, because she won't have any more smog allergies. Gladys, really, is like most people. There's always a better place to go, a larger house, a nicer neighborhood, a more suitable park. It's only a matter of finding it.

Sit. Stay. Heal: One Dog's Response to 9/11

Lee Forgotson

ALTHOUGH MY HUSBAND TED AND I LIVED ONLY A FEW MILES from the World Trade Center, most of my initial experiences of September 11 came from the television set. Ted, a producer at *CBS News,* left our Brooklyn apartment late that morning and didn't come back for days. I couldn't get to my own office, because the city had shut down, and outside, the streets were filled with a thick, unbearable smoke that adhered chemically to the back of your throat. So I stayed inside alone, with my faithful dog, Rex, and watched the world turn to ash.

Now, our television is positioned such that if you're lying on the sofa with your head on a decorative pillow, the screen is at eye level. This is also the level of Rex's head. So all morning, as I lay there watching over and over again the towers fall, Rex kept inserting his face between me and the television, plying me with a variety of facial expressions as if to get a response. We have a system of communication, Rex and I, that involves eye movements and a diverse range of barks. If he's hungry, he looks pointedly from me to his food dish. He barks at his leash if he wants to go for a walk. But by the seventh hour of my nonstop, no-commercial-break, planes-crashing-into-towers paralysis, he simply stared straight at me, head cocked, with his mouth slightly open, as if he were trying to find the right thing to say.

And what can one say that hasn't been said already? I kept hearing that the role of the media was to "create a narrative"; but I was having a hard time believing that anyone who wasn't a firefighter, a police officer, a nurse, doctor, or rescue worker truly had a role. I mean, *who needs* another writer when the city is on fire? What could I do?

Every hour or so, I would get off the sofa, and go to the windows to gaze in disbelief toward the nontowers, and then I would pace, and Rex would follow me like, well, like a puppy, and match my every stride. He'd follow me into the bedroom, and watch me with his head cocked as I rifled through my chest of drawers looking for donatable clothes. And he would follow me yet again into the kitchen, and sit and watch while I gazed trancelike into the cabinets and debated the global usefulness of a single can of French onion soup. And always, always, I would shuffle back to the sofa and the television set, wanting, *needing* for some reason, to see the planes hit the towers.

Soon Rex began to paw at me, crawl on top of me, lick my mouth. When that failed, he brought me toys and tuggy ropes, and held them before me with his tail a-wagging and a big dog-smile on his face. But I just couldn't see how Rex's stuffed-animal cuteness, or the goofy way in which his lips stretched around a tennis ball, had a place in a world in which severed limbs could smash into Starbucks; in which a human jaw could get lodged into concrete.

Rex remained undeterred. He began to nudge my hand that held the remote, and nudge and nudge until that hand would rest on his head. Then we would sit like that, my hand holding the remote on top of his head. We'd watch firefighters hoisting flags atop the rubble, we'd watch distraught mothers holding up missing-persons flyers, we'd watch that endless black smoke swallow all hope, and soon Rex would try to flip my hand off his head into a new position—onto his belly, if he got it right. But I was too catatonic to scratch dog bellies. I'd tell Rex, sharply, to *cut it out!* and shove him off the sofa with my foot. Poor Rex would sigh, creep into a corner, and place his head between his paws.

Meanwhile, Bernadine Healy of the Red Cross had been appearing on every channel, admonishing viewers to stop watching so much television. "Avoid repetitive viewing of the terrible images," she said. "Go out and do something. Give blood. Volunteer." And then they'd show the planes crashing into the towers.

By Tuesday, I finally realized if I really wanted to be useful I should start by being kind to my own dog. "Do you want to go for a walk?" I said. "A real walk?" (Up 'til then I'd merely sent him into the courtyard for a quick poop and a pee.) Rex barked and spun in circles, thrilled to hear that things might finally be getting "back to normal." I, too, felt a sense of purpose. Lost, shell-shocked people would pass by in taxis and on buses and say, "Look, there's a woman walking her dog."

So off we went, out into a day so incongruously beautiful and autumnal I had to shield my eyes with my forearm like a vampire unused to the sun. Before me, Rex trotted: tail up, nose down, pulling forward, always forward, toward Prospect Park. He didn't notice that, above us, four fighter planes circled the city. He didn't notice that our local diner had posted a sign that said FREE COMFORT FOOD. He didn't even seem to notice the burnt-electrical-equipment smell, or the way the endless debris in the air sometimes caught the sunlight and sparkled to the ground in a not entirely unpleasant way, like tiny flickers of hope. Idiot children, some people call dogs. I'd call them blessed.

Our usual midday route takes us past a fire station, and I have to confess that before September 11 I had barely even noticed it. The giant garage door was always closed, so I had given no thought to the people behind it: the men whose job it is to save and to serve. Once, on a rainy day, I had even gotten miffed because a fire truck blocked the sidewalk, and Rex and I had to wait like two minutes to get across. *Two minutes* I could not give these men. And now the firehouse had become a shrine to their missing Twelve. I'd already seen it on TV—the flowers, the candles—but standing before the firehouse was like entering a vacuum of sorrow and silence. No one spoke. Nothing could be heard except a crying woman's sniffles and the slight wind-tossed rustling of dried-up flowers. Rex tugged, to keep us moving, to get to where he'd spotted a cat the week before. "Wait," I whispered. "Show some respect." Next to me, two teenage boys in Limp Bizkit getups leaned against one another, as if each were the other's supporting beam. One openly wept.

In the summers I teach creative writing to boys like this—boys who'd bring in Eminem lyrics during poetry week and convincingly compare him to Frost. Now, they faced the final photographs of their dads.

It was all too much, and I gave Rex the okay command to lead us home.

Back at my apartment, Ted was finally able to get through to me on the telephone.

"How are you?" he asked. "What are you doing with yourself?"

"Nothing. I mean I'm doing nothing. I can't write, I can't read, I can't eat. All I can do is cry."

Ted offered some words of comfort, then asked about Rex.

"He's sulking in a corner because I'm not paying enough attention to him."

"Put him on the phone," Ted said.

I placed the receiver underneath the flap of Rex's left ear. The television was on mute and, while Ted talked to Rex, I read the text banner. AMERICA UNDER ATTACK, it had said the first day. Now it said, AMERICA RISING. "You take care of your mother now," Ted was saying. "You hear?" And Rex must have heard, because after Ted hung up, the dog had a look on his face like that of Colin Powell at a White House briefing: confident, capable, in charge.

That night, I fell asleep on the sofa, and when I came to, MSNBC was airing an amateur videotape of the second tower's collapse. In the background was a horrible noise—shrill beeping, like tiny sirens. I would later learn that the noise came from dozens of personal alarms of firefighters, but in my half-awake state that noise became the very sound of terror. Plus, there was a horrible weight on my chest that had no explanation, until I regained full consciousness and realized that the weight was of course Rex. He had positioned himself like a Sphinx on top of my torso and his elbows had managed to wedge their way irrevocably between my ribs. But still, I let him stay.

That morning, I vowed to get out and do something. To avoid repetitive viewing of the terrible images. To visit my local animal shelter and walk some dogs. My first charge was a Shepherd mix named Amy. "She just came in today," the volunteer coordinator told me. "Owner surrendered. He's been calling us for months asking us to take her, and suddenly we had a space. So he dumped her off and left her. She's really freaked."

When they brought her out, Amy didn't acknowledge me or any of the other humans. Instead she simply pulled me, the keeper of the leash, toward the door. We hurried down the sidewalk, heading west. The East River was lined with stupefied onlookers, who could do nothing but stand and stare. The smoke downtown was still too thick to reveal what lay beneath it, too dense to prove the towers really were gone. So they watched. And waited. Meanwhile, Amy rushed up to sniff every doorway, alley, and parked car. She pulled me across the street toward strange men, only to veer away in a new direction once she realized she had to keep looking. And I know—we all know—she was looking for her Person, but what could I do? Across the river, thousands of people were checking lists outside the Armory, looking for their Persons, too.

At the next intersection, Amy walked in circles, as if trying to get her bearings, as if trying to figure out where she last saw Him. I tried to comfort her, to sweet-talk her: I stroked her flank and said her name. But Amy didn't want my love. She wanted the person she had been assigned to. The person with whom she had an agreement—to love and to serve. Frantically, Amy dragged me in the direction of the shelter again—the point at which all things in her life started going wrong. In a last-ditch effort, she jumped onto a windowsill and peered into someone's apartment. Inside, a woman was watching television. Get outside, I wanted to tell her. The real emotions are out here.

I walked other dogs that evening but I couldn't stop thinking about Amy. I wondered how long it would take Amy to "accept" that her Person is gone. How long it would take her to become like other dogs at the shelter—a little less determined, a little more resigned. And how do you mourn someone who has vanished, as it were, into thin air?

Back at the apartment, Rex was waiting for me at the doorway. I knelt down and gave him a good belly rub, and promised him a big turkey dinner with a gingersnap for dessert. When we first took Rex home from the shelter four years earlier, he had hated us. He tried to run away all the time. It had never occurred to me until now that Rex may have been looking for his Person back then. Perhaps he still was.

Friday night, Ted finally came home and the three of us went to a local, dog-friendly bar for a beer and some food. Ted and I sat at our usual table in the corner and let Rex do his thing, which is to tool around the bar and sniff under all the tables in search of french fries. Tonight, however, Rex could not move about so quickly, for the place was crowded and the air was thick with disbelief and concern. Our beers came, and Ted and I lifted our glasses and acknowledged how lucky we were that no one we knew directly was killed, and how guilty we felt to feel lucky at all, and how strange it was to mourn something so large and abstract, and when I looked around to check on Rex, I saw that he was sitting at the feet of a stranger. The man—young, handsome, in his twenties—sat alone, and his eyes moved robotically from CNN to his glass. Rex just sat there, waiting for something from him it seemed, that Colin Powell look on his face. I tried not to stare; I tried to pay attention to what Ted was telling me about his day and his job, but each time I looked toward their corner, Rex and his friend were getting more intimate. First the man was stroking Rex's flanks and talking to him. Then he was scratching Rex behind the ears. His face was getting closer and closer to Rex's head. I was worried. Rex, as former shelter dog (whom we suspect had been abused), still had a tendency to lunge at strangers. But now the man was on his knees, hugging Rex and crying into his fur.

Ted and I used to joke that Rex would never make it as a therapy dog. He would vivisect the stuffed animals at Children's Hospital and try to play tug with a cancer patient's IV. But I realized, that night in that Brooklyn bar, that by depriving Rex of his need to comfort me, he had brought his comfort elsewhere—to a needy stranger. I realized that he would never stop giving and loving, because, in Rex's dog mind, that was his job. As Ted and Rex and I walked home that night, we passed an ash-covered car that glowed a ghostly white in the light of the streetlamp. It seemed frozen in space and time, like something from Pompeii. And on the front windshield someone had scrawled: *You are not alone.* I gripped Ted's hand and Rex's leash and felt this.

Comfort

Abigail Thomas

I FELL IN LOVE WITH ROSIE LAST OCTOBER. I'D BEEN TO THE Blessing of the Animals at the Cathedral of St. John the Divine, and a crowd was gathering around the booths and tables set up outside in the parking lot. I noticed her from half a block away, sitting under a table with two other dogs up for adoption. It was love at first sight, although she looked like a handful—high-strung and nervous. Half-Dachshund, half-Whippet (a union that must have come with an instruction sheet) she was simply the most beautiful dog I'd ever seen. A small deer, a gazelle, or a Dachshund's dream come true, as someone remarked, looking at Rosie's long legs. Is she housebroken? Spayed? I asked a few unnecessary questions. I knew I wanted her no matter what. I knelt down and stroked her silky brown coat, and looked into a very nervous pair of brown eyes. Her slender body quivered. I had been thinking about a second dog, and here she was.

My Beagle, Harry, didn't exactly jump up and down for joy when

Rosie arrived. In fact he growled. He was occupying his half of the sofa (which he takes in the middle) and Rosie's approach was unwelcome, to say the least. But he looked a little more alive, I was happy to see. Harry and I had both been leading a reclusive life for a long time, neither of us inclined to leave the house unless we had to. My husband had been struck by a car some eighteen months before and suffered a traumatic brain injury. I had begun to realize he would never get better, never be able to live at home again. Since the accident Harry had refused to go out. I had to carry him trembling into the elevator, through the lobby, across the street into Riverside Park, and once I put him down, he lunged toward home.

Harry had been with us only four months when the accident happened. We had gotten him through a friend who'd found him starving in the woods. The day he arrived we were worried: We gave him food, but he wouldn't eat; we put down water, but he wouldn't drink; we took him for walks and he skulked close to the ground, his tail between his legs. If we approached him, he tried to make himself as small as possible in a corner of the sofa. Finally, despairing, we went to bed. Ten minutes later we heard the click of toenails across the bare floor and then there was Harry, in bed with us. It was going to be all right. It was going to be better than all right. And then one night in April Rich had taken Harry for his nighttime walk when Harry's leash broke and he ran into Riverside Drive, headed home. It was a quarter to ten. Rich stopped an oncoming bus, but he didn't see the car coming on the other side. Harry came home alone, and shortly afterward I heard that Rich had been hit.

"How do you feel about your dog now?" I recall someone asking soon after the disaster. "I love my dog," I said. It seemed a peculiar question. "I couldn't get through this without Harry." In the first weeks of Rich's hospitalization I would often wake in the night to reach for him only to find that the warmth I felt at my side was Harry's small body. In those moments grief and gratitude combined in a way I have since gotten accustomed to.

After some initial squabbling over property rights, Harry and Rosie reached a détente. The only real fight they had was over a glazed doughnut I had foolishly left within reach, but it was an Entenmann's doughnut, well worth fighting for. Within days of Rosie's arrival, Harry was out and about, his tail held high. Now we head off for the dog-run every morning. Walking Rosie is like having a kite on the end of a leash while Harry stumps along maturely, a small solid anchor. In the dog-run Harry and I sit on the bench watching as Rosie runs, leaps, bounds, races any dog who will follow her, and outruns all of them except two—a Saluki named Sophie and an Afghan named Chelsea. They are the only dogs faster than Rosie, but most days are too elegant to run at all.

Rosie got us out of our slump, but she sleeps with one eye open; if I so much as sigh, she is alert. If I look up from my book, or take off my reading glasses, she is tensed to follow. I found out that her owner died in the World Trade Center, and she had been without him about a month before I adopted her. Whoever he was, he must have loved her as I do; he trained her, and when I tell her to sit and she sits, I swear I can feel his ghost hovering nearby. I want to tell the people who loved him that his dog is part of a family now, that she is doing fine.

I visit my husband once a week. He is cared for in a facility upstate that specializes in traumatic brain injury. The accident was more than two years ago now, and I still can't get my mind around it. He is there and not there, he is my husband and not my husband. His thoughts seem to break apart and collide with each other, and I try not to think at all. On good days we sit outside. We don't talk, we just sit very close together and hold hands. It feels like the old days, it feels like being married again. When I get home at night, my dogs greet me, Rosie bounding as if on springs, Harry wiggling at my feet. Sometimes I sit right down on the floor before taking off my coat.

If you were to look into our apartment in the late morning, or early afternoon, or toward suppertime, you might find us together sleeping. Of course a good rainy day is preferable, but even on sunny summer days, the dogs and I get into bed. Rosie dives under the quilt on my right, Harry on my left, and we jam ourselves together. After a little bit Harry starts to snore, Rosie rests her chin on my ankle, the blanket rises and falls with our breathing, and I feel only gratitude. We are doing something as necessary to our well-being as food or air or water. We are steeping ourselves, reassuring ourselves, renewing ourselves, three creatures of two species, finding comfort in the simple exchange of body warmth.

My Dog, Roscoe: A Story

Bonnie Jo Campbell

AS MY SISTER'S PRISON LUNCHROOM TEA LEAVES PREDICTED, I became pregnant early into my marriage to Pete the electrician, and just when I was starting to show, a stray dog—bigger than a Cocker Spaniel, smaller than a Retriever, white with black pepper spots—appeared at the back door of the house that we were renting with an option to buy. The dog's faded red collar had no identification tags, but "Roscoe" was written on the fabric in alcohol marker. At first I tried to shoo him away, but he stayed nearby, and I quickly became fond of his lopsided face—one ear hung down lower than the other. Pete suggested we wait and get a puppy after the baby was born. Usually I appreciated Pete's long-term view, but here was a living, breathing creature who needed me, now. For a week, I reminded Pete of how lonesome I was when he worked late, and all the while I fed the dog breakfast cereal and meatloaf under the back-porch stairs where I had built him a nest of blankets. When Pete finally agreed to our adopting Roscoe, I bathed his coat with coal tar shampoo, took him to the veterinarian for shots, and, on Dr. Wellborn's advice, made an appointment for the surgical neutering.

Once he was cleaned up, I began noticing a worldly light shining in Roscoe's dark eyes—his soulful expression revealed that he had known pain—if not in this life, then in a previous one. Perhaps we had suffered together in times past. Maybe we'd been on a Roman slave ship, chained side by side to our oars. Or if I had been Cleopatra, then he might've been some Nile-side employee whom I'd hardly noticed, but who had died by throwing his body between me and an assassin's blade.

Roscoe was somewhat wary around Pete, perhaps because Pete was so tall, but when the dog and I were alone, he had a habit of rolling onto his back and opening his legs in a way that reminded me not of a fellow slave or an Egyptian, but of my old fiancé, Oscar, may he rest in peace. Two years ago, Oscar fell headfirst from a hayloft, where he was nakedly comingling with a Galesburg girl, who at the funeral claimed Oscar had been *her* fiancé and had some proof to back it up. My sister Lydia, who was, then as now, serving her jail sentence for growing and selling marijuana, should have been more respectful of the dead, but she never even let me speak Oscar's name wistfully without reminding me of the ways I'd been betrayed. In the eight years we were together, Oscar had twice given me chlamydia (both times he swore it came from an exercise bicycle) and in the last few years had taken to disappearing for hours or days without explanation. Life with handsome Oscar had a lot of ups and downs, but I had fallen for him in the tenth grade and had loved him as a girl can only love her first love.

One day as I scratched Roscoe's chest, which was surprisingly muscular for a little mongrel, his tongue snaked out and he began to lick the underside of my wrist. It gave me a shiver. Only two people in this life had ever known that my wrists were my most romantically sensitive body part—perhaps Roscoe had been studying Pete and me in our intimate moments. Or perhaps this dog and I had been very close in our previous life together. Maybe those slave-ship captains had severely whipped Roscoe when he voiced his opinions about human rights, and maybe I revived Roscoe with fresh water from my own meager rations before we found ourselves in profound and passionate embrace.

Roscoe turned from me to administer to his own privates. When he tired of that, he headed toward the kitchen, but he paused in the doorway to look over at me and puff up his chest and, if I wasn't mistaken, to suck in his little belly, exactly the way Oscar used to. I followed him into the kitchen and kneeled to look into his face. Couldn't be. Ridiculous. Plenty of dogs had brown eyes. Plenty of dogs licked people's wrists and inflated their chests. How could I even think such a thing? Roscoe took a nugget of dry food in his mouth and crunched it distractedly, pretending not to notice I was looking at him—but that was another of Oscar's postures!

When I undressed to get into the shower, I looked down and saw Roscoe gazing at my breasts with his tongue hanging out. "Stop it," I scolded. The dog stopped smiling and lowered his eyes with a look of guilt I knew all too well. I'd felt proud of the way my stomach was swelling, but Roscoe made me embarrassed. I wrapped my bathrobe around myself and stepped over him. Later, while waiting for Pete to get home from his double shift, I reclined on the couch and opened a bag of Be-Mo sour cream and onion potato chips. Although Pete preferred plain salted chips, he found no fault with my eating these or any other snacks—recently he had allowed me to spell out the letters of baby names on his bare stomach in cheese doodles while he read a paperback, *The Water People of the Bright Planet.*

Roscoe's eyes followed my hand as I lifted each chip from the bag to my mouth. When I finally offered him a chip, Roscoe stretched up and took it in his teeth. I breathed a sigh of relief. Oscar had always hated chips, and he had especially hated the sour cream and onion kind. But this dog liked them, and that was that, and all the rest had been my imagination. Roscoe sauntered into the kitchen, and I leaned off the couch and caught sight of him spitting out the chip, then lapping water from his dish, as if to wash away the taste. Next he puffed up his chest and sat ignoring me.

"Oscar?" I said.

The dog turned my way and sucked in his stomach.

"Is that you?" I asked.

The dog trotted back to me and tilted his head sideways, which made a darling gesture. Dr. Wellborn had said the droopy ear was probably frostbite damage, but now I knew better. Oscar had departed this world as a result of falling from that barn's loft onto a threshing spike, which had entered his brain through his right ear.

Roscoe opened his mouth and let his tongue hang over his small bottom teeth.

I said, "You couldn't live without me, could you?"

The dog pushed his nose under my hand, and I smoothed the fur on his head, then patted the couch cushion beside me. "Come up here, big fella." The dog jumped onto the couch and laid his head on my stomach. He watched my face for a while, then focused on the television. I pushed him away only when his drool soaked through my nightie.

Over the course of the next few days, I noted how much my old boyfriend had changed. Oscar had always been a prime rib and filet mignon man, yet Roscoe dutifully ate his Waggy Meals and Chew Bites in both beef and poultry flavors. To my relief, he had also mellowed in his television habits—Oscar used to roll his eyes whenever I turned on my ten o'clock police and lawyer dramas, but Roscoe seemed content to watch with me, never suggesting that he'd prefer news or wrestling. On the negative side, while Oscar had been fastidious about his personal cleanliness, Roscoe never missed an opportunity to rummage through neighbors' garbage bags or to roll on the carcasses of raccoons or squirrels he discovered along the road. But most important was the fact that Oscar now realized he'd treated me badly—after all, here he was, eager to make up for his past crimes.

That night I lay in bed beside my husband, with Roscoe's nose on my foot. Pete's work clothes were laid out on the chair. The timer on the coffeemaker was set, the doors and windows were all checked and locked. The bills were all paid. Living with Pete had seemed safe and sensible all these months, but lately the security was making me feel a little restless.

"Maybe we shouldn't get him neutered," I said.

"What?" Pete looked away from his paperback, *The Star Clouds.*

"Is that really fair? What if he wants to have a family? What gives human beings the right to impose their wills on other species?"

"Sarah, you're not imposing your will on him. You're rescuing him. If not for you, he'd probably have gotten hit on the road or gassed at the pound already."

After I kissed Pete off to work the following morning at 6:45, I called the dog to me. During the sleepless night, I had come to the conclusion that my restlessness wasn't from missing Oscar—after all, here he was. Rather, it arose from a need for resolution. His sudden death in the arms of another woman (another fiancée!) had been such a shock that I hadn't gotten closure. Oscar needed to know exactly how wounded I had felt. "You've been very bad," I said, pointing into his face. At length I reminded him of some of his worst behavior, including his frolic with that mean librarian. Oscar always denied any such encounter—and at the time I had believed him—but after the evening in question, the woman continually renewed his books so he never had to pay late fees, while she required of me the strictest compliance. She let him check out reference books, for crying out loud. "You've been very, very bad," I concluded.

Roscoe finally closed his mouth and whined.

"Hah!" I said, "At last you admit your guilt!" Now he couldn't explain away all those hours he claimed to be at the nursing home with a nonexistent grandmother, and he certainly couldn't deny dirty dancing in that hayloft. And because he couldn't reach the doorknob, he couldn't storm out in an indignant huff. He gazed at my finger with regret, until suddenly his head whipped around and he gnawed at his back leg, pretending to bite a flea.

"Look at me when I talk to you," I said, grabbing his nose. "You can't avoid me, Oscar, Roscoe, whatever you call yourself." When I let him go, he lay his speckled nose between his paws.

"That's better," I said. "Now that I'm loved by a man who is true, I know how badly you treated me. For the next eight years, I'm going to have a little control in this relationship."

Still, neutering him seemed over the top, unreasonably cruel, not to mention stupid should I ever want Oscar to become human again, say if something happened to Pete while he was installing cable on the twelfth floor of a new office building. Who knew what kind of deal Oscar had made with the powers of the universe in order to be reincarnated as my dog.

When my sister Lydia called me at work later that morning, I told her that Oscar had come back to find me.

"You told me he died in a farming accident," she said. "You sent me the obituary."

"He stayed gone for two years."

"And now he's come back, sniffing around your door?"

"Sort of," I said.

"Listen, Sarah, this is bad," Lydia said. "The reason I'm calling is that I did the tarot for you this morning."

"You mean the toilet-tissue tarot?" After Lydia's cell mate reported on Lydia's so-called satanic activities, the prison authorities took away her tarot deck, and she had to make a new one from the materials at hand.

"Listen, the lovers appeared prominently, upside down. I drew it last night too, with the fool." The lovers card was not necessarily bad, but it suggested temptation, choice, the struggle between sacred and profane love, and upside down it warned of the wrong choice. "Don't you worry, though," she said. "I'll put a curse on Oscar to get him out of your life for good."

"You don't understand," I protested. "He's come to me in the form of a stray dog." I presented her with all the evidence. "He's really sorry for what he did to me."

"Get a grip!" she demanded. My sister was usually an open-minded person, but she became harsh with me on the phone. "Your Pete is a light shining above the rabble. You have found true love with a good man and now you're going to have a baby, so shut up about Oscar and shut up about that damned dog."

I clutched the phone in silence, wondering if maybe they'd slipped lard into the crust of her vegetarian potpies again.

"And your potato chip test is stupid," she said. "If I could bust out of here, I'd drive across four states just to kick your ass."

I'd intended to say I was depositing money in her jail account and that I'd bought her a book about improving the Feng Shui of very small spaces. Instead I told her thanks for being so supportive, next time I'd consult with the Psychic Friends Network, and I hung up. On Wednesday afternoon I called the clinic and canceled the Friday neutering.

Thursday morning, Roscoe whined to go outside earlier than usual, while Pete was showering. I dragged myself out of bed and fiddled to straighten the leash. As I opened the door, a cramp took hold of me, and in my moment of inattention, Roscoe took off. He pumped his legs faster and faster across our yard, dragging his leash around the basswood tree and through our neighbor's tomato plants. I ran after him but was slowed by my slippers and robe. Roscoe took the road at a shallow angle. If he'd been paying any attention, he'd have noticed the approaching menace of the blue car that braked and swerved but couldn't avoid slamming—whomp—into him. His body flew through the air and landed on the dirt shoulder. In pursuit, I didn't hesitate to run right in front of the car, which halted within a foot of me. My heart stopped momentarily, and the world took on a greenish tinge as I realized I had just risked extinguishing not only my own light but also the five-month-old spark inside me.

At the sight of Roscoe's lifeless body, however, I once again forgot about the future. I kneeled beside him. Before us, in a kennel opening out of a garage attached to a ranch-style house, perched the object of Roscoe's desire—a black female Chow with lush fur and a ridiculously curly tail. She was rubbing her haunch against the side of the pen. Three other neighborhood dogs scratched and whimpered at the chain-link, and as I watched, a loopy-gaited Irish Setter crossed the road safely and joined the other males.

The woman who'd hit Roscoe got out of the car and stood beside me in the kind of ugly, padded shoes librarians wear. "He just ran out in front of me," she said. "I'm so sorry. I have two dogs of my own. Golden Retrievers. I love dogs."

I put my face into the lifeless fur and began to weep. I wept until a rough tongue unrolled itself onto my neck.

"You're alive!" I shouted.

Roscoe maneuvered himself slowly to a sitting position, then pulled his body up with great difficulty and stood shaking on three legs. When I touched the fourth leg, he winced, and I noticed blood was pooling beneath it. "Go get my husband," I yelled to the woman. "Down that little road, the yellow house on the left."

Roscoe heaved a sigh and sank to the ground again.

"You just couldn't be true, even as a dog," I said. Momentarily, Roscoe's ears both drooped, but then he sniffed the air in the direction of the cage and the one good ear lifted. I was thinking that it ought to be illegal to let females out when they smelled that way—they were little more than death traps—but in my heart I knew it wasn't the bitch's fault.

Roscoe continued to watch the cage even after somebody called the female dog inside. As the other males dispersed to sniff stupidly around the yard, Roscoe turned and looked at me through the most regretful, guileless eyes in the world, and I knew that at last he did understand.

"Sarah, honey, we'd better get him into the truck," said Pete from behind me. "I called Dr. Wellborn's office, and she's coming in early for us. Looks like he's lost some blood."

I hadn't heard Pete's truck pull up, and I somehow hadn't even registered the amount of blood soaking into the dirt shoulder. Now that Oscar truly understood the error of his ways, I was losing him. If something happened to Pete, if he was shocked with twenty thousand volts in a freak power surge, Oscar would not be able transform into a man and take me back. Pete and I lifted Roscoe into the truck as the lady who had hit him watched patiently—she could probably stand there all day in those comfortable shoes. Though Pete argued it was unsafe, I insisted on riding in the truck bed with my dog. Pete drove slowly, and I stroked Roscoe's head.

As we coasted to a stop outside the clinic, I opened the tailgate and lugged myself out, feeling the heaviness of pregnancy for the first time. I pulled Roscoe toward me and was grateful when Pete grabbed hold and helped me carry him. The veterinarian's blond assistant held the door for us.

"He's bruised and traumatized," said Dr. Wellborn after the examination. She was a serious dark-eyed woman with her thick hair pulled back, a Queen of Pentacles, rich with practical talents, probably a Capricorn, too. "But nothing seems to be broken. He's almost stopped bleeding, but I'd like to stitch that gash."

"Thank you, Doctor," I said.

"He'll do it again, though, unless he's neutered." She studied a yellow chart. "It says here you canceled your Friday appointment."

"You canceled the appointment?" Pete turned to me.

"I just couldn't bring him in at that time," I said.

Pete stared at me, genuinely puzzled. While I may have misled him slightly on occasion, while I had failed to mention the Oscar-Roscoe affair, I'd never told Pete an outright lie before.

"Your aura or horoscope or something?" Pete suggested. He wanted to believe me.

"We've still got a surgical opening for tomorrow morning," said Wellborn. "You can leave him here overnight. That way we'll keep an eye on his wounds."

Castration. It seemed so very final. Even if Oscar could transmigrate to a body like his old one, the residual effects would remain on his soul, and he would never ever forget I'd been the one who did this to him.

Until death do us part, I'd told Pete. I thought I'd already committed to him, but there I was, thinking about life with another man.

"It's up to you," Dr. Wellborn said.

The truth was that the last few weeks with Roscoe had been happier than any I'd spent with Oscar in our years together. As a dog, he was devoted and companionable, and he listened when I talked to him. And I knew in my heart that even if, God forbid, something happened to Pete, I could never return to the frustration and insecurity of being Oscar's girl.

Pete was screwing up his eyes, as if waiting for me to explain—to confess to being an adulterer or to sprout red feathers from my forehead.

Roscoe whimpered, but it was just too late. However he'd gotten to be a dog, his well-being was now in my hands.

"Of course we'll take the appointment," I said.

I smiled at Pete and placed one of my hands on my belly, where I felt a tiny sigh of relief.

Navajo

Nasdijj

MY THEME SONG. OFTEN, THE PLACES I HAVE LIVED ARE, TOO, places I have worked. I walk through these places like some ghost who haunts the wind, a sullen pianissimo of melting whispers mingled with the leaves. My dog, Navajo, an echo caught faintly in the cricket sounds before me.

I work with children.

You are thinking, Sounds like laughing and screams on playgrounds. Swings.

You would be right to think that.

Group homes. Psychiatric treatment centers. Foster facilities. University intensive care units. Residential programs. State institutions. Places with time-out rooms and bars on the windows. Juvenile detention facilities. Classrooms. Prisons.

Places where the sounds bounce off the walls like discord is cacophony. Even children at the margins reverberate.

Romp. Even children at the margins romp with dogs.

Tonight I sit mindless in the haggard shadows of the boy's room and watch my kindred babies breathe. I never quite trust them enough to do it right. Who knows of madness, whether it is divine or whether it be of the blacker pit? The lunatic, the lover, the father, and the poet are of imagination all compact. A sober light spills through the window with expedient lucidity.

The dog's dark eyes glisten like the river glitters on a midnight moon. There is always something about this room, no matter the boy, that smells of puppy milk.

What toys are here belong to my dog, Navajo.

Mr. Devil is blue, and the squeaker gone long ago. Mr. Duck is pink. Mrs. Smurf is purple. Navajo, herself, is color-blind.

She plays tennis, too. Run, fetch.

Navajo, my Blue Heeler mongrel, knows I am here among the lightless places. Watching my babies breathe. She pretends to sleep at the foot of the bed of the boy who now occupies this room. She will growl, too, if I move too quickly. The boy asleep belongs to her. She has claimed him with her rescued wisdom.

He has been adopted.

Even I, the master of the house, a shadow of visions, must not be rash in transit. She knows better than to growl at me, and keeps her protest to a minimum.

Oh, it's him again, the watchman, me.

She will not share the boy, and in his sweaty sleep, she holds the quiet hill of sheets and blankets, stillness undisturbed, maintaining her anchor like a pilgrimage.

My wife misses me in these sleepless moments, but she knows I have to do this. The watchman's rounds.

The lighting of the streetlamps.

The boy asleep in his pajamas is but the latest of my Heeler's wandering charges. His sweat has soaked the pillow. His black hair is wet. I love him and the dog he sleeps with.

She knows them for the vagrant children that they are. Most come to us in noise, tumultuous, yet this one is a silent visage. They come to us as adoptive placements, foster children, children in between, children with emergencies, birdmen, Icarus, refugees; they arrive with baggage even if they have none.

Wings of wax.

Sometimes you are the teacher, but always you are the parent, too, as there seems to be no escape from that cohesive fragility.

Your job is to protect them. Mostly from themselves.

The dog is but the bargeman, and the wizard of the other side. Usually, the children do not know, not being as wise as the dog, that there even is a river, and that they are in it. That the river has granted them a passage.

The boy is twelve. Twice as old as the dog. Yet light-years younger. He has arrived a wastrel stray. His windmills are somnambulant. His family history is common and irrelevant. What is important is that he breathes. Do it. Do it for me.

His parents lost to some gray place that passes in succession from death to grief. This one has been abused. Raped. Hush. Nothing new to the story of abuse. Hunger unmoved. The rape of children is an ordinary thing. A house where hollow rocks retain the dreaming sounds of screams. A grinding away at the diamond of his spirit and the residue of dreams.

I was driving down the highway once. Someone in the car in front of me threw a puppy out the window. Now, I do this work.

With boys and dogs.

It is revenge. Mine.

The boy is mute. His world is one of a self-induced silence. He has seen far more than most of us will ever know or ever want to. He has survived the loss of his family, a major surgery, and now he battles AIDS.

We can no longer work in any of these places with any of these kids, children from the margins, places that not only hem them in, but squeeze them, too, in strangulation, without assuming, now, that they do not come to us with this disease. Because they do.

Navajo, the sphinx, silly dog, knows all the secrets of the prison house. She knows this: If you love her, she will love you hard, in return.

We are each other's business. I stand here in the dark and watch them, wondering what I will do if they die. The boy. The dog. Knowing all of us will die, that is the way of it, and knowing, too, that it's what I do with their living in these moments that we have that count.

When the boy is awake, and not too sick, we watch the crazy TV shows from Australia where the crazy guy in his L.L. Bean shorts rescues crocodiles.

He adopts them.

What is adoption? You take one in. To accept as one's own. To appropriate. To restore. You take one in, into a particular environment. Sometimes, you take one in to nothing more complicated than a classroom. Learning as a positive, nurturing experience. Like birth, adoption comes with blood.

When I touch him now, I must be careful to use the rubber gloves. Universal precautions come with hugs.

When Navajo was small, she'd go outside to poop, and she'd shake and quiver because any sound or noise whatsoever scared her half to death. Cleaning poop just comes with the territory, and cleaning the boy, now, too, comes with fatherhood. A tenderness and he cries.

Adoption, like birth, is a giving back.

As I touch him, as I am allowed to do (someone has to do it), the intimacy of the thing is not unlike the messy intimacies of birth. To be unborn again. The river. The letting go. Touching him, too, is not unlike those times of holding her, under your coat in the cold with her shivers, and she's peeking out and sniffing at the cold, clear, New Mexico snow.

We were adopted. By Navajo. She just moved in. She saw the futon, and that was it.

The notion of the family must adopt a new perspective. A dog, a boy with AIDS, will teach you to see new things. Navajo was a damaged animal, afraid. Today she's a little skeptical but fundamentally giving, even if she limps.

Question is, as you sit there in the dark, petting the dog, and touching the wet hair of the sweating boy, Can we adopt ourselves? Can we exist? How do we return them to the world? Working with these kids (and dogs) is living with them as family regardless of the place, the setting, the institution, or the marble halls. We are connected, conflicted, and compelled to touch. Sometimes even rubber gloves are, indeed, too much.

There are no barriers between the father, the son, or the dog. We are all wrestling crocodiles.

The children and the dogs have always arrived with the deafening bangs of death and thunder. From thunder comes the rain. From rain, the rivers flow.

I was working at the Sangre de Christo Animal Hospital in Santa Fe. I do not know why. I did not need the money. I think it was about that dance I do with death.

It walked through the door on clicky legs almost every day.

The dog was almost gone. The family sat outside in the waiting room. The entire family. Mother. Father. Children. Grandparents. Choked. Sobbing. Weeping.

Holding hands.

The veterinarian (one of the most compassionate people I have ever met) had me hold the dog.

The needle.

I did not know what to do. Loss itself slipped from my mouth like frost. The vet just talked warmly to the dog. About time.

About how it was time to go now.

Time.

That was why I was there. To learn about time. Almost half a million Americans have died from AIDS. Six hundred thousand people in the United States alone are living with HIV. It is the height of fantasy to assume that kids in pseudo-parenting situations do not have it. Big Bird is a person inside a costume. More than one million Americans have been infected with HIV. We are not isolated from the world around us. Children from the margins, where survival is a day-to-day proposition, come to us infected with everything from tuberculosis to full-blown AIDS.

They are in classrooms. They are in (supposedly) SRO hotels. They are in schools. They are in group homes. They are in homeless shelters. They are on the bus. They are in day-care centers watching Big Bird count.

Who from the wet bedsheets of invisibility has come to learn and love alone? Who among us can say with accuracy we, too, would speak? To die is nothing. To lose your voice to monsters is the world. The boy just stopped speaking, and that was the end of it. He had been raped. Now this.

Life was just too much. He withdrew into an ear-splitting rip through the cosmos. The rest is always silence. The only one who seems to reach him now is the animal on his bed.

My Cattle Dog with her own broken places.

Hush. When she kisses him with her wet dog tongue, you wonder, and you let it go. There is no rubber glove that would fit her tongue. The dog is perhaps the only one to kiss him, ever. She knows all the children's stories without having to be told.

She makes him laugh. To hear him laugh is *la milagra.* Music.

She quivered in my coat. Kisses are not dangerous and he needs them. Now more than ever.

She knows when something is hurt. She does not like the thunder. It is too loud. I never thought to have her work with these kids. I never thought her cut out for it. She comes to them in the same way she came to me. An accident. She is not your textbook dog. She does not fit the mold. *Milagra.* She would never pass the helper tests. Her temperament is apprehensive with concern.

There was the blind boy she herded. Like he was a sheep. Whenever he came even remotely close to bumping into things, she'd use her entire body (and bark) to nudge him back. She cannot stand to see them injured.

There was the boy who signed. He taught her, too, to watch.

There was the one with seizure disorders who could not fool her. She could see a seizure coming. Her advance warnings were never wrong.

She barked.

There were the ones who had autism. She saw them like she sees ducks at the lake, and she gets upset if someone breaks the chain and isn't holding hands. No one wanders. No one is allowed. We have seen the world together. It is our home.

She was found a few weeks old in a cave on the Pecos River in New Mexico. She had a broken leg. We figured someone had kicked her. The sight of men in hats made her tremble. She had surgery. The vet again. Pins in bones (the vet working miracles, which is this vet's specialty). We did not know if the surgery would take. Navajo uses that leg, but not a lot, and mainly she limps.

No hopping, we command.

She was the animal hospital's resident refugee. She would not eat. The dog had reached that point where she was almost (but not quite) giving up. The ghost. I took her home. I would feed her by hand if I had to. She was a scraggy dog. Ribs. People said, Oh, she'll eat when she's hungry, but people are sometimes wrong. She was skin and bones. I had to put food down her throat.

It took three years. Three years of being force-fed. Like a bird with worms. Finally, after three years of this, she began eating on her own. Tentatively. Hush.

She would not walk on roads with traffic.

She would not pee if there were birds around.

Her wings were wax.

We were living in Navajoland. There was an old Anasazi trail that meandered through the mesa. Children liked to follow us as they had never seen a dog on a leash before. One young Navajo boy, about seven, was most intrigued. Because you want her to be safe, he said.

Just safe.

Because being safe is very important, I explained. This boy considered this concept deeply. We discussed it every day. This being safe. I had seen the reservation cop cars at his house.

So no one gets hurt, he noted. It was a revolutionary concept.

A great hush would descend upon the mesa, and in the distance, I swear you could hear the Anasazi drums.

So no one gets hurt, I said. Including and especially her. Two years on that trail. Up one way and down the other. Always the same walk. Always the same Navajo boy. Always the same concern about what was (and what was not) safe, like something in him had unthawed. In North Carolina, Navajo has a professional trainer. Barbara Long in Chapel Hill is her teacher and her friend. Navajo has come a long way, Barbara says. Navajo has made big strides. Initially, the animal was always expecting bad, bad things to happen, and her body language was suspicious, the head was always down. But Navajo has started enjoying things. There is a lot more looking at me. She has better coping skills than even a year ago. There's a more relaxed posture; she's not assuming she will be challenged all the time. She lets you rub her now. They do get better. She feels safe, but she does have issues.

She knows when your leg is short, Awee, the current boy child in her life, writes. Awee at twelve is writing now. His words in print. To communicate with me. It is not talking. Yet. But we watch Crocodile Hunter and we laugh.

The secrets of the prison house. His disease receding like an underbreath. They call it hope. The medications work. His voice elusive. It would be a mistake to push. Just hush. You clean him, and you love him, too, like giving birth, a messy thing of blood and loss.

His stories (about boys who lose everything and terrible things happen) set in caves. He puts Navajo under the covers with him, but she prefers the end of the bed, ever alert to the possibility of thunder. Birds might come. Or the garbage truck. The boy, like the dog, replenishes his sweetness, set at naught, and squalls, above the pitch, out of tune, off the hinges, breathing baby like a yawn, minded to the devil daggers drawn.

Both the boy and the dog are making progress. They are alive. They are adopting crocodiles. *La milagra.*

Progress facilitated by what is fundamental to that nebulous thing we call friendship. The father and the son and the dog are about a friendship. Without it, the cave.

Even their eyes are quick, and blacker than the ash buds in the front of March, the fires of memory that sustain them, parhelion scars, dog stars, fade away into the dim, and I am left standing here, the watchman, too, obscured by what the future holds in the dead vast and middle of the night, the queen of sleep, the dawn. Time. I am still the student.

The surge and the thunder of the odyssey, a boy, twelve and sick, a dog, six and healing, none so deaf as those of us who fear to watch them breathe, just breathe, my victories like daybreak, my babies gentle as suckling doves. Who from invisibility has come to learn and love alone? None of us here sitting in the dark waiting for the light to illuminate our home.

Drenched in sweat's downpour and time like a conduit.

I never knew how much the dog had yet to give to such an animal as the boy. A pianissimo down the marble halls. A barking at the places that will break. They will break you, too. I had never trusted the dog to give as much as she does. I had always drawn her back, and stuffed food down her throat for three years. She simply waited. Trembling as is her way. Through an eternity of marginal children. All of them derelict in one way or another. My eternal hushing them. Her pilgrimage to calm, and in her eyes she is very small.

To keep such watch on stones of boys, and catch them when they fall.

Saying Good-bye to Shelby

Thom Jones

A BOXER'S GREETING IS A JOY TO BEHOLD. THEY JUMP INTO THE air in such a jubilee of delight, it's as if your return to hearth and home were the most noteworthy event of the century when all you've done, say, is walk to the mailbox and back. Return after an hour or more and you'll get backflips, trumpets, and a procession of drum-beating pageantry befitting a king.

But this last time, my Shelby outdid herself with the circus greeting, and a few moments later, her hind legs began to falter. As she tried to recover, her front legs failed, too. She staggered about the house slamming into furniture and walls, wagging her tail all the while. Was she having a seizure? Had her heart failed to pump enough blood to her hindquarters? Or had the cancer already spread to her brain?

She was eleven years old, this big brindle beauty to whom I was not going to get too attached. I was *certainly* not going to let myself love her the way I'd loved the one before her. When my previous Boxer died in my arms at age fifteen, I felt as if a part of myself had died, too. I emerged from the vet's office into a black-and-white world, a world literally devoid of all color. An hour went by before my color vision returned. I vowed right then and there: Never again.

But dogs have a way of finding the people who need them, filling an emptiness we don't even know we have. So it was for Shelby, who took all of five minutes to stake her claim to my bruised heart. At nine months, she was big and bold, bright and brash, the daughter of two champions. My wife didn't want another dog, and my daughter, then seven, was wary of this bumptious intruder. They held out only slightly longer than I had before they, too, were summarily seduced.

As canine crimes go, Shelby's were all misdemeanors—in nine years' time she had three accidents, chewed one shoe, and swallowed a single bar of bath soap. That was her entire rap sheet. At the first light of day, with an exuberance she never outgrew, she'd come bounding into my bedroom to play. My friends and associates dare not wake me before noon ("I don't care if it's nuclear war, don't ever call me in the morning!"), yet I understood the natural world and couldn't blame my little angel for her uncontainable high spirits at the first rays of dawn. It took me more than sunbeams to get on with my day, but when I'd finally consumed enough coffee to come back to life, Shelby and I shared our invariable breakfast: a can of King Oscar sardines. She got the three biggest. Next up: Quaker oatmeal. I served Shelby hers on a plastic Ronald McDonald plate that I set just outside the back door.

On cool days, she would run fifteen miles with me. She shredded three cotton ropes a month playing tug of war. She ran down Frisbees; she wrestled and boxed with me. In hot weather, she could dive and retrieve in depths that exceeded six feet. Like me, she was at home in the water. On a visit to my mother's summer cottage in Wisconsin, I heard a child say, "Daddy, look at that duck." It was Shelby, of course, a quarter-mile out on the lake, swimming after a mother duck and her flock. One large, square head surrounded by little round ones; a sort of Loch Ness Boxer, I guess you could say.

When I became diabetic, and had to walk off high blood-sugar readings in all kinds of weather (mostly rain), Shelby splashed through the puddles beside me, nearly pulling my arm out of its socket. Our neighbors referred to us as "the two thugs." That was outdoor Shelby.

Indoors, she was delicate as a cat, taking great care around my young daughter. She calibrated her strength according to each customer, sensing precisely how much each could endure. We had similar tastes in people. Friendly but discriminating, Shelby liked the same visitors I liked, but merely tolerated the people I only pretended to like.

Fun and games are all well and good, but like most dogs, Shelby liked to work, too. To stave off boredom and enhance her self-esteem, I devised various duties for her, appointing her chief of security. It wasn't until later that I would realize she'd already taken on the job of looking after me. The fact that I'm still here is a testament to how well she did it, despite all those dog IQ ratings that place Boxers somewhere in only mid-range.

I've read that 50 percent of all dogs can smell epilepsy and warn their owners of impending seizures. I have simple partial seizures—twitches and jerks that come on toward the end of the day. Before I switched medications and got them under control, Shelby would throw her shoulder against the back of my legs, as if to say, "Hey, pay attention!" Sure enough, within minutes, the seizures would start.

Shelby was still a young dog when, as a writer with a hot book, I got a call from ABC's *20/20*. The producer asked me to appear on the show. He was under the impression that I had grand mal epilepsy and wondered how long it would take after I quit my medication to have a fit in front of a camera crew. Seizure dogs are trained to sit near their masters to protect them in the event of grand mal seizures. The well-intentioned producer pointed out that millions of people watch the show, and suggested I could sell lots of books. I politely declined in light of the stigma attached to epilepsy, to say nothing of the fact that I had a personal life. Besides, I was just having twitches, which I doubted would make for thrilling TV.

I was teaching in Iowa City at the time, and had just written a *Village Voice* piece. Having eaten a fairly small breakfast, I drove downtown to fax them a revision. The forecast called for heavy snow that day, so instead of going straight home, I stopped at the market to stock up. By the time I unloaded my groceries, I had a vague sense of my blood sugar dropping, and realized I needed to eat. It was my last conscious thought before I hit the floor in what proved to be a diabetic coma.

I'd always assumed that a coma was akin to sleep. It is not. Soaked in sweat, my teeth chattering like joke-store choppers, I was essentially paralyzed. I felt as if I were being strangled. Meanwhile, the insulin pump attached to my body was delivering drop after drop of insulin, putting me in deeper trouble. I needed sugar and each succeeding drop of insulin became a kind of poison.

As I lay there immobilized on the kitchen floor, I became aware of Shelby licking my face and bumping me with her snout, then leaping onto the couch and sounding her deep bass alarm out the window, then coming back and licking me some more. A neighbor heard her barking and looked inside, saw me lying there, and called the paramedics. Saved by my boisterous four-legged nurse, the one with the mid-range IQ.

When we left our subdivision for a house in the country, Shelby took on expanded duties. She was never happier than when she was chasing deer from our clover field. She also kept close watch on the horses next door. I was standing in the kitchen eating a sour apple one day when I spotted one of them back by the fence. I fed him my apple and after he'd eaten it, I got him another one out of the fridge. It must have been mighty sour; the horse took a bite, then spit it out. Shelby, who had been standing there taking this in, suddenly took off for the gate like a brown cruise missile. She was soon a mere BB on the horizon. I watched in amazement as she crawled through the gate. She was soon standing on the other side of the fence wolfing down the sour apple. From then on, I waited till my jealous darling was asleep before venturing out to feed the horses their treats.

My life—the writing life—has its fair share of perks. It's a stay-at-home job, for one thing. It allows me to sleep until noon, for another. And given that I like to write—at least *some* days—I haven't had to "work" for a living for more than a decade. Shelby was at my side for most of those years. She watched me write countless stories, lending moral support. She rode shotgun in the passenger seat of my Saab or my daughter's Checker whenever I drove to the video store, or made a library run. We lived our lives side by side, me and this singular dog to whom I was not going to get attached.

I used to travel the world at the drop of a hat, but that, too, changed when I acquired Shelby. Book tours, visits to relatives—any trip that involved breaking out a suitcase—induced separation anxiety in us both. It got worse as she aged; the older dogs get, the more they seem to like their routine. I put Shelby on Sinequan, an antidepressant. There were times when I took it myself. It helped us both some, but it wasn't until I walked through the front door that her sense of well-being was fully restored.

A few weeks ago, as the long, rainy Washington winter gave way to a rare sunny day, Shelby and I drove downtown to the park. We took a leisurely stroll, then sat on a bench for a while soaking up sun. I couldn't help but think back to the days when our "walks" had been runs. We were both slowing down. At the same time, however, we were still in sync, keeping the same, steady pace, stride for stride.

An old dog has a beauty and dignity all her own, with her graying muzzle and soft, knowing eye. Her silliness gives way to serenity; more time is now spent in sleep than in play. In a perfect world, we would die, man and dog, as we lived: side by side, simultaneously. No one who's given his heart to a dog should have to walk in the door to this deafening silence. Or come upon a faded Ronald McDonald oatmeal plate. Or a chair whose cushions are forever imprinted with the shape of the slumbering dog.

But the world isn't perfect. And so, the end came—much too soon, the way it always does. She did not succumb to her lymphoma, an incurable cancer that led to four surgeries over her final six months. Shelby's faltering legs turned out to be a sign of low blood sugar, caused by a tumor on her pancreas. While I've long heard it said that dogs come to resemble their owners, I never knew it could happen to such a degree. The condition that led to my Boxer's demise was in fact the mirror image of my own.

I am still in the early stages of grieving, still disoriented, still easily brought to tears. She is gone, but somehow, she's still with me, her invisible presence watching my every move. I can't open the door, or a can of sardines, without feeling her like some phantom limb—severed but still part of me, always here. As she will be for as long as I live.

My Colter

Rick Bass

YOU NEVER KNOW WHEN THE LAST HUNT IS GOING TO BE. YOU certainly don't expect it at four years. If you think about it at all, it is with the vague pleasure of distant daydreams, and imagining only the good things age brings: the deepened layers of stored memories—the thousands of hunts, rather than mere hundreds. If you do imagine a last hunt, you picture it at season's end, amidst snow and ice, and with the hunter, the dog, barely able to creep, but still pushing resolutely forward, nearly blind and shivering but with his blood still as hot as when he was born.

You do not picture early September, full of health and power, and still in his ascendancy.

How many grouse killed? It doesn't matter. Perhaps a hundred, out of God knows how many—surely a thousand?—flushes. How many pheasants? Never mind. A dozen, more or less; and maybe a thousand flushes there, too, counting the hens.

I do not want to write this. I do not want it to end already.

He is gone. Here is how it happened.

The day before, I had cut my knee badly with the chain saw, while thinning brush. The blade had torn through almost to the kneecap, slicing open the bursa over the patella, so that it would not stop bleeding: not in torrents, but in pulses, as if weeping. I finally had to go in that night for stitches.

If I had not messed up—or if I had messed up on any other day, at any other moment—perhaps things would be different.

The next day, a Friday, I worked in the cabin all day. The leg was stiff and I could barely walk. It rained all day but broke to clearing sun shortly before dusk.

What I wonder—though am not sure I want to know the answer—is how much knowledge we have before we know it? Last summer, the day before my old Mississippi Hound Ann died suddenly, I was gripped all day by an almost paralyzing, totally inexplicable depression—a sadness whose depth was all the more amazing for the seeming lack of any reason for it, beforehand.

This September, did I cut my leg—as if trying to cleave a part of my body from me—because some part of me knew Colter would be vanishing, or did things happen in a more linear fashion, so that the sawing of my leg was but the first step to loss, preceding and setting up that which was to follow?

Are we traveling along the arc of a circle, sometimes easing forward then slightly backward, or are we moving forever forward in a straight line?

It used to always seem to me that Colter had all the world's knowledge already in his body: that that was how he could go straight to a bird, every time, regardless of wind or scenting conditions. One, two, three quick casts, like the slashes of some giant sword, and then he'd charge straight for the bird. Every time. Some irreducible part of him, which had been wedded to the birds at birth, already knew. He had only to be turned loose into the field to rejoin them.

I was supposed to keep my foot, my hurt leg, elevated. Like some old man, I was lying upstairs on my bed reading and watching that autumn light on the aspen. I put the book down and dozed. It was about six o'clock. Elizabeth and the girls were downstairs. I heard a tremendous baying—the sound the dogs make whenever a car comes down the long gravel driveway—but then I heard nothing else, and so I got up and went to the window.

The pups were on their chains, looking up the driveway. Old Homer came walking stiff-legged down the drive, the way he does after a car or truck has left—after he has vanquished it.

I didn't see Colter. I figured it was a false alarm—a sound out on the main road. I figured Colter was down by my writing cabin. I went back and lay down. The doctor had said no hunting for ten to fourteen days, but I was hoping it would have to be only two or three.

If I had not cut my leg, we would have been out hunting in that gold light.

An hour later, I knew he was gone. Alone, he never left the space between the house and the writing cabin. The pups would run rabbits whenever they got loose together, but never Colter.

I waited up all night that first night, as I did for many nights running. My knee healed quickly, I scoured the woods with the other dogs for a lion or wolf attack, but found nothing.

He had his name and number on his collar. All I can guess is that someone drove down the drive, stopped, turned around when they saw our house—a lost tourist, perhaps, mistaking our driveway for a back road—and that for some reason, Colter followed that vehicle. Believing, somehow, that that vehicle was going hunting. He'd never done such a thing before, but there must have been something different about this one. Perhaps it had another dog, or dogs, in it.

Vanished.

Earlier that afternoon, when Elizabeth and the girls had gotten back from town, I had lifted the baby out of the truck, despite my knee, and carried her a short distance before setting her down to walk. Colter had come running up and had darted all around us, licking the heck out of her, like a puppy, and making her laugh. It was funny for a while, but then he kept licking us, and wouldn't stop, and surely my last words to him were something inattentive, as I helped bring Lowry and the groceries inside—something like, "Go on, now."

Why does luck end?

You remember every hunt—every moment, every tree, every bush. You remember the plucking of every bird; you remember examining every crop, and you remember what each bird had been eating. The memory of these things enters your blood slowly, day by day, as it has always been in your dog's blood. Slowly, you move forward to join him.

The dog creates, transcribes, a new landscape for you. And then when he is gone, it is as if that world is taken away.

Memory is no substitute for the future—for possibility, and for more learning, and the certainty of knowing that tomorrow you and your dog are going to head out to one of the same stretches of woods that you have always hunted.

A hunting dog—a hunter like Colter—sharpens your joy of all the seasons, and for a while, sometimes a long while, such a dog seems capable, by himself alone, of holding time in place—of pinning it, and holding it taut.

Dogs like that are young and strong for what seems like a very long time.

There is a magic in the world, a knowledge we will never know. I knew for certain he was gone when on the second day, unable to bear the waiting, I took his younger brother Superman up the road, hobbling on a cane, but carrying the gun. I was grieving already—weeping, as I watched Superman try to work the same woods Colter had raced through, and knowing he could never, ever be the dog Colter was.

Just as I was thinking that—at that precise moment—I saw that Superman had gone on point, and that in front of him a young ruffed grouse was fanning. The late-day sun was shining on the bird and I knew then that someone, somewhere, was telling me Colter's hunt was over—perhaps Colter himself—but was trying to do so with some semblance of mercy or grace.

The bird flushed and I hit it and Superman ran over to examine it, though again with a kind of professionalism—not the gonzo wild-eyed glee of Colter. I suspect Superman will be a perfect little grouse dog, based on that point I saw there in the sunlight just as I was giving up hope, but I realize that now that I have one—a perfect grouse dog—that that is not what I wanted, though all along, it is what I believed I wanted.

I'll work the pups: Point and Superman, Colter's younger brothers. I grieve. What can fill such an absence? I know one day I won't grieve, but I cannot imagine it—I cannot see through to that knowledge, from where I am now. No way can I imagine that.

I'll work the pups. We'll start all over. But once you have lost a dog—your first, and the one you trained alone, from a pup—the one you first set sail into the world with, you never fully give all of yourself to the next dog. You never again can look at a dog you love without hedging even a tiny bit, and only if subconsciously, against the day when that dog, too, must leave. You can never again entirely hunt or enter the future so recklessly, so joyously, without that weight of knowledge or forethought.

Jarrett, who helped train Colter—who worked with him two summers, and helped light the fuel within him—wanted to use Colter as a professional guide dog. Jarrett often compared Colter to Michael Jordan. Unlike Superman, Colter didn't hunt so much to please me, in those first years, as to please the universe; and even as he began to mature, there was still always that feeling, that knowledge, that it was between the bird and him, and that I was merely fortunate enough to get to watch it.

He was irreducible. He was never "built up," in his training, nor was he whittled down. Jarrett and I tried to bring in his borders and focus, bit by bit, year by year, and bird by bird, but that was all. His joy, his fury to be in the field, was pure and irreducible. His two little brothers possess his talent but not his genius. Point is more like Mike Tyson than Michael Jordan, and Superman, of course, is like the Professor on *Gilligan's Island.* They are only three years his ghosts—twelve seasons—though of course it could be ten thousand years, too.

I have to admit something. Because I believe he is still somewhere out there—perhaps a long way from Montana, and perhaps hunting for someone only on the occasional weekend, or perhaps simply being a yard dog, and sweet with children—I have the hope, I cannot shake the hope, that someday he might yet show up on the porch, ready to hunt again, or that I might yet get a phone call from someone who says, "I have a dog that sounds like he might be yours." Because he just vanished, I will always probably believe and hope that—for a long time, anyway, until it has been so many years that his natural time has passed, or should have passed: though with a dog like the Brown Bomber, who can say, for sure, when that time might be?

He lay in the dry autumn yellow grass at the edge of the marsh outside my writing cabin, and snoozed in the sun, brown as chocolate. He followed me down to that cabin each morning, waited hours, then followed me back up to the house when I was done: He attended, guarded the door, of my every word.

He could tell, by scent alone, whether the pheasants he chased were roosters or hens. When you called his name, he would grin and show all his teeth. He would sneak in the open windows of trucks and eat the lunches in those trucks: sandwiches, cupcakes, baklava, everything. Once when he was a pup, my friend Tim and I gave him a rest and took Tim's Retriever, Maddie, out for a run, and left Colter in the back of Tim's truck. We heard Colter screaming, wailing his disapproval, and then there was a brief silence, after which he came bounding up to join us, having torn his way through the screen window of Tim's camper-shell to get out.

There is no closure. One way or the other, he is still out there running. He will never rest. There will exist between us always this small gulf; I will always want him to know a moment's rest, and peace, and he will always know in his hot heart that the only peace to be gotten is by never resting, by always pushing on.

As I sleep restlessly, night after night, or more often, as I lie there awake, he runs, and I feel guilty that I am not there to honor the birds he is finding; that I am not there to shoot them for him, as he keeps finding them.

He is my Colter. Someone else may have fallen into possession of him—perhaps not knowing of his past—but when he runs, I am still his, and he is still mine.

Dog Years

Tom Junod

IT WAS, OF COURSE, AN EXECUTION: DEATH BY DECREE. WE killed him, or had him killed, with an overdose of barbiturate suspended in a solution pink as peppermint, drawn into a syringe the size of a rich man's cigar. The end was apparent at the beginning, when we saw the nurse clutching the pink syringe in her fist at the door of the room we had been assigned—the tiled and antiseptic room we had been hustled into, carrying our condemned cargo. The nurse was wearing white sneakers and scrub pants and a flowered smock. She had a bow in her hair, and the syringe she prepared was like the gun introduced at the start of Act One that must be discharged by the end of Act Three. She passed it to the doctor, discreetly, without our seeing the lethal exchange, and from that moment on, time itself had an almost tangible quality, measured not by the ticking of a clock but by the number of breaths left to something beloved. The doctor, with the syringe held loosely at her hip, was patient, but at the same time determined, and so she seemed to be drawing closer and closer, eliminating time as she eliminated distance, until she was squatting beside us, and a shocking effulgence of color rose suddenly from the neutrality of the room—a blooming stain of terminal brightness—as she began searching Marco's hind leg for a receptive vein.

I had seen this intensity of color once before, six years earlier, when Marco was one and a half and I nearly drowned in my backyard. My wife and I live on a lake—well, a pond, really—in suburban Atlanta, and one winter day I decided to paddle out to its center in the slovenly old canoe we had inherited with the house. I left my dogs alone on the shore, even though at that time they tended to fight in my absence; even though the water was cold enough to be skeined with ice two days earlier, and Marco had a tendency to swim after me whenever I took out the canoe. Dressed in a fleece pullover, and a couple of sweatshirts, and sweatpants, and heavy boots, I paddled hard against a stiff wind; then, as I came around, I heard a heavy concussive splash, as of something launched from a springboard, and twisted around awkwardly in the canoe to tell Marco to go home. The canoe tipped, and dumped me into the lake in my winter clothes; then it sank, right in front of me, in fifteen or twenty feet of winter water, its ghostly prow settling a foot below my boots. I heard the dogs barking—Hawk's round hound-dog howl, and, an octave below, Marco's gruff guttural chop, falling with the rhythm of a distant tradesman's hammer—and I heard the wind's insinuating whisper over the water whose taste was now in my mouth. With my house still in sight, I was all alone, out in nature, a dot on its indifferent green surface, and I thought to myself: I can die out here. Though already waterlogged, I did not stop to take off my boots or my pullover; I simply swam as hard as I could to the closest shore, about fifty yards away, not realizing how exhausted I was until I grabbed the pole of a dock and heard the high pleading bleat of my breath and tasted the salt of my lungs in my throat. I was in the yard of someone I had never met. His dog came out to greet me, then pulled up as I rose streaming out of the water, and began barking. The homeowner followed the alarm, and saw a blue-faced man—me—advancing on his back door. He threw up his hands and turned around without a word, in a kind of burlesque of polite suburban panic; in a few seconds, he reappeared and threw a blanket over my shoulders in a sudden and heartfelt embrace. He drove me home and told me to go inside, to my wife and a hot shower, but I was in shock, and feeling weirdly ebullient I strolled into the yard to collect my dogs, and there saw Marco, coming toward me with his lip curled in fear and apology and his sopping orange fur puckered with flamelike extrusions. Indeed, it was as if he had exploded into flame in my absence; he had acquired a kind of mystical plumage, and stood at the center of a world unbearably bright, and it was in seeing him—his preternatural effect—that I came to realize how close I'd come to dying.

Janet and I had lost pets before we lost Marco. We had lost, in the course of our lives together, three cats and a dog—one by disease, and three by vehicular homicide. The first was a black cat we had taken in when we were really just kids. We were living together, but not yet married, and so there was something sacramental about the cat, whose name was Cassius. He was the first living thing whose ownership we shared, and so he became our first little envoy in the world—a fleshly standard-bearer for what we imagined ourselves to be. He embodied our fledgling wishes for ourselves, beyond ourselves, and at the same time . . . well, he was still a cat, you know? With our best wishes, we left him in our apartment building when we went on vacation, and when we came home, one of our neighbors informed us that he had been run over by a car the second night we were away. She was a young woman who had mastered the old woman's art of savoring the announcement of misfortune—she could have been an Italian widow—and so perhaps she got a taste of her future, as we got a taste of ours. We went out that night to drink away our sorrows with the couple who were becoming our best friends in Atlanta—the couple we had selected as our best friends, because we liked them and because they mirrored us, not only in their pasts, but also in their ambitions for the future. They were not Southerners. Named Sue and Neil, they were both from New Jersey, and indeed, one of the first bonds Sue and I shared when I met her at my job was a common history in Catholic schools. Though lapsed as a Catholic, I was drawn to Sue for her doctrinal certainties, expressed most often in her observance of obscure holy days, and the swift admonitory theology she mustered in response to the sin of self-pity. I was not self-pitying that night, in the bar, when I found out our cat died. I was sad—obdurately sad, and sick at heart, a spectacle which Sue found at first tiresome, and then morally indulgent. "I know he was a great cat," she whispered to me, at the end of the night, in the tone of corrective confidence she had picked up at the confessional. "But you have to remember, he had no soul."

I have thought of those words often, over the ensuing—could it be?—nineteen years. I thought of them when I dug the grave of our next cat, the great Gomez, in the backyard of our apartment building, after he began suffering with feline leukemia, and then when I took him to be "put to sleep" and surprised myself with the blinding extent of my own tears. I thought of them when I found the body of Buddy, the stray who one day followed Gomez through our front door, garishly squashed on the double yellow line. I thought of them when Sue and Neil molted in our estimation from friends to family, and began fulfilling, on their own, the ambitions that we as two connected couples had once shared. The division between flesh and spirit was nowhere more apparent than in our respective fates, for when Sue and Neil began having children, Janet and I were left to the tenuous consolation of pets. We experienced the iron pangs of infertility, and on the day when Willie—the Rottweiler we'd bought as precursor to children—and then loved as substitute—ran out in front of a sporty red car in front of me and in front of the little white house that was dedicated to the dream of family and wound up standing like a tombstone at dream's end, well, I felt almost biblically cursed, for the worship of false idols, for the pagan misunderstanding between what was truly sacred and what, upon death, reverts by law to meat.

I bought Marco for Janet. I bought him because I already had a dog, the indomitable and indomitably optimistic Hawk, whom I had salvaged from bad ownership when he was nearly two, and who in return was pledged to follow me everywhere I went, from the mailbox to the bathroom. Hawk I got for a couple of hundred bucks. Marco was three years younger, and so laughably expensive that when I bought him I was clearly in the grip not only of the sin of overestimating the worth of animals but also of attempting to buy perfection.

We saw him first in a video sent by his breeder in California. Like Hawk, he was a Cane Corso Mastiff, a so-called "rare breed" pushed by its advocates as an example of uncorrupted Italian breeding, harking back to the bloody glories of Rome, but in reality probably a hodgepodge of Mastiff, Pit Bull, and Bloodhound, with strong jaws, short snouts, skulls broader than the stretch of a human hand, unnervingly vigilant eyes, whorls of loose flesh, cropped ears, and docked tails—the works, when it comes to guard dogs. In the video, he was sullen and drowsy, but identified as the pick of the litter because of what the breeder called his massive bone and because of his color. A litter of Cane Corsos is like a litter of cats: They come out in all colors, from black to blue to chestnut brindle. Marco was red, or what is known as red in the parlance of the breed—he was really closer to solid orange—but I had always wanted a red Cane Corso, so the breeder shipped him to an associate in Pennsylvania, and I flew up from Atlanta to get him. He was still sullen and drowsy—nine weeks old, he growled when I tried snatching his bowl of food—but I figured that nurture would overcome nature, and wrote the check.

The breeder had named him Marsalis. We renamed him Marcello, and called him Marco. Then, by some trick of the tongue, we called him Marcus. Then we called him Macho. Then Magus. Then Maggo. Then Maggo Cheese, to rhyme with the snack-food flavor; also, as a derivation of "Macheesemo." Then Head Cheese, because, as it turned out, he was sullen even when he wasn't drowsy. Then sometimes Cheese Head, but most often simply The Cheese. We also called him Little One, to distinguish him from Hawk, who was always bigger, if only in his own estimation. Then we cinched up the vowel, and called him Leetle One. Then Lee. Then Lee Roy. Then Roy Lee. The LeeLee. Then MaggoLee. Then Machu Picchu, like the lost Inca city. Then Peach. I also called him Butterscotch Pudding for the way his ill-fitting orange coat pooled up when he laid down, and so, from there, Pudding, and Pookie, and Pook, though I did not share these appellations with Janet, but spoke them in private, as tokens of a kind of intimacy. I say all this—reveal all this—not to make readers squirm, by the way; nor to strike a note of cuteness or sentimentality; nor to embarrass myself or my wife. I say this to avow what anyone involved in a long marriage has to know: that love, at least love of the domestic and domesticated sort, operates on the level of language, because language is the necessary instrument of reinvention. We fall in love with perfection; we stay in love with fallibility, by virtue of our ardor and imagination—by the language we lavish upon it, by the words we bestow. As such, the cadences of marriage and the cadences of dog ownership are uncomfortably similar: First, we make up pet names for our partners, then we make up names for our pets. The Bible tells us that

Adam, the first married man, was also the man given the task of naming the animals; what it doesn't tell us is that after the Fall, he kept on naming them, because that was the only purchase on perfection that his angry God would allow.

Marco was not perfect, you see. He was as fallible as any fleshly creature could be. He had a black birthmark on his pink spatulate tongue, and a kind of windowpane—an icon in the shape of the Microsoft logo—staining one of his bovine brown eyes. His temperament was spotty, at best: mostly, he was gloomy and disconsolate, or as Janet and I would both say, with a singing affection that assigned stress to every syllable, "miserable." As a guard dog, he was spoiled beyond repair, beyond functioning, with such scant tolerance for pain that he wound up a terrifying coward, so fierce behind a pane of glass that he made our minivan shake when anyone walked by, and so docile in person that he sought safe harbor between my legs when guests made loud noises, and hiccuped uncontrollably when I yelled at him. He was irredeemably dog-aggressive, so that we couldn't take him to the park for communal canine frolic. He remained in the unbreakable habit of growling at us to express his nagging dissatisfactions, although he never bit anyone—well, he never bit anyone except me, when I tried to break up a battle between him and Hawk, and wound up going to the local doc-in-a-box for a stitch in my forefinger. At his heaviest, he weighed 120 pounds; at his healthiest, 100; and he was so strong in both incarnations I had trouble controlling him when he got worked up at the end of the leash. For a big dog, he was extremely physical and athletic, happiest when he was chasing a ball, but even this—his one consistent source of pleasure, when I think about it—brought him ruin, because his body was as fragile as his psyche. He always had goop in his eyes; he had a thyroid condition that scrawled a kind of brand on his flank; his front elbows were dysplastic, and his joints began crumbling with arthritis. Oh, hell, he was a mess, but we loved him, not despite his flaws but because of them: We were the kind of pet owners who, when their imposing beast closed his jaws around a guest's forearm, exclaimed, "That just means he loves you!" and chose to see, in his persistently and charismatically curled lip, a smile. Indeed, Janet would go out of her way to elicit the curled lip by tickling Marco around the snout—she called the resultant gesture his "Elvis"—whereupon she would rain kisses upon his helpless velvety head, and sometimes gaze into his eyes with such cross-species passion that I would tell her to get a room. For all his entrenched sorrow, he was a vocal dog, with a kind of gruff eloquence that crossed a cow's moo with a sow's grunt when he was angling for affection; and so, while to his silence we imputed the usual values of love and loyalty and forbearance, in his vocalizations we heard a break not just in his silence but in all silences—the silence of God—and made a fetish of the pink split that appeared under his black nose and parted his black muzzle when he prepared to speak.

But enough. It is noble to sing of a lost child and it is poetry to sing of a lost lover, but to sing of a lost dog is merely pathetic, except in country music. And yet I—we—loved Marco to such a degree that when I try to imagine what it is like to love a child, I wonder how much more love is possible in the human heart and the human soul—how much more room in the human heart and soul it is possible for a child to uncover. The answer, I know, is this: plenty. The answer, I know, is that I don't know love unless and until I experience the love for a child. At the same time, however, I suspect that the process must be similar, if not the product—the dream of perfection surpassed by the embrace of fallibility, until love exists for its own sake, oblivious to its object. The difference is that when you love a dog, or animal, you can never escape the awareness that your love is cursed, and mortal, and ultimately doomed—love of a lower order. A child is our purchase on the future, and so teaches us about the demands of immortality. A dog teaches us precisely the opposite. A dog teaches us about the demands—and possibilities—of our mortality, meted out in the remarkably useful actuarial equation apportioning seven "dog years" for every one "human year." A child is meant to outlast us. We, however, are meant to outlast our dogs, and so we share with them, from the start, the most shameful secret of any creature—the secret every creature wants to hide—which is that it is born and meant to die. If we are lucky, we will have many dogs in a lifetime, and if we are very lucky, we will take each of them to the vet, and, in a ritual that is not at odds with this kind of love but somehow aligned with it, we will ask the vet to prepare a pink needle and respectfully kill it.

I grew up not many blocks from a venerable and somewhat famous pet cemetery. Located in Wantagh, Long Island, right across the street from Wantagh High School, it is called Bide-A-Wee, and has provided the final resting place for many noteworthy dogs, from—as a matter of rumor—Rin

Tin Tin to, as a matter of fact, Nixon's Checkers. Janet and I went there, not long ago, on a visit home, before Marco died, before we even knew he was sick. I hadn't visited in many years. I hadn't visited, in fact, since I was very small and my mother told me a fib when the family dog died—when she took me to one of the freshly dug graves, and said that's where Ginger was, although Ginger was probably interred in a Dumpster behind the local animal hospital. My brother was a gravedigger there when he was in high school, and I always remembered him talking about confectionary old women trying to clamber into the cold ground in pursuit of their departed Poodles, so I stayed away. Now that I had returned, however, I couldn't get over how weirdly familiar the place was—here was a place I somehow recognized, as I suppose I would recognize the ancient face of a grade-school teacher I thought I'd forgotten. The cemetery was surprisingly old, full of ornamental cherry trees beautifully gnarled in their maturity, and graves dating back to the '20s and '30s. It was both bucolic and ghostly, conjuring up not just missing creatures but entire missing worlds: Some of the tombstones had been overturned, and on the faces of others the fading porcelained portraits of cats and dogs had been chipped away with rocks or hammers, so that in stretches the place had the look of a cemetery vandalized for sectarian cause. Visitors had even placed a line of stones on top of Checkers's tombstone, as though the dog that had saved Richard Nixon's political ass deserved the same tribute as Oskar Schindler at the end of *Schindler's List.* But although there were dead dogs everywhere—and dead cats, and dead parakeets, and dead fish—the ghosts that haunted me were not the ghosts of Rex and King and Max and, yes, Fido and Rover, but rather the ghosts of those humans who had buried them. They had loved these animals enough to memorialize them, often in family plots, but now that they themselves were long dead, who remembered them, or, more to the point, their hopeful and hopeless and ultimately perishable love? Who remembered the man who, back in the '40s, had asked the stonemason to carve HE CAME WHEN CALLED on his dog's stone; or the woman who, in the '50s, believed that her canine companion had gone WHERE THE GOOD DOGS GO; or the heartbroken wretch who, back in the '60s, was moved to forgive his dog for dying, in the words HE ONLY MADE ONE MISTAKE? They had all vanished, even more thoroughly than the beasts whose bones still fed the soil, for if human love is an effort at persistence—an attempt to extend oneself beyond oneself—

their love had failed utterly. The love of a child can persist for generations, as that child loves in turn. The love of an animal, however, always drags behind it the anchor of mortality, and so although stone after stone advertised the deceased as FOREVER FAITHFUL, I couldn't help but think that we cling to such sentiments in error, for dogs are only faithful up to a point. I couldn't help but think that we love in error—that my wife loves in error, that I love in error—and that now I was strolling through an entire garden of erroneous human love, beautiful because it was doomed to a vandal's hand, beautiful because it celebrated what was misplaced, beautiful because it is not only the object of our love that is fallible: It is love itself.

It has always felt dishonest to say that Marco died on November 6, because such words imply that he—or his body—made the decision by simply expiring. He didn't. He died at the moment we ordained. He had gotten sick after our late return from summer vacation. He was strong, then he was weak. We took him to the vet, who diagnosed him as the victim of something called cardiomyopathy. His big heart had grown even bigger, swelling to the point of uselessness. It is not only a big dog's disease; it is a human disease, and to retard its progression, we fed him human pills—many of the same pills, in fact, taken by my father. It cost a lot of money, but of course if we could have paid for his survival we would have paid most anything. When it comes to dying, however, dogs seem to know what humans don't: that death doesn't want your goddamn money, and so, when after two days of last-ditch care in the hospital, the canine cardiologist—yes, there are canine cardiologists, and yes, we used one—called us in to "have a look at him," we knew he was a goner. He was under a blanket, in a wire cage, his head pillowed next to an uneaten pile of fresh chicken, and when he saw us he stretched his neck and widened his eyes and wagged his usually recalcitrant tail, but he didn't move. He couldn't. We carried him out, like a coffee table, and when we asked the cardiologist, when we'd have to "put him to sleep"—a preferable euphemism, in my mind, to "put him down"—she said, "You'll know. He'll tell you."

I'd always hated language like that, sentiments like that. They always seemed as dishonest as any other aspect of the anthropomorphism we pour into our love for animals, as any other palliative that helps us get on with their dying. But then, after we got home, we lifted him out of the van and placed him on the ground, and he collapsed—as if his legs weren't screwed in anymore, as if his bones were unconnected to his muscles, and had been grotesquely liberated, under his skin. And, just as the doctor had said, we knew. We carried him inside, placed him on his bed, called the vet, and began listening to the last of Marco. His breathing was labored: he sounded like he was breathing by machine. His lips were cold and gray. His nose was caked with mucus he could no longer process or expel or lick away, and had gone from black to a fishy brown. He had a smell, and after lying with him for nearly an hour Janet announced that his eyes had gone blank—that the alien and incomprehensible eyes that had always managed somehow to answer her were locked in some kind of irrevocable stare. It was a rainy afternoon, dark and cold and wet, and in the shadows of our house there was a sense of time slipping away, hurtling forward in some paradoxically dilatory fashion, transformed by the addition of a terrible terminus. Then it was ten minutes to five, and as we stood up to ferry Marco to his five o'clock appointment, the doorbell rang, and standing like a messenger in the oblong glass was a young girl in outlandish retro bell-bottoms selling coupons to a local pizza place. Mercilessly, I told her that she had come at the worst possible time—that she had caught us in the process of taking our dog to his termination—and she raised her hand to her forehead in a sudden panicked gesture and fled back down the walk. We let Hawk—at once wise and uncomprehending—sniff one last time around the brother we had forced upon him, and hoisted Marco into the van. We parked, as instructed, in the back of the veterinary clinic, and saw, for the first time, in its faceless brick and featureless steel doors, how close it was to an abattoir, except that now the doors sprung open, and the nurse came out—she looked exactly like the girl selling pizza—and the vet, and they embraced us. I was crying, of course, strangling in it, really, but Janet and I took Marco inside, past a woman who was carrying her dog back out, who was crying because her dog had been given a reprieve, and who looked at us in horror as we were led to a room whose twinned stainless-steel surgical tables beckoned with a sinister gleam.

Then the vet, a woman deeply kind and deeply Southern, was upon us, with her big pink gun. She prodded Marco's hind leg, so that she wouldn't get in our way, so that only Janet and I would figure in Marco's final glimpse of the world, but she came up painfully dry, and crowded next to us as she attended to his front paw. After all our waiting, time now was turning on a big cog, and moving so fast that when the pink solution inside the syringe blackened with a storm cloud of Marco's blood, I was compelled to ask, "Is this it?" The vet nodded, and went on slowly with her work, speaking to us in the same tone as she spoke to our dog—in a kind of cooing singsong.

Marco lasted the extent of the needle: At first there was no difference in his breathing, and my mind stirred with a weird apprehension of miracle; then he took three sippy hiccuping breaths, and stopped. He just stopped, right there in front of us; he was finite and finished; and in the backwash of his final silence I had to bite my knuckle to quell the blubbering opera of my tears. Did I say how beautiful a dog he was? He was beautiful. Did I say how beautiful my wife is? She is beautiful, and now in the transporting color that rose from the room—from the locus of Marco's body—I saw, for the first time, and also for the last, that her blond hair was nearly half gray. Her eyes were almost unbearably blue, and her cheeks were almost unbearably pink, slicked with the syrup of her tears, as Marco, her dog, burned once again with a red flame. It was strange, and totally unexpected: He had almost become ugly, in his dying, but now it was as if he was restored to us in his death, and for once the hated euphemism seemed proper and just. He had been put to sleep. Well, not really, but it looked that way, for his ears bracketed his usual whorled and stubborn frown; the only difference was that they didn't twitch when I called him—and, by God, I did call him. Of course, he didn't come; what came in his place was a consuming sense of peace, in regard to our past and in regard to our future. After years of dithering, Janet and I had finally sent applications to an adoption agency, and in our dog's departure, there was also a sense of arrival. We were living in dog years now ourselves; by even the most optimistic estimate, we had pushed beyond the magic halfway point in our lives, and so with Marco, we had shared our own mortal secret. Did he have a soul? Maybe not. But we did, and it was our soul's job to give him a soul, to assign him one, by language and by love. That's what we—we humans—do. Our dog was gone now, but the light that went out, and then rose again in final tender flourish, was our own.

Credits

Grateful acknowledgment is made to the following for permission to reprint previously published material.

LYNDA BARRY: "Dogs!" from *One Hundred Demons* first appeared on Salon.com, 2000. Copyright © 2000 by Lynda Barry. Reprinted by permission of the artist.

RICK BASS: "My Colter" first appeared in *The Bark,* Spring 2000, and appeared in *Colter: The True Story of the Best Dog I Ever Had,* Houghton Mifflin, 2000. Copyright © 2000 by Rick Bass. Reprinted by permission of the author.

BONNIE JO CAMPBELL AND INTERNATIONAL CREATIVE MANAGEMENT, INC.: "My Dog, Roscoe" by Bonnie Jo Campbell first appeared in *Witness* magazine. Copyright © 2001 by Bonnie Jo Campbell. Reprinted by permission of the author and International Creative Management, Inc.

COUNTERPOINT PRESS: "The Children Are Very Quiet When They Are Away" by Maeve Brennan, from *The Rose Garden.* Copyright © 1999 by Maeve Brennan. Reprinted by permission of Counterpoint Press, a member of Perseus Books, L.L.C.

ALICE ELLIOTT DARK: "Watch the Animals: A Story" first appeared in *Harper's* magazine, 2000. Copyright © 2000 by Alice Elliott Dark. Reprinted by permission of the author.

MARK DERR: "Darwin's Dogs" first appeared in *The Bark,* Winter 2000. Copyright © 2000 by Mark Derr. Reprinted by permission of the author.

THE DIAL PRESS/DELL PUBLISHING: "The Color of Joy" from *Pack of Two* by Caroline Knapp. Copyright © 1998 by Caroline Knapp. Reprinted by permission of The Dial Press/Dell Publishing, a division of Random House, Inc.

LEE FORGOTSON: "Sit. Stay. Heal: One Dog's Response to 9/11" was originally published in *The Bark,* Winter 2001. Copyright © 2001 by Lee Forgotson. Reprinted by permission of the author.

HARPERCOLLINS PUBLISHERS, INC.: "Accident" from *Heaven's Coast* by Mark Doty. Copyright © 1996 by Mark Doty. Reprinted by permission of HarperCollins Publishers Inc.

HEATHER HOULAHAN: "Trust" was originally published in *The Bark,* Winter 2001. Copyright © 2001 by Heather Houlahan. Reprinted by permission of the author.

CATHERINE RYAN HYDE: "Bloodlines: A Story" first appeared in *Ploughshares,* Spring 2001. Copyright © 2002 by Catherine Ryan Hyde. Reprinted by permission of the author.

ERICA JONG: "A Woman's Best Friend" was originally published in *Cigar Aficionado* magazine, June 2000. Copyright © 2000 by Erica Jong. Reprinted by permission of the author.

TOM JUNOD: "Dog Years" originally appeared as "Marco Died" in *Esquire* magazine. Copyright © 2002 by Tom Junod. Reprinted by permission of the author.

MAXINE KUMIN: "Mutts" originally appeared in *Women, Animals and Vegetables: Essays & Stories,* published by Ontario Press Review. Copyright © 1994 by Maxine Kumin. Reprinted by permission of the author.

STEPHEN KUUSISTO AND IRENE SKOLNICK LITERARY AGENCY: "Blind Date" by Stephen Kuusisto, from *Planet of the Blind,* published by Delta, 1998. Copyright © 2002 by Stephen Kuusisto. Reprinted by permission of the author and Irene Skolnick Literary Agency.

DONALD MCCAIG: "Uncle Harry" first appeared in its entirety in *The American Border Collie.* Copyright © 2002 by Donald McCaig. Reprinted by permission of the author.

NASDIJJ: "Navajo" first appeared in *The Bark,* Fall 2001. Copyright © 2001 by Nasdijj. Reprinted by permission of the author.

PAMELA PAINTER: "Confusing the Dog: A Story" originally appeared in *Ploughshares,* Fall 1989. Copyright © 1989 by Pamela Painter. Reprinted by permission of the author.

ANN PATCHETT: "This Dog's Life" was originally published in *Vogue* magazine, March 1997. Copyright © 1997 by Ann Patchett. Reprinted by permission of the author.

MICHAEL PATERNITI: "Neighbors" was originally aired on Public Radio International, WBEZ-FM's *This American Life,* April 1999. Copyright © 1999 by Michael Paterniti. Reprinted by permission of the author.

CHARLES SIEBERT AND DARHANSOFF, VERRILL, FELDMAN, LITERARY AGENTS: "Citizen Canine" by Charles Siebert originally appeared in *The New York Times Magazine,* March 26, 2000. Copyright © 2000 by Charles Siebert. Reprinted by permission of the author and Darhansoff, Verrill, Feldman, Literary Agents.

ELENA SIGMAN: "The Existence of Dog" originally appeared on Salon.com, March 2002. Copyright © 2002 by Elena Sigman. Reprinted by permission of the author.

BILL VAUGHN: "Living in Dog Years" originally appeared in *Outside* magazine. Copyright © 2001 by Bill Vaughn. Reprinted by permission of the author.

Acknowledgments

We owe a debt of gratitude to the editorial expertise of Lee Forgotson for her help in assembling this project. Thanks also to the editorial assistance provided by Gerry Gomez Pearlberg, Susan Tasaki, and Douglas Clark. We offer a nod of appreciation to Louise Rafkin, Jennifer Peale, Donald McCaig, and Michael J. Rosen for their invaluable introductions.

Special thanks to all the writers, artists, and dog people who have contributed their work to the pages of *The Bark,* and to our dedicated staff, Alice Jurow, Deborah Lewis, Dirk Walter, and Ruth Wightman.

Our gratitude to those who were there at the start: Anita Monga, Peter Moore, Jessica and Richard Behrman, Douglas Gordon, Rebecca Kidd, and the Friends of César Chavéz Park. As well, a thank-you to *The Bark*'s true believers, Helene Rubinstein, Al Shugart, Nion McEvoy, Ruth Silverman, Greg Kidd, Douglas Evans, Mark Grasso, and Susan Woelzl. Cheers to Brig. Gen. Robert L. Scott, Jr. (Ret.), author of *God Is My Co-Pilot,* for blessing our motto "Dog Is My Co-Pilot." Thanks to Peter for the clever twist.

We are grateful for the support and guidance of our editor at Crown, Annik La Farge. Annik's enthusiasm and unflagging commitment to the project was a source of inspiration. We thank our good fortune at teaming with our literary agent at International Creative Management, Lisa Bankoff. Her keen insight and judgment have been indispensable.

We would like to acknowledge the dedication and tireless efforts of the many people who strive to improve the lives of dogs and their human companions through their work with animal shelters and rescue and humane organizations everywhere.

And, finally, our heartfelt thanks to Leslie Sullivan for introducing us to Nellie, our founder dog and the girl who started it all.

We dedicate this book in loving memory of Hirk Williamson.

About the Contributors

LYNDA BARRY'S cartoon strips have been collected in *The Freddie Stories, The Greatest of Marlys,* and *One Hundred Demons.* She is also the author of *The Good Times Are Killing Me* and the novel *Cruddy.*

RICK BASS has authored more than sixteen books of fiction and nonfiction, including *The Watch,* a short story collection for which he won the PEN/Nelson Algren Award; *Where the Sea Used to Be; The Sky, the Stars, the Wilderness: Novellas;* and *Colter: The True Story of the Best Dog I Ever Had.*

LOUISE BERNIKOW is the author of several books, including *Among Women, The American Women's Almanac: An Inspiring and Irreverent Women's History,* and *Bark If You Love Me.* Her work has appeared in the *New York Times, Playboy,* and *Esquire.*

JON BILLMAN is a former wildland firefighter and seventh-grade teacher. His work has appeared in *Esquire, Outside,* and *The Paris Review.* He is the author of *When We Were Wolves.*

MAEVE BRENNAN contributed to *The New Yorker*'s "The Talk of the Town" from 1954 until 1981. Her columns were gathered in a book, *The Long-Winded Lady.* Her short stories were collected in *In and Out of Never-Never Land, Christmas Eve, The Springs of Affection,* and a posthumous volume, *The Rose Garden.* She died in New York, in 1993, at the age of seventy-six.

BONNIE JO CAMPBELL is the author of a collection of short fiction, *Women and Other Animals,* and a novel, *Q Road.* She is also coeditor of *Our Working Lives: Short Stories of People and Work.* Her work has appeared in *The Southern Review* and *The Pushcart Prize 2001.*

MARGARET CHO is a comedian and writer. Her successful 1999 off-Broadway show, *I'm the One That I Want,* was made into a film and was the basis for her bestselling book of the same name. Her second ground-breaking show, *Notorious C.H.O.,* culminated with a concert at Carnegie Hall and was also released as a feature film. She has been honored by the National Organization for Women, the Gay and Lesbian Alliance Against Defamation, the National Gay and Lesbian Task Force, and the Asian American Legal Defense and Education Fund. Her most recent tour, *Revolution,* started in the spring of 2003.

CAROLYN CHUTE is the author of *The Beans of Egypt, Maine, Letourneau's Used Auto Parts, Merry Men,* and *Snow Man.* She has received a John Simon Guggenheim Memorial Foundation Fellowship and a Thornton Wilder Fellowship. Her short stories have been published in *Shenandoah, Ploughshares,* and *The Ohio Review.*

ALICE ELLIOTT DARK is the author of *Think of England, In the Gloaming,* and *Naked to the Waist.* She is the recipient of numerous awards, including a National Endowment for the Arts Fellowship. Her work has appeared in *The New Yorker, Harper's,* and *The Best American Short Stories of the Century.*

MARK DERR is the author of *Dog's Best Friend* and a contributing editor to *The Bark.* His articles have appeared in the *New York Times* and a number of periodicals. He is at work on a book about the role of dogs in American history.

MARK DOTY is the author of six poetry collections, including *Sweet Machine* and *My Alexandria.* His memoir, *Heaven's Coast,* won the PEN/Martha Albrand Award for First Nonfiction. He is the recipient of the Witter Bynner Prize for Poetry from the American Academy of Arts and Letters and the National Book Critics Circle Award.

LEE FORGOTSON'S series "Rex and the City" appears regularly in *The Bark;* she is a contributing editor to that magazine.

HEATHER HOULAHAN is a search-and-rescue dog handler and canine director of Allegheny Mountain Rescue Group in Pittsburgh, Pennsylvania, and is the proprietor of LapWolf Dog Training, specializing in challenging dogs.

PAM HOUSTON is the author of *Cowboys Are My Weakness, Waltzing the Cat,* and a collection of autobiographical essays entitled *A Little More About Me.* Her stories have been selected for *The Best American Short Stories* and *The O. Henry Awards: Prize Stories,* as well as *The Pushcart Prize.* Her new novel, *Sighthound,* will be out in April 2004.

MICHELLE HUNEVEN is the author of two novels, *Round Rock* and *Jamesland.* Her short stories have appeared in *Harper's* and *Redbook.* She is also a journalist and restaurant critic whose work has appeared in the *Los Angeles Times, LA Weekly,* and *Gourmet.* She received the Whiting Writer's Award for fiction in 2002.

CATHERINE RYAN HYDE is the author of *Pay It Forward, Funerals for Horses, Electric God, Walter's Purple Heart,* and the story collection *Earthquake Weather.* Her work has appeared in *The Antioch Review, Michigan Quarterly Review,* and *Ploughshares.* Her writing has been honored by the Raymond Carver Short Story Contest, the Tobias Wolff Award, and *The Best American Short Stories.*

THOM JONES is the author of the short story collections *Cold Snap, The Pugilist at Rest* (a National Book Award finalist), and *Sonny Liston Was a Friend of Mine.* His stories have appeared in *The New Yorker, Playboy, Esquire,* and *Harper's.*

ERICA JONG is the author of several bestselling novels, including *Fear of Flying, Any Woman's Blues,* and her latest, *Sappho's Leap;* seven books of poetry, including *Ordinary Miracles* and *Becoming Light;* and memoirs, including *The Devil at Large: Erica Jong on Henry Miller* and *Fear of Fifty.*

TOM JUNOD is a writer-at-large for *Esquire,* where "Dog Years" first appeared, in slightly amended form, as "Marco Died." He has also written for *GQ, Life,* and *Sports Illustrated.* He has won two National Magazine Awards for feature writing.

JON KATZ is the author of a dozen books, including *A Dog Year: Twelve Months, Four Dogs, and Me* and *The New Work of Dogs.*

DONNA KELLEHER is a holistic veterinarian whose practice includes the use of acupuncture, herbs, and nutrition to heal animals. She is president of the Washington chapter of the American Holistic Veterinary Medical Association. She is the author of *The Last Chance Dog and Other True Stories of Holistic Animal Healing.*

CAROLINE KNAPP is the author of *Drinking: A Love Story, Pack of Two,* and *Appetites: Why Women Want.* She was a regular columnist at *The Boston Phoenix* and wrote for *New Woman, Mademoiselle,* and the *New York Times.* She died in 2002 at the age of forty-two.

MAXINE KUMIN is the author of twelve books of poetry, most recently *The Long Marriage* and *Selected Poems 1960–1990.* Her fourth book, *Up Country,* won a Pulitzer Prize. She has also published several novels, collections of essays and short stories, and more than twenty children's books, several of them in collaboration with the poet Anne Sexton.

STEPHEN KUUSISTO is the author of *Planet of the Blind: A Memoir* and *Only Bread, Only Light,* a collection of poems. He is a Fulbright scholar and teaches creative writing at Ohio State University. He is at work on a new book about knowing the world by sound.

DONALD MCCAIG is the author of *Nop's Trials, Nop's Hope,* and *Eminent Dogs, Dangerous Men.* He, his wife, Anne, and their dogs work a sheep farm in the mountains of western Virginia.

PATRICIA B. MCCONNELL, PH.D., is an adjunct associate professor of zoology at the University of Wisconsin–Madison and a certified Applied Animal Behaviorist. She is the author of *The Other End of the Leash: Why We Do What We Do Around Dogs* and writes a column for *The Bark,* "Both Ends of the Leash."

NASDIJJ is the author of *The Blood Runs Like a River Through My Dreams* and *The Boy and the Dog Are Sleeping*—memoirs of his life as a Native American. His essay "The Blood Runs Like a River Through My Dreams" was first published in *Esquire* and was named a finalist for the National Magazine Award. The inspiration for much of his writing comes from the support group he runs for boys with AIDS.

ALYSIA GRAY PAINTER'S work has appeared on PBS and in *McSweeney's Internet Tendency, Modern Humorist,* and the anthology *More Mirth of a Nation.*

PAMELA PAINTER is the author of the story collections *Getting to Know the Weather* and *The Long and Short of It.* She is a coauthor of *What If? Writing Exercises for Fiction Writers.* Her stories have appeared in *Atlantic Monthly, Harper's,* and *The Kenyon Review.* She is a founding editor of *StoryQuarterly* and teaches at Emerson College in Boston.

ANN PATCHETT is the author of four novels, *The Patron Saint of Liars, Taft, The Magician's Assistant,* and *Bel Canto,* which was awarded the PEN/Faulkner Award and the Orange Prize for Fiction. Her work has appeared in *The New York Times Magazine, The Village Voice, Gourmet,* and *Vogue.*

MICHAEL PATERNITI is the author of the bestselling book *Driving Mr. Albert: A Trip Across America with Einstein's Brain,* which first appeared as an article in *Harper's,* winning a National Magazine Award. He is a frequent contributor to NPR's *This American Life* and has written for various publications, including *The New York Times Magazine, Esquire, Outside, Rolling Stone,* and *GQ,* where he is a writer-at-large.

MICHAEL J. ROSEN has created some fifty books for both adults and children, including *Kids' Best Dog Book* and the anthologies *Dog People* and *21st Century Dog,* which benefit animal welfare efforts through a fund he began in 1990. He is a frequent contributor to *The Bark.*

CHARLES SIEBERT is the author of *Wickerby: An Urban Pastoral* and *Angus.* His poems, essays, and articles have appeared in *The New Yorker, The New York Times Magazine, Harper's, Outside,* and *Esquire.*

ELENA SIGMAN is a writer whose work has appeared in *Elle* and *Money Magazine,* on Salon.com, and in the *International Herald Tribune.*

GEORGE SINGLETON is the author of two short story collections, *These People Are Us* and *The Half-Mammals of Dixie.* He teaches fiction writing at the South Carolina Governor's School for the Arts and Humanities. His work has appeared in *Harper's, Playboy, Atlantic Monthly,* and *The Southern Review.*

SUSAN STRAIGHT is the author of *I Been in Sorrow's Kitchen and Licked Out All the Pots, Blacker Than a Thousand Midnights, The Gettin Place,* and *Aquaboogie,* a collection of short stories that won the Milkweed National Fiction Prize. Her novel *Highwire Moon* was a National Book Award finalist for fiction. Her work has appeared in *Harper's* and *The New York Times Magazine* and on Salon.com.

ALEXANDRA STYRON is the author of *All the Finest Girls.* She is at work on her second novel.

LAMA SURYA DAS is the founder of the Dzogchen Foundation, based in Cambridge, Massachusetts, and the author of *Awakening the Buddha Within: Tibetan Wisdom for the Western World, The Snow Lion's Turquoise Mane: Wisdom Tales from Tibet* and *Awakening the Buddhist Heart;* and a coauthor, with Nyoshul Khenpo Rinpoche, of *Natural Great Perfection.*

ABIGAIL THOMAS is the author of several works of fiction and nonfiction, including *Safekeeping: Some True Stories from a Life, Good Evening and Other Poems,* and *Getting Over Tom,* and the children's books *Lily* and *Herb's Pajamas.*

ELIZABETH MARSHALL THOMAS is the author of *The Tribe of Tiger, The Hidden Life of Dogs, The Social Lives of Dogs,* and the novels *Certain Poor Shepherds, Reindeer Moon,* and *The Animal Wife.*

MARK ULRIKSEN, who created the cover and interior art for this book, is an artist and illustrator whose work often features dogs. He is currently illustrating his first children's book, *Dog Show* by Eizabeth Winthrop. He is a regular contributor to *The New Yorker* and *The Bark.*

BILL VAUGHN is a contributing editor at *Outside* magazine, and the author of *First, A Little Chee-Chee,* a sporting collection, and a novel, *bluelight.*

ALICE WALKER'S novel *The Color Purple* won the American Book Award and the Pulitzer Prize. She is the author of *Possessing the Secret of Joy, Meridian, The Way Forward Is with a Broken Heart,* and a biography for children, *Langston Hughes: American Poet.* Her books of poetry include *Absolute Trust in the Goodness of the Earth: New Poems, Horses Make a Landscape Look More Beautiful,* and *Revolutionary Petunias.*

About the Editors

Claudia Kawczynska is editor-in-chief and Cameron Woo is the creative director of *The Bark,* which they cofounded in 1997 in Berkeley, California. Created initially to rally support for a local off-leash area, *The Bark* quickly grew from a modest newsletter into a glossy, award-winning magazine, championed for its intelligence, wit, and design. Acclaimed as "*The New Yorker* of dog magazines," *The Bark* chronicles every aspect of our life with dogs, exploring the special bond between canines and humans. *The Bark* has garnered numerous honors, including a Folio Gold Award and Best Alternative Press Award and was recognized as one of the Most Notable Magazine Launches of 1999. *The Bark* is available at newsstands and in bookstores everywhere, and online at www.thebark.com. The editors live and work in Berkeley with their three dogs and five cats.